CYBER LAWS AND COMPUTER CRIMES

CYBER LAWS AND COMPUTER CRIMES

RAJAN NAGIA

CYBER TECH PUBLICATIONS
4264/3, Ansari Road, Daryaganj, New Delhi-110002 (India)
Ph.: 011-23244078. Fax: 011-23280028
E-Mail: cyberpublicationsdelhi@yahoo.com

Cyber Laws and Computer Crimes

First Edition 2009

Reprint 2025

Published by G.S. Rawat
For CYBER TECH PUBLICATIONS
4264/3, Ansari Road, Daryaganj, New Delhi - 110 002
E-mail : cyberpublicationsdelhi@yahoo.com
Phone : 011-23244078,
Fax : 011-23280028

Printed at
Asian Offset Printers

Preface

There is a saying that if a village is developed, the first ones to arrive there are the thieves. So, for every new technology developed there are people who are there to misuage it too. The same applies to the computers too. There are lots of thieves there also, who try to steal your data, your valued files, money from your accounts, money from ATMs, etc. All these come under the various Cyber Crimes.

Sensing the problem which was bound to occur, the Information Technology Act, 2000 was developed. It put the guidelines for keeping a check on these crimes and if caught, how to deal with the culprits and what sections to be applied on them.

Various type of crimes covered are:

- Cyber Terrorism
- Invasion of Privacy
- Pronography and Pedophilia
- Spam
- Cyber Stalking
- Hacking
- Obscenity and Vulgarity
- Computer Viruses

Various aspects of the Information Technology Act, 2000 is also discussed in the various other chapters.

Crimes relating to Online business is also discussd.

I am indeed debited to the staff of Cyber Tech Publications for their suggestions and encouragement in producing this book in this form.

Suggestions for improvement are always welcomed.

Author

Contents

1

Introduction to Cyber Laws

Introduction to Cyber Laws

Since the beginning of civilization, man has always been motivated by the need to make progress and better the existing technologies. This has led to tremendous development and progress, which has been a launching pad for further development. Of all the significant advances made by mankind from the beginning till date, probably the important of them is the development of Internet. To put in a common man's language, Internet is a global network of computers, all of them speaking the same language. In 1969, America's Department of Defense commissioned the construction of a Super network called ARPANET. The advanced Research Projects Agency Network (ARPANET), basically intended as a military network of 40 computers connected by a web of links & lines. This network slowly grew and the Internet was born. 1981 connected over 200 computers connected from all around the world. Now the figure runs into millions.

The real power of today's Internet is that it is available to anyone with a computer and a telephone line. Internet places at an individual's hands the immense and invaluable power of information and communication.

Internet usage has significance increased over the past few years. The number of data packets, which flowed through the Internet, has increased dramatically. According to International Data Corporation ("IDC"), approximately 163 million individuals or entities will use the Internet by the end of this year as opposed to 16.1 million in 1999. If left to its own measure, it is highly unlikely that such a trend can reverse itself. Given this present state of the Internet, the necessity of Cyber Laws becomes all the more important.

Need for Cyber Laws

When Internet was developed, the founding fathers of Internet hardly had any inclination that Internet could transform itself into an all-pervading revolution, which could be misused for criminal activities and, which required regulation. Today, there are many disturbing things happening in cyberspace. Due to the anonymous nature of the Internet, it is possible to engage into a variety of misusing this aspect of the Internet to perpetuate criminal activities in cyberspace. Hence, the need for Cyber Laws.

What is Cyber Law?

Internet is believed to be full of anarchy and a system of law and regulation therein seems contradictory. However, cyberspace is being governed by a system of law and regulation called Cyber Law. There is no one exhaustive definition of the term "Cyber Law". Simply speaking, Cyber Law is a generic term, which refers to all the legal and regulatory aspects of Internet and the World Wide Web. Anything concerned with or related to or emanating from any legal aspects or issues concerning any activity of netizens and others, in Cyberspace comes within the ambit of Cyber Law. The growth of Electronic Commerce has propelled the need for vibrant and effective regulatory mechanisms, which would further strengthen the legal infrastructure, so crucial to the success of Electronic Commerce. All these regulatory mechanisms and legal infrastructures come within the domain of Cyber Law.

Importance of Cyber Laws

Cyber Law is important because it touches almost all aspects of transactions and activities on and concerning the Internet, the World Wide Web and Cyberspace. Initially it may seem that Cyber Laws is a very technical field and that it does not have any bearing to most activities in Cyberspace. But the actual truth is that nothing could be further than the truth. Whether we realize it or not, every action and every reaction in Cyberspace has some legal and Cyber legal perspectives.

Cyber Law and Common Man

Yes, Cyber Law does concern me. As the nature of Internet is changing and this new medium is being seen as the ultimate medium ever evolved in human history, every activity of yours in Cyberspace can and will have a Cyber Legal perspective. From the time you register your Domain Name, to the time you set up your web site, to the time you promote your web site, to the time you conduct electronic commerce transactions on the said site, at every point of time, there are various Cyber Law issues involved. You may not be bothered about these issues today because you may feel that they are very distant from you and that they do not have an impact on your Cyber activities. But sooner or later, you will have to tighten your belts and take note of Cyber Law for your own benefit.

For example, you may knowingly or unknowingly book a Domain Name, say www.xyx.com, which may be the trade mark of any other company, person or legal entity in any part of the world, say B. Domain Names are given to you on first come first served basis. But you may be involved by the other party being B in a Cyber legal dispute, which may allege that you are deliberately involved in the practice of Cyber squatting (the practice of knowingly registering the trade mark of any legal entity, company or person with the intention of holding on to handsome premium).

You may also be involved in Cyber litigation as the concerned party, B, may approach the World Intellectual Property Organization (WIPO) for adjudicating the matter and WIPO by a summary procedure may direct you to relinquish and release the said Domain Name to B, the concerned party. Needless to say, it shall be incumbent on the concerned party, B, to produce all documentary and other evidence to substantiate its claim to the concerned

Domain Name. This is just one of the many examples that show the importance of Cyber Law for you.

General Awareness about Cyber Law

Today, the awareness about Cyber Law is beginning to grow. Many technical experts in the beginning felt that legal regulation of Internet is not necessary. But with the rapid growth of technologies and Internet, it is crystal clear that no activity on Internet can remain free from the influence of Cyber Law. Publishing a Web page is an excellent way for any commercial business or entity to vastly increase its exposure to millions of persons, organizations and governments worldwide. It is that feature of the Internet, which is causing much controversy in the legal community.

Cyber Law Evolving Constantly

Yes, Cyber Law is constantly being evolved. As new and new opportunities and challenges are surfacing, Cyber Law, being a constantly evolving process, is suitably modifying itself to fit the call of the time. As the Internet grows, numerous legal issues arise. These issues vary from Domain Names, to Intellectual Property Rights to Electronic Commerce to Privacy to Encryption to Electronic Contracts to Cyber Crime to Online Banking to Spamming and so on. The list is very long.

Stage of Development of Cyber Law

Cyber Law today, on a global scale, is at an early stage of development. Just as different civilizations and societies in history have taken time to develop and refine their legal systems, in the case of Internet too, it will take some time for Cyber Laws to be fully developed and refined. Different countries in different parts of the world are adopting their own strategies to this new field.

Domain Names

Introduction to IP address

The Internet is a network of computers. Each computer on the said network has its own distinct entity and presence. That is the reason why every computer is given a distinct Electronic Address called the Internet Protocol address or in short IP address. This IP address is given by numerical values like 202.54.15.75. The IP address is just like any telephonic number, which renames a particular computer on the Internet.

What is a Domain name?

Since it is not possible to remember each and every numerical value of an IP address, the system of domain names evolved. Internet domain names, in a common man's language, are used as an easy-to-remember alias, which point to a specific IP address. The domain purpose of the domain name is simply to provide an easy method for remembering another's electronic address.

It's a unique name used to identify, among other things, a specific Web site. Thus, a typical domain name would be http: //www.indiainfoline.com/.

Components of a Domain Name

Any domain name consists of two components, namely, the top-level domain name (TLD) and a second level domain name. Thus, in the said example, http://www.indiainfoline.com, and ".com" would be the top-level domain name while "indiainfoline" would be second level domain name.

Different Categories of Top Level Domain Names (TLDs)

As on date, there are two categories of top-level domain names. In the first category come the domain names .com, .net, org, and .edu. When the system of registering domain names began, the norms were that the .com name is to be given to commercial organizations, while others such as org, .net, .gov and .edu are to be assigned to non-commercial organizations, network providers, governmental agencies and educational institutions respectively. However, as time has passed, due to the enhanced volumes of domain name registrations, the said norms have been abandoned and today anyone can, without any restriction of any kind whatsoever, register any domain name.

The second category of top-level domain names is the country code TLDs denoted by a two letters country code. For instance, the top-level domain name for India is **in**. The responsibility for assigning the same is given in each country to a specified country domain name registrar. In India, the TLD.in is registered by NCST at Bombay.

Who registers Domain Names?

The domain names were initially registered by Network Solutions only, who had the sole monopoly to register the said TLDs. This monopoly of Network Solutions continued for many years and only in 1999, the Internet Corporation Assigned Names and Numbers (ICANN) allowed other accredited registrars to register domain names. Today there are more than 100 registrars with whom one can register a TLD.

Unique feature of Domain Names

On "first come, first served" basis. This feature of domain names gives rise to numerous legal issues and disputes. Thus, the important thing in domain names registration is speed. To take an example, the domain name www.microsoft.org was available and was registered by Amit Mehrotra much before Microsoft Corporation could think of it. This led to numerous ticklish legal issues. Microsoft Corporation, despite having the trade mark Microsoft, could not get the domain name www.microsoft.org because of the "first come, first served" criteria of domain name registration.

How are Domain Names different from Trademarks?

To put it simply, Domain names are indeed different from trademarks. While it is possible that the same trade mark may be registered by different persons in different categories and different lines of business, it may be possible to only register one domain name corresponding to such trade mark. This aspect of domain names has led to numerous legal problems.

Cyber Squatting

Another legal issue surrounding domain names is that of Cyber squatting. Cyber Squatting is the practice by means of, which a person or legal entity books up the trade mark, business name or service mark of another as his own domain name for the purpose of holding on to it and thereafter selling the same domain name to the other person for valuable premium and consideration. Cyber Squatters book up domain names of important brands in the hope of earning quick millions.

Recent trends relating to tackling Cyber squatters

The Internet history has shown that while some corporate players have been willing to and have indeed coughed up money to get back their legitimate domain names, the recent trend is more towards taking the cyber squatters by the horns and fighting them out by legal processes. Courts throughout the world, including in India, have been pro-active and have been granting injunctions to stop cyber squatters from operating their web-sites.

Effective Remedy against Cyber squatting

The latest breath of fresh air in the fight against Cyber squatting has been the Uniform Domain Name Dispute Resolution Policy, which has been duly approved by ICANN. Under the said Domain Names Dispute Resolution Policy, a summary procedure is adopted to adjudicate the complaint of any complainant relating to any domain name on payment of processing fees. This policy has been in operation since the end of last year.

Indian Scene

Legitimate domain names. The domain name www.theeconomictimes.com and www.timeesofindia.com have been won back under the said policy. Two recent successes for Indian Companies under the said policy include winning back the domain names www.tata.org and www.philipsindia.com by TATA and Philips India respectively.

Cyber Crime

What is Cyber Crime?

When Internet was developed, the founding fathers of Internet hardly had any inclination that Internet could also be misused for criminal activities. Today, there are many disturbing things happening in cyberspace. Cyber Crime refers to all the activities done with criminal intent in cyberspace. These could be either the criminal activity in the conventional sense or could be activities, newly evolved with the growth of the new medium. Because of the anonymous nature of the Internet, it is possible to engage into a variety of criminal activities with impunity and people with intelligence, have been grossly misusing this aspect of the

Internet to perpetuate criminal activities in cyberspace. The field of Cyber Crime is just emerging and new forms of criminal activities in cyberspace are coming to the forefront with the passing of each new day.

Exhaustive definition of Cyber Crime?

There can be no one exhaustive definition about Cyber Crime. However, any activities, which basically offend human sensibilities, can also be included in its ambit. Child Pornography on the Internet constitutes one serious Cyber Crime. Similarly, online pedophiles, using Internet to induce minor children into sex, are as much Cyber criminals as any others.

Various categories of Cyber Crimes

Cyber Crimes can be basically divided into 3 major categories being Cyber Crimes against persons, property and Government.

Cyber Crimes against Persons

Cyber Crimes committed against persons include various crimes like transmission of child pornography, harassment of anyone with the use of a computer such as e-mail, and cyber-stalking.

The trafficking, distribution, posting, and dissemination of obscene material including pornography, indecent exposure, and child pornography, constitutes one of the most important Cyber Crimes known today. The potential harm of such a crime to humanity can hardly be overstated. This is one Cyber Crime, which threatens to undermine the growth of the younger generation as also leave irreparable scars and injury on the younger generation, if not controlled.

Is Cyber Harassment also a Cyber Crime?

Cyber Harassment is a distinct Cyber Crime. Various kinds of harassment can and does occur in cyberspace, or through the use of cyberspace. Harassment can be sexual, racial, religious, or other. Persons perpetuating such harassment are also guilty of Cyber Crimes.

Cyber Harassment as a crime also brings us to another related area of violation of privacy of netizens. Violation of privacy of online citizens is a Cyber Crime of a grave nature. No one likes any other person invading the precious and extremely touchy area of his or her own privacy, which the medium of Internet grants to the netizen.

Cyber Crimes against property

The second category of Cyber Crimes is that of Cyber Crimes against all forms of property. These crimes include unauthorized computer trespassing through cyberspace, computer vandalism, transmission of harmful programs, and unauthorized possession of computerized information.

Is Hacking Cyber Crime?

Hacking and cracking are amongst the gravest Cyber Crimes known till date. It is a dreadful feeling to know that a stranger has broken into your computer systems without your knowledge and consent and has tampered with precious confidential date and information. Coupled with this, the actuality is that no computer system in the world is hacking proof. It is unanimously agreed that any and every system in the world can be hacked.

The recent denial of service attacks seen over the popular commercial sites like E-bay, Yahoo, Amazon and others are a new category of Cyber Crimes, which are slowly emerging as being extremely dangerous. Using one's own programming abilities as also various programmes with malicious intent to gain unauthorized access to a computer or network are very serious crimes. Similarly, the creation and dissemination of harmful computer programs are virii, which do irreparable damage to computer systems is another kind of Cyber Crime. Software piracy is also another distinct kind of Cyber Crime, which is perpetuated by many people online who distribute illegal and unauthorized pirated copies of software.

Cyber Crime against Government

The third category of Cyber Crimes relates to Cyber Crimes against Government. Cyber Terrorism is one distinct kind of crime in this category. The growth of Internet has shown that individuals and groups to threaten the international governments as also to terrorize the citizens of a country are using the medium of Cyber Space. This crime manifests into terrorism when an individual "cracks" into a government or military maintained web site.

Comprehensive law on Cyber Crime

Development has to take place in terms of putting into place the relevant legal mechanism for controlling and preventing Cyber Crime. As of now, there is absolutely no comprehensive law on Cyber Crime anywhere in the world. This is reason that the investigating agencies like FBI are finding the Cyberspace to be an extremely difficult terrain. These various Cyber Crimes fall into that Grey area of Internet law, which is neither fully nor partially covered by the existing laws and that too in some countries.

A Recent Case

The most recent case of the virus "I love you" demonstrates the need for having Cyber Laws concerning Cyber Crimes in different national jurisdictions. At the time of the web publication of this feature, Reuters has reported that "The Philippines has yet to arrest the suspected creator of the 'Love Bug' computer virus because it lacks laws that deal with computer crime, a senior police officer said". The fact of the matter is that there are no laws relating to Cyber Crime in the Philippines. The National Bureau of Investigation is finding it difficult to legally arrest the suspect behind the 'Love Bug' computer virus. As such, the need for countries to legislate Cyber Laws relating to Cyber Crime arises on an urgent priority basis.

US Courts regarding Cyber Crimes

The Courts in United States of America have already begun taking cognizance of various kinds of fraud and Cyber Crimes being perpetuated in Cyberspace. For the victims of various Cyber Crimes, there is no one healing remedy. They can either file for civil damages or wait for the culprits to be nabbed and then to be tried under provisions, existing or envisaged, which are not comprehensive at all. However, a lot of work has to be done in this field. Just as human mind is ingenious enough to devise new ways for perpetuating crime, similarly, human ingenuity needs to be channeled into developing effective legal and regulatory mechanisms to control and prevent Cyber Crimes.

Fighting Cyber Crime

We all remember that Cyberspace is a common heritage of ours, which we have inherited in our life times from the benefits of ever growing technologies. This Cyberspace is the lifeline of the entire universe and given its irreversible position today, it is the duty of every netizen to contribute toward making the said cyberspace free of any trouble or Cyber Crime. To rephrase the famous words of Rabindra Nath Tagore in today's context, "Where the Cyberspace is *****tireless striving stretches its arms towards perfection into that cyber heaven of freedom. 0 my father, let our humanity awake."

2

Cyber Terrorism

Cyber Terrorism-Fact or Fancy

"We are at risk. Increasingly, America depends on computers. They control power delivery, communications, aviation, and financial service. They are used to store vital information, from medical records to business plans to criminal records. Although we trust them, they are vulnerable to the effects of poor design and insufficient quality control, to accident, and perhaps most alarmingly, to deliberate attack. The modern thief can steel more damage with a keyboard than with a bomb".

Thus, began the opening chapter of one of the foundation books in the computer security field. This book, commissioned by the National Academy of sciences, was the product of twenty-one experts in their field and was a proposed blueprint for future computer security in the United States. In the six years since this was written, computers and information technology has exploded. But most people, including those in the computer field, believe the above statement to still be true.

The combination of two of the great of the late twentieth century is combined in the term "cyber terrorism". The fear of random, violent victimization segues well with the distrust and outright fear of computer technology. Both capitalize on the fear of the unknown. It is easy to distrust that, which one is not able to control.

Terrorism, with its roots in the periphery of mainstream society, is feared. It is perceived as being random, incomprehensible and uncontrollable. Groups with obscure names and origins impact catastrophically on the innocent. It is in fact, designed to be feared. That is its real power.

Technology is feared from two perspectives. First it is by definition arcane. It is complex, abstract and indirect in its impact on individuals. Because computers do things that used-to-be-done by humans, there is a natural fear related to a loss of control. People believe that technology has the ability to become the master and humanity the servant.

The popular press has further the fifes by "hyping" the concept of convergence. According to the press, one is led to believe that all of the functions controlled by individual computers will all converge into a singular system. Further support for this scenario is the increase in "connectivity". Many people conclude that the entire world will soon be controlled by a single computer system.

Ironically, these same people subjectively understand that since computers are products of, and operated by, human being; they are not reliable in either a mechanical or logical sense. Certainly, there can be no doubt as to immense automobiles there is risks. Most risks can be managed. It is the unmanageable risks that we fear. This paper will address what risks and possibilities are of combining terrorism and computers.

Before we can discuss the possibilities of cyber terrorism, we must have some working definitions. The word cyber terrorism refers to two elements cyberspace and terrorism.

Another word for cyberspace in the virtual world. Barry Collin defines the virtual world as symbolic true, false, binary, metaphoric representations of information-that lace in, which computer programs function and data moves.

Terrorism is a much-used term, with many definitions. For the purpose of this presentation, we will use the United States department of state definition.

The term terrorism means premeditated, politically motivated violence perpetrated against noncombatant targets by sub national groups or clandestine agents.

If we combine these definitions, we construct a working definition such as the following:

Cyber terrorism is the premeditated, politically motivated attack against information, computer system, computer programs, and data, which result in violence against noncombatant targets-by, sub national groups or clandestine agents.

This definition is necessarily narrow. For the term cyber terrorism to have any meaning, we must be able to differentiate it from other kinds of computer would suggest that the letter is an offensive function of governments.

In United States v. Morris, "Robert Morris was charged for preventing authorized use of computers and loss caused thereof".

Reasons for Cyber Terrorism

These traditional tools of terrorism explosive bullets and especially nuclear, chemical and biological weapons are dangerous not only to terrorists target to but to the terrorist himself.

Terrorism and the Internet are related in two ways. First, the Internet has become a forum for terrorist groups and individual terrorists both to spread their messages of hate and violence and to communicate with one another and with sympathizers. Secondly, individuals and groups try to attack computer networks, including those on the Internet what has become known as cyber terrorism or cyber warfare?

At this point, terrorist is using the Internet more than they are attacking it. At least 12 of the 30 groups on the state department's list of designated foreign terrorist organizations maintain. Web sites on the Internet, While U.S. terrorist, most groups appear to use the Internet to spread their propaganda. Report that As long as they don't specifically engage in criminal acts, they can do anything they want to aid and abet their activities. This is a safe haven for them.

Some Israeli and U.S. officials believe that terrorists from Hamas and Islamic Jihad use the Internet to provide specific instructions to fellow terrorists including maps, photographs, directions, codes and technical details of how to use explosives.

In addition to terrorist sites, the World Wide Web also contains dozens of sites run by domestic white supremacist and militia groups using the information superhighway to promote their radical anti U.S. government terrorists and activities as well as would be secessionist groups such as the self proclaimed Republic Texas.

According to the Bureau of Alcohol, Tobacco, and Firearms, Federal agents investigating at least 30 bombings and four attempted bombings between 1985 and June 1996 recovered bomb-making literature that the suspects had obtained from the Internet. Among the many examples in February 1996, three junior high school students from Syracuse, NY were charged with plotting to set off a homemade bomb in their school based on plans they had found on the Internet. While many have called for laws restricting the publication of bomb making instructions on the Internet, others have pointed out that this material is already easily accessible in bookstores and libraries.

Responding to terrorist Web sites is an extremely sensitive and delicate issue most of the rhetoric disseminated on the Internet is considered protected speech under the first amendment. Furthermore, although web sites belonging to terrorist groups are public the FBI is precluded from keeping files on them. Agents may surf the Internet but they cannot save material from a Web site on a regular basis unless they are conducting a criminal investigation.

In October 1998, Pennsylvania Attorney General Mike Fisher filed a complaint against the white supremacist group Alpha HQ, of Philadelphia, for publishing terrorist threats, harassing messages and ethnic intimidation on its Internet Web page. Among other things, the group published a picture depicting the bombing of Pennsylvania's Reading Berks Human Relations Council office and featured a picture of the Assistant Director at the Pennsylvania Human Relations Commission on the same page as the exploding building.

Abroad cyber crime has already assumed a political agenda. In August 1997, a group calling itself the Internet black tigers affiliated with the Liberation Tigers of Tamil Eelam claimed responsibility for E-mail harassment of several Sri Lankan missions around the world. The group claimed in Internet postings to be specialists in suicide-e-mail bombings with the goal of countering the Sri Lankan Government.

Elsewhere, Internet saboteurs defaced the Home Page of, and stole E-mail from India's Bhabha Atomic Research Center in May and June 1998. The three anonymous saboteurs claimed in an Internet interview to have been protesting recent Indian nuclear blasts. In July, the leader of a Chinese cracker group (a cracker is someone who breaks into a computer or system).

In the fall of 1997 the president COM mission on critical infrastructure protection concluded that the U.S. infrastructure is increasingly vulnerable to attack and that local, stage and federal officials are not prepared to deal with the problem.

A major ongoing debate related to terrorism and the Internet is the question of encryption. Encryption is software technology that locks computerized information to keep it private. Only those with an electronic key can deciphered the information.

Encryption protects individual and corporate privacy and is a fundamental building block of electronic commerce. But police and intelligence agencies oppose denying the government accesses to electronic information because terrorists and other criminals can use encryption technology to conduct illegal activities while avoiding government monitoring. World Trade Center bombing mastermind, Ramiz Ahmed your self for example utilized encryption technology in his foiled plot to blow up 11 U.S. airlines in the Far East.

While the motivations of terrorists might essentially remain the same, we are now facing new and unfamiliar weapons. The intelligence systems, tactics, security procedures and equipment that were once expected to protect people, systems, and nations, are virtually powerless against a new and very devastating classification of weapons. Also, many of the methods of counter-terrorism honed over the years and ineffectual against this enemy.

New Perspectives for Cyber Terrorism

Cyber Terrorism requires some new perspectives. The following concepts must be considered in order to fully understand cyber terrorism threats:

1. The motivations behind a cyber terrorist may be the same as any other type of terrorist attack. Cyber Terrorism is another tool, as are explosive and automatic weapons.
2. The individuals or organizations executing these acts may not necessarily be those committed to the outcome of the act. Cyber Terrorism can require technical expertise that exists outside the realm of a terrorist organization.

   Frequently, a system cracker may be hired to execute the cyber terrorism act. This may be a professional looking for money. Or it may be a teenager, looking for a challenge. The recruitment process may or may not include the cause.
3. Like many terrorist attacks there may not be warming. However, with Cyber Terrorism one may not even know that the act has taken place until sometimes after the attack. Attack on computer systems can go unnoticed, even after penetration. Cyber terrorists may be in the system several times before the act takes place for reconnaissance or experimentation. Also, the act may tied to a delay, much like a bomb timer, set to execute when a certain time span or a certain event takes place.
4. The cost of such an act is minimal, and the tools and information are ubiquitous. While tracing terrorist payloads is often possible with nuclear, biological, or even

some chemical weapons. Cyber Terrorism requires only an inexpensive personal computer, modem, phone line, and software tools-tools, which are available free and in multiple locations on the Internet. Tracing a terrorist equipment or even his activities are complex and frequently near impossible to accomplish in real time.

5. Intelligence gathering on Cyber Terrorism is difficult. Tradecraft and Intel gathering is complicated by virtual meetings, drops-sites, encryption, and stenography discussed later in this chapter.
6. Finally, the prevention of attacks requires more co-ordination than almost any other form of terrorism. The explosion of inter networks the connection of trusted to non-trusted systems, and myriad other factors, along with reliance and dependence on computerized systems, makes cyber terrorism one of the most difficult threats to prevent.

What is the bottom line? As cyber terrorism relates to traditional counter-terrorism, while many of the players may be the same, the playing fields, and some of the rules of the game, have changed.

Where do Acts of Cyber Terrorism occur?

When we speak of where a cyber terrorism act may occur, we are not specifically referring to a physical location.

Geography is limitless and irrelevant when dealing with cyber Terrorism threats. We must think in terms of cyber terrorists acts as happening in cyberspace, regardless of locale or origination or target. The systems that are most likely to be attacked are at the-point where we are most vulnerable, the point at, which the physical and virtual worlds converge. Let us first define these two domains.

The political world is matter and energy-light, dark, hot and cold, all physical matter-that place in, which we live and function.

The virtual world is symbolic-true, false, binary, metaphoric representations of information-that place in, which computer programs function and data moves.

The physical and virtual worlds are inherently separately worlds. However, it is at the interaction, the convergence, of these two worlds that stands as the most likely location of a cyber terrorist's acts.

United States v. Carlia Communications, Inc., 815 F. 2d 1367.

Which upheld that a federal state prohibiting the interstate transmission of only tangible objects, not intangible objects.

Attack on World Trade Center

The September 11, 2001 attacks on the World Trade Center and the Pentagon made it tragically obvious that terrorism has reached a new level of sophistication. Without the use of traditional weapons or tactics, a network of terrorists gained access to intellectual and physical resources and used them in an incredibly effective fashion as weapons of destruction against the civilian population. The terrorist familiarity with the hijacked aircraft U.S. flight procedures and regulations carrier schedules payloads and distances all indicate careful and deliberate research planning and execution. The Internet has provided terrorists with a deadly new weapon in their arsenal. The web contains a virtual encyclopaedia of information that terrorists can use to plan and execute every aspect of attacks. It also furnishes them with a vast global network over, which they can communicate and exchange information hack into sensitive databases and procure resources Federal Aviation Administration (FAA) information on flight and pilot procedures and training also are accessible on the internet. Access to flight training facilities might easily have been researched and arranged via Internet long before they entered the country.

As per the Federal Bureau of Investigation terrorism is defined as 'the unlawful use of force or violence against persons or property to intimidate or coerce a government the civilian population or any segment thereof, in furtherance of political or social objective". Cyber-terrorism could therefore be defined as the use of computing resources to intimidate or coerce others instead of using the traditional methods of killing taking hostage and guerrilla warfare terrorists now use the Internet to cause much wider damage to a country. Instead of disabling a country's military defenses and shutting off the power in a large city, the terrorists can affect more people at much less risk to them. As an example, one can hack into the computer network of a Bank and leave an encrypted threatening message for senior directors saying that if they do not pay desired amount of money they would use anything from logic bombs to high emission radio frequency guns to destroy the Bank's files Stored in their computers. Most of the Banks would rather pay the money than letting the public know how vulnerable they are.

Another example of cyber-terrorism could he hacking into a hospital computer system and changing the patient's medicine prescription to a lethal dose as an act of revenge.

There are many such examples of cyber terrorism in its many forms. It sounds a far-fetched activity, but such things can and do happen. Computer users and the professionals should he aware of possible areas of weakness to such terrorism, to protect their computer Systems. The US Commission of Critical Infrastructure Protection, instituted during 1996 to create cyber terrorism awareness, found that the combination of electricity, communication and computers are necessary to the survival of the US, all of, which can be threatened by cyber warfare Zeran v. America on Line, 129 f.3d 327.

The outlined the reason of such immunity by saying that congress recognized the internet and interactive computer services as offering a forum for a true diversity of political discourse, unique opportunities for cultural development and myriad avenues for intellectual activity.

Cyber Warfare

The Internet has created the biggest threat of being exposed to the cyber warfare also known as information warfare. Information warfare is defined as the offensive and defensive use of information and information systems to deny, exploit, corrupt, or destroy an adversary's information, information-based processes and computer-based networks while protecting one's own. The weapons used in this warfare are simple, a personal computer, a keyboard, a mouse and an Internet connection. This war could also be found from a cyber cafe. With these weapons an adversary can play havoc with a country's economy, business and state secrets including defense. The Cyber war threatens not only the traditional military targets but also the IT-enable economic lifeline of a country, which were out of bounds for enemy attacks during a conventional war.

Many countries have established complex IT infrastructures to manage electricity generation and supply banking air traffic control, oil and gas and various other information based civic amenities, which could become easy targets of cyber attack. The Internet makes these Systems within the reach of hostile person(s) anywhere in the world. Such critical system should be isolated from outside connection or protected by adequate firewalls, use best practices for password control and protection and use protected action logs. The CIA has also created its Information Warfare Center, with 1000 people and a 24-hour response team, to deal with cyber terrorism. The US Air Force has created Electronic Security Engineering Teams (ESET) to proactively handle cyber-terrorism.

Cyber war can be against a nation, a corporate house or an individual. At the individual level the attacker may be engaging in this warfare for revenge, financial gains, mischief's, blackmail or for some other darker motives. At the corporate level, the cyber war goes much beyond the attacks associated with corporate espionage. The target of warfare at the corporate level is business through the information stored on the corporate computer system, essential to perform daily operations pertaining to the image or reputation of the company. It involves theft of secrets from a company and releasing the secrets, or even falsified secrets, that can damage the company in such a way that its survival is at stake.

India has also been a victim of the cyber war from across the borders and the cyber-space has become another flash point after Kashmir. Hackers, reportedly from Pakistan, have been hacking and defacing Indian sites with alarming frequency. During the last two years hackers who claim to have Pakistani affiliations have attacked more than 40 Indian Web sites. During December 2000, a notorious group of hackers, called G-Force Pakistan, hacked a site Zeetv.com and posted a message on Kashmir as well as derogatory remarks on Indian Army and Indian Government. G-Force has also hacked to sites of Indian Science Congress Asian Age newspaper, National Research Center, Agricultural University of Maharashtra, Indian Institute of Management, Ahmedabad, the Gujarat Government, Center for Electronics Design and Technology, Indian Institute of Technology, Madras, among several others. Pakistan Hacked Club, reportedly led by Doctor Nuker, who claims to be its founder, has hacked web sites of Indian Parliament, Ahmedabad Telephone Exchange, Engineering

Export Promotion Council and United Nation (India). Nightman, another active group of hackers has hacked and defaced the Web sites of the government and the Indian companies, viz., Lal Bahadur Shastri National Academy of Administration, Blue Star Info Tech., and Mahindra and Mahindra.

As per the report appeared in The Times of India, during October, 2001, hackers in USA are waging a cyber war against Osama Bin Laden and his allies, despite warning from the US Government and security experts that this activity may be counterproductive. Kim Schmitz, a German hacker turned security consultant, reportedly launched a Web site to recruit hackers for tracking down funds and other evidence linking Bin Laden to the September 11, 2001 terrorist attacks. Schmitz launched group called Young Intelligent Hackers Against Terror (YIHAT), which now has 34 people from 10 different countries and 3 Arabic language translators. It is claimed that these hackers have already tracked down Bin Laden's Bank accounts in a Bank in Sudan. Another US-based hacker group, known as 'The Dispatchers' has also launched a campaign against the sites deemed-to-be linked with Osama Bin Laden and Taliban regime in Afghanistan. This group claims to have shut down the Web site of the presidential palace of Afghanistan as well, as some Iranian and Palestinian sites.

United States V. Rice, 1992 U.S. App. LEXIS 9562.

The fraud of Rice did not cause any pecuniary loss but involved unauthorized access and unauthorized disclosure of confidential information. Rice was convicted by a jury of computer fraud for accessing the computer system of a government agency without any authority and his conviction was later on confirmed.

Examples of Cyber terrorism Act

Let's take a look at a few examples of potential cyber terrorist acts. These examples are not potential acts we may see in the future. These are all situations that could happen today, with today's technology.

A cyber terrorist will remotely access the processing control systems of a cereal manufacturer, change the levels of iron supplement, and sickness and kill the children of a national enjoying their food.

That cyber terrorist will then perform similar report alternations at a processor of infant formulates. The key the cyber terrorist does not have to be at the factory to execute these acts.

A cyber terrorist will place a number of computerized bombs around a city, all simultaneously transmitting unique numeric patterns, each bomb receiving each other's pattern. If bomb one stops transmitting all the bombs detonate simultaneously.

3

Cyber Stalking

Introduction

The Oxford dictionary defines stalking as "pursuing stealthily". Stalking or being 'followed' is a problem that many people, especially women, are familiar with. Their privacy is invaded; their every move is watched. It is a form of harassment, and can disrupt the life of the victim and leave them feeling very afraid and threatened.

Sometimes these problems (harassment & stalking) can occur over the Internet.

This is known as cyber stalking. Cyber stalking is when a person is followed and pursued online. Cyber stalking involves following a person's movements across (he Internet by posting messages (sometimes threatening) on the bulletin boards frequented by the victim, entering the chat-rooms frequented by the victim, constantly bombarding the victim with e-mails, etc.

The Internet mirrors the real world. That means it also reflects real life and real people with real problems. Although it is rare, Cyber stalking does occur. Cyber stalking usually occurs with women, who are stalked by men, or children who are stalked by adult predators or pedophiles. A cyber stalker does not have to leave his home to find, or harass his targets, and has no fear of physical violence since he believes he cannot be physically touched in cyberspace. He may be on the other side of the earth or a neighbour or even a relative. And stalker could be of either sex.

Typically, the cyber stalker's victim is new on the web, and inexperienced with the rules of netiquette and Internet safety. Their main targets are mostly the females, children, emotionally weak or unstable, etc. Sometimes men are also stalked, but it is believed that over 75% of the victims are female on assumed basis and the actual figures can really never be known since most crimes of such nature go unreported.

Fagan v. Metropolitan Police Commissioner, (1969) 1 QB 349; Venna, (1976) QB 421; Sevage, (1992) 1 AC 699, 740).

Assault, in its technical or "psychic" sense is any act by, which D intentionally or recklessly causes P to apprehend immediate and unlawful personal violence.

Cyber stalkers can be categorized into 3 types

(1) The common obsessional cyber stalker

The common obsessional stalker refuses to believe that their relationship is over. Do not be misled by believing this stalker is harmlessly in love.

(2) The delusional cyber stalker

The next type is the delusional stalker. They may be suffering from some mental illness like schizophrenia, etc. and have a false belief that keeps them tied to their victims. They assume that the victim loves them even though they have never met.

A delusional stalker is usually a loner and most often chooses victims who are married women, a celebrity or doctors, teachers, etc. Those in the noble and helping professions like doctors, teachers, etc. are at often at risk for attracting a delusional stalker. Delusional stalkers are very difficult to shake off.

(3) The vengeful cyber stalker

These cyber stalkers are angry with their victim due to some minor reason-either real or imagined. Typical examples are disgruntled employees. These stalkers may be stalking to get even and take revenge and believe that 'they" have been victimized. Ex-spouses can turn into this type of stalker.

Kinds of Cyber Stalking

Two different kinds of cyber stalking situations, which can occur: -

1. Online harassment and cyber stalking that occurs and continues on the Internet.
2. Online harassment and staling that begin to be carried on off-line too. This is when a stalker may attempt to trace a telephone number or a street address. Always be careful what details you give out over the web and to whom.

The Times, May 14, 1996 cited from Allen, R. v. Johnson (Anthony Thomas), a panel of the Court of Appeal affirmed the conviction of the appellant of public nuisance based on his numerous obscene telephone calls over a period of five and a half years to thirteen different women in a particular area.

What Motivates a Cyber Stalker?

(1) Sexual Harassment

This should not surprise anyone, especially women, since sexual harassment is also a very common experience off-line. The Internet reflects real life and consists of real people. It's not a separate, regulated or sanctified world. The very nature of anonymous communications also makes it easier to be a stalker on the Internet than a stalker off-line.

(2) Obsession for love

This could begin from an online romance, where one-person halts the romance and the rejected lover cannot accept the end of the relationship. It could also be an online romance that moves to real life, only to break-up once the persons really meet. Then, that person again can not accept the NO. Sometimes, this obsession stalking can even start from real life and then move over to cyberspace.

One of the problems with obsession stalking is that since it often starts as real romance, much personal information is shared between persons involved. This makes it easy for the cyber stalker to harass their victim. Some users online enjoy "breaking hearts" as a pastime, and so may well set up obsessions for their own enjoyment-games that they may later regret having played.

Sometimes, an obsession can also be a fixation by a stranger on another user for no valid reason. Since these obsession stalkers live in a dream world, it is not always necessary for the target to have done anything to attract her (or his) attention in the first place. Obsession stalkers are usually jealous and possessive people.

Death threats via e-mail or through live chat messages are a manifestation of obsession stalking.

(3) Revenge and Hate

This could be an argument that has gone out of hand, leading eventually to a hate and revenge relationship. Revenge vendettas are often the result of something you may have said or done online, which may have offended someone. Vendettas often begin with arguments where you may have been rude to another user.

Sometimes, hate cyber stalking is for no reason at all (out of the blue)- you will not know why you have been targeted nor what you have done, and you may not even know who it is, who is doing this to you and even the cyber stalker does not know you. In fact, you have not been individually targeted at all-someone that does not know you have chosen you as a random target! This stalker may be using the net to let out his frustrations online.

(4) Ego and Power Trips

These are harassers or stalkers online showing off their skills to themselves and their friends. They do not have any grudge against you-they are rather using you to 'show-off' their power to their friends or doing it just for fun and you have been unlucky enough to be chosen.

Most people who receive threats online imagine their harasser to be large and powerful. But in fact the threat may come from a child who does not really have any means of carrying out the physical threats made.

It is estimated that there are about 2,00,000 real-life stalkers in America today. Roughly one in 1,250 persons is a stalker-and that is a large ratio. Of course, no one knows the truth, since the Internet is such a vast medium, but these figures are as close as it gets to give statistics.

Out of the estimated 79 million population worldwide on the Internet at any given time, we could find 63,000 Internet stalkers travelling the information superhighway, stalking approximately 4,74,000 victims.

How do they operate?

(a) Collect all personal information about the victim such as name, family background, Telephone Numbers of residence and work place, daily routine of the victim, address of residence and place of work, date of birth, etc.

If the stalker is one of the acquaintances of the victim he can easily get this information. If stalker is a stranger to victim, he collects the information from the Internet resources such as various profiles the victim may have filled in while opening the chat or e-mail account or while signing an account with some web site.

(b) The stalker may post this information on any web site related to sex services or dating services, posing as if the victim is posting this information and invite the people to call the victim on her telephone numbers to have sexual services. Stalker even uses very filthy and obscene language to invite the interested persons.

(c) People of all kind from nook and corner of the world, who come across this information, start calling the victim at her residence and/or work place, asking for sexual services or relationships.

(d) Some stalkers subscribe the e-mail account of the victim to innumerable pornographic and sex sites, because of, which victim starts receiving such kind of unsolicited e-mails.

(e) Some stalkers keep on sending repeated e-mails asking for various kinds of favors or threaten the victim.

(f) In online stalking the stalker can make third party to harass the victim?

(g) Follow their victim from board to board. They "hangout" on the same BB's as their victim, many times posting notes to the victim, making sure the victim is aware that he/she is being followed. Many times they will "Flame" their victim (becoming argumentative, insulting) to get their attention.

(h) Stalkers will almost always make contact with their victims through e-mail. The letters may be loving, threatening, or sexually explicit. He will many times use multiple names when contacting the victim.

(i) Contact victim via telephone. If the stalker is able to access the victim's telephone, he will many times make calls to the victim to threaten, harass, or intimidate them.

How would you protect yourself?

A cyber stalker looks for weaknesses in people. He or she is cunning and crafty. People looking for sympathy or wanting to make friends, find romance online, etc. are an open invitation to many types of stalkers.

NO ONE has a right to harass, threaten and disturb you. Once harassment becomes a threat against you, then the harasser has also broken the law and there are a number of steps you CAN take to deal with it including taking help of the Police department.

Trying to work out what you have "done" to deserve this will get you nowhere-the attack or harassment will often appear as motiveless and you may have difficulty understanding the psychology of the harasser. With some kinds of online harassment it is better not to waste time trying to work out "why" and to concentrate rather on what you can do to protect yourself and how to end this nightmare.

Case of Cyber Stalking

Abrar Ashraf Khatri, a student of class 7th and resident of Kidwai Marg, Wadala, was a regular visitor to Internet cafes. In May, he came into contact with Pens Williams, a resident of Apurva building, Opposite Recreation Club, Andheri (W), through the Net. They became close friends and started meeting each other after working hours.

His father, Ashraf, got wind of the friendship in July when Abrar did not attend school one day and remained missing the entire day. He was finally located loitering in Wadala and brought back home.

On November 2, Abrar left home again. Ashraf lodged a missing person complaint with the Rafi Ahmed Kidwai Marg police station under Sections 363 and 368 of the Indian Penal Code.

He also informed the police of Abrar's friendship with Williams. When the police questioned Williams, she refused to co-operate and asked them to produce a search warrant. Meanwhile, Abrar kept passing on message to his parents through his cousin Naseer.

Finally, the case was transferred to Deputy Commissioner of Police (Prevention) Dr. Pradnya Sarvade, who directed the MPB to investigate. The MPB approached Videsh Sanchar Nigam Ltd. (VSNL) and found that Abrar used to frequent Ganesh Birazdar Cafe in Dombivli (E) to keep in touch with his cousin. They then nabbed the boy on one of his visits to the cafe.

Senior Inspector Kiran Kacheshwar Pagare said "After interrogating Abrar, we found that he was likely to be taken to Pakistan as Williams had asked him to bring his passport along with him when he left his home on November 2. Williams had kept the boy at her Andheri home from November 2 to 4.

Later, she shifted him to a friend's place in Kalyan. She told him to assume the same Ajay Sharma, gave him expensive clothes, shoes, a gold chain, Rs. 2,000 and her mobile phone and promised him that she would send him to Pakistan and make him rich." Pagare said that the case had been handed back to the RAK Marg police and that Williams is likely to he arrested.

4

Invasion of Privacy

Introduction

Today whenever you visit a site and want to get yourself to he part of that web site, let it be any site like e-mail account, business online, enjoyment site, etc. you have to register yourself on that site by entering your personal information like name, your address, telephone number, your hobbies and like information. Many companies make money of that information by selling it to other companies or firms online so as they further can use information for their own business sake. These credit companies and other organizations collect this data on millions of citizens daily. Much of the data is created while interacting with government and private organizations. Exactly, these thing organizations know about you.

- Credit history
- Income
- Personal data (Social security number, age, family history, ethnicity, religion, etc.)
- Reading material (magazines, books, etc.)
- Reading material (magazines, books, etc.)
- Listening preferences
- Motor vehicle information
- Federal, state, and private loans
- Telephone calls
- Medical information
- Insurance information
- Schools records
- Employment history
- Legal hearing and judgments
- Marital history

Sometimes consumers supply data knowingly, but do not realize how the data may be used later. Unlike the government, private organizations depend on information for profit. This personal information ends up being recorded in many different places as businesses sell information to other private organizations.

The federal government is about the biggest data collector of all and information collected on an individual can be retrieve by keying in the person's social security number. Does the government really need so much data on individuals?

Some of the hottest buzz about the Internet is the issue of privacy. Everyone on the Internet deserves privacy. Concerns about privacy are the leading reason non-Internet users stay off the Web.

Inset Systems, Inc. v. Instructions Set, Inc., 937 F. SUPP 161.

The Court held that advertising over the Internet was purposefully directed towards the Forum State.

Invasion of privacy can take various forms on the Internet:

- Spam-unwanted e-mails
- Cookies-lead web sites back to your computer
- Hackers-access computer stored information

Electronic mail is a wonderful way of communicating but it is often abused. The constant filing of their e-mail boxes with unwanted information usually annoys people.

Depending on what you do when visit a site, you may provide information about your visit to the web site's owner. It is important to know what a site's privacy policies are. If the site does not say, then perhaps you should ask. As web sites for major companies need to be secured against hackers or persons with malicious intent.

The Internet is a huge technological issue, but due to the privacy issue some people are afraid to make purchases on the net, government needs to make laws to protect these privacy issues. In the US, the law is not doing much to protect your privacy. But in Europe, legislators have passed a law called the "European Union Protection Initiative for the same".

Martiz, Inc. v. Cyber gold, Inc., 947 Supp. 1328.

Finding that it had jurisdiction over a California defendant in a trade mark infringement case where the defendant's only contact with the state was through its California-based web site, which was accessible in Missouri.

5

Hacking

Introduction

Hacking in simple terms means an illegal intrusion into a computer system and/or network. There is an equivalent term to hacking, i.e., cracking, but from Indian Laws Perspective there is no difference between the term hacking and cracking.

"Every act committed towards breaking into a computer and/or network is hacking."

Hackers write or use ready-made computer programs to attack the target computer. They possess the desire to destruct and they get the kick out of such destruction. Some hackers hack for personal monetary gains, such as to stealing the credit card information, transferring money from various bank accounts to their own account followed by withdrawal of money. They extort money from some corporate giant threatening him to publish the stolen information, which is critical in nature. Government web sites are the hot targets of the hackers due to the press coverage it receives because hackers do enjoy the media coverage.

Motives behind the Crime

- Greed
- Adventure
- Destructive mindset
- Power
- Wants to sell n/w security services
- Desire to access forbidden information

Indian hackers always thought they were too sophisticated to fall into the hands of the rough cops in this country, whom various human rights groups routinely accused of brutality. But that feeling evaporated after one of the four people arrested recently in connection with a hacking incident, one of who accused Mumbai police of breaking his hand during interrogation.

Jurisdiction

Bensusan Restaurant Corp. v. King, 126 F 3d 25, 29.

No personal jurisdiction was found where a web publisher in Missouri published a general access web page that contained ticketing and event information about a jazz dub known as "the blue note" in Columbia, Missouri.

Resuscitation Technologies Inc. v. Continental Health Care Corp., 1997 US Dist. Lexis 3523.

"The New York defendant had extensive communication with the Indian plaintiff, including 80 e-mails the Court in Indiana found the level of activity directed to Indian was substantial, thus giving Indiana personal jurisdiction over the defendant".

The Hacking case in Indian and action against it:

While the charge hasn't been substantiated, hackers in Mumbai admitted to being petrified. And the police, while denying the incident, don't sound too apologetic.

"Let hackers know that some tough people are out here", said Senior Inspector.

It all started when 23 year old Anand Khare, who calls himself Dr. Neukar, gained control over ccicmumbai.com the site of Mumbai cops' Cyber Crime Cell, or CCC. He pasted abuses and challenged them to catch him. Three others were arrested and charged with helping Khare. One of them, Mahesh Mhatre, said an officer broke his hand during the interrogation. He also accused the police of torturing him. Mhatre owns the cyber cafe from where Khare executed the hack. "I have approached the State Human Rights Commission asking them to look into the matter", said Mhatre's father, Subash. "I am waiting for their response."

The deputy commissioner of police, Manoj Lohiya, denied the allegation. "It's not our job to get personal", said Lohiya, who is also chief of the CCC. Mhatre's hospital report confirmed that there were no bone injuries and according to a CCC (Cyber Crime Cell) official who took part in the interrogation, said that the accused was only slapped and giving it a name of torture is an exaggeration. But with a report that the State Human Rights Commission was investigating the death of a man, who died in police custody, was still fresh in their minds, the hackers were really scared.

The effect of this punishment for the hackers scared many others and ultimately the result was that some hackers called the CCC asking, if they could join the CCC as technical hands. They want to be a part of the official side of Internet security now because they are scared. But some hackers have a different view over this, one said that, punishment should fit the crime. A slap on the writ is understandable, but if a programmer is treated as a criminal then it leaves an unpleasant taste. Another hacker naming himself as Prince said that even the only rumour of heavy-handed police tactics has been enough to send hackers diving for cover. He said that Indian hackers don't have a strong united community, so they are lying low. Nobody wants to mess again.

The hacker namingly L-20 blamed the policeman for messing with law enforcement. But that may have a positive effect on the hackers like a 21-year-old engineering student and "Web security enthusiast", plans on taking the high road. He said, "I am joining CCC to help out the cops in detecting hackers. That seems to me both safe and exciting."

6

Pronography and Pedophilia

Introduction

The Internet is being highly used by its abusers to reach and abuse children sexually, worldwide. The Internet is very fast becoming a household commodity in India. Its explosion has made the children a viable victim to the cyber crime. As more homes have access to Internet, more children would be using the Internet and more are the chances of falling victim to the aggression of pedophiles.

The easy access to the pornographic contents readily and freely available over the Internet lower the inhibitions of the children. Pedophiles lure the children by distributing pornographic material, and then they try to meet them for sex or to take their nude photographs including their engagement in sexual positions. Sometimes pedophiles contact children in the chat rooms posing as teen-agers or a child of similar age, and then they start becoming friendlier with them and win their confidence. Then slowly pedophiles start sexual chat to help children shed their inhibitions about sex and then call them out for personal interaction. Then starts actual exploitation of the children by offering them some money or falsely promising them good opportunities in life. The pedophiles then sexually exploit the children either by using them as sexual objects or by taking their pornographic pictures in order to sell those over the Internet.

In physical world, parents know the face of dangers and they advise their children to keep away from dangers. But in case of cyber world, most of the parents do not themselves know about the basics in Internet and dangers posed by various services offered over the Internet. Hence, the children are left unprotected in the cyber world. Pedophiles take advantage of this situation and lure the children, who are not advised by their parents or by their teachers about what is wrong and what is right for them while browsing the Internet.

Burris v. Azadani, (1995) 1 WLR 1372.

The Court both affirmed that the plaintiff had a cause of action in nuisance and, in addition, under the tort of harassment as the plaintiff had a 'legitimate interest' in receiving protection from behaviour, "which might be highly stressful and disturbing".

How do they operate?

(a) Pedophiles use false identity to trap the children/teenagers.

(b) Pedophiles contact children/teens in various chat rooms, which are used by children/ teen to interact with other children/teen.

(c) Try to be friend of that child/teen and extract personal information from him by winning his confidence.

(d) Gets the e-mail address of the child/teen and starts making contacts on the victim's e-mail address also.

(e) Starts sending pornographic images/text to the victim including child pornographic images in order to help child/teen shed his inhibitions so that a feeling is created in the mind of the victim that what is being fed to him is normal and that everybody does it.

(f) At the end of it, the pedophile set up a meeting with the child/teen out of the house and then drags him into the net to further sexually assault him or to use him as a sex object.

New, Largest But Not Forever

Sex on the Net is the quickest big business in the world. It attracts tens of millions of users. "Respectable" Web businesses rely on it for ad dollars. Online pornography was the first consistently successful e-commerce product and played a major part in the Internet's explosive growth. And adult sites gave us technological advances in advertising, user tracking, and e-commence that have now spread throughout the Web.

But thanks to societal disapproval and fear of legal prosecution, the porn industry on the Internet remains largely underground. Most mainstream analysts don't comment on it, and accurate statistics are extremely hard to come by (for instance, estimate range from 20,000 to 7 million active X-rated sites on the Net). (Burstow), (1996) Crim LR 331. The judge held that there was no reason for giving "inflict" a narrow or restrictive meaning.

In 1998, pornography made up 11 per cent of the $ 9 billion consumer e-commerce pie. In 1999, porn will make up 8 per cent of the total $ 18 billion in consumer e-commerce. (Estimates from Forester Research).

In an attempt to understand this cryptic segment of the Internet, it was decided to follow the money from start (the photographer) to finish (the viewer). It was talked to content providers, entrepreneurs from all parts of the adult industry, analysts, and even programmers taking a stance against filtering software.

What we found is that sex on the Web is still a very big business indeed, but as mainstream e-commerce grows, pornography is no longer the major player.

We also discovered that the Wild West days when anybody could create an adult site and made a lot of money is gone; the money is increasingly in the hands of a few big players. And nearly everybody is bracing for a crackdown.

The Times, 16 December 1994 cited from Allen, (In Gelder). The Court of Appeal while quashing a conviction for inflicting Grievous Body Harm (GB H) contrary to the Offences Against the Person Act, 1861 Section 20 arising from obscene telephone calls to the victim, which had resulted in psychiatric illness declined to consider the separate ground of appeal in, which the appellant claimed that it was impossible to inflict GBH over the telephone.

Where Does Porn Come From

Anyone with a camera and a dirty mind can create an X-rated image. Amateur porn is common, but the vast majority of adult sites are professional outfits. Rick Muenyong, who offers information and resources to adult Webmasters through his YNOT Adult Network, estimates that 90 per cent of free porn sites, and nearly all porn sites, buy their material rather than create it themselves.

Under the Lights

As long as the money's right, there's no shortage of people willing to take their clothes off and perform in front of a camera. Photographers with connections in the traditional adult industry have the easiest time finding subjects: models actively seek them out, hoping to move up to better-paying jobs in adult films or magazines. New players advertise for models in magazines and trade weeklies and often use individuals who already work for strip clubs or escort services.

In any legitimate adult shoot, every model must show proof of age and sign a release giving the photographer the rights to sell the pictures. In the last two years, self-regulation has become an accepted reality, and most photographers can no longer sell material without the right paperwork. The risks to Webmasters-lawsuits for copyright infringement or a visit from a child porn crackdown squad-are too high to ignore.

Behind the Lens

Although many Net porn photographers have a background in the traditional about industry, demand is enormous, and many camera clickers with no previous adult background now made money doing sex shoots. But it's not a job for the squeamish. Florida photographer Bruce Zell, who began selling CD-ROMs of his Z-rated shots directly to Webmasters in early 1998, has found that it's much easier to sell "anything with some oddity to it".

The fact is, anybody can snap pictures of attractive people in simple poses. But in order to stand out, adult sites must appeal to every conceivable fetish. If Webmasters can find services selling unusual images, they're likely to buy more typical items from the same sources at the same time.

Distributing the Material

The shoot is done. The material is ready. Next, it has to get to the people who want to put it online.

In the early days of the Net, individuals would simply scan dirty pictures from magazines and video-box covers, then post them to bulletin boards and news groups. Many of the first adult sites consisted of this hijacked material, copied and passed from site to site.

The Web Posse Cracks Down

Then, in 1997, the Association for the Protection of Internet Copyright (APIC), also known as the Web Posse began policing adult material. The group, consisting, costly of photographers and copyright holders from the traditional porn industry, sent threatening letters to Webmasters, pressured ISPs to boot offending sites, and encouraged local district attorneys to bring infringement charges.

APIC's aggressive tactics worked, and professional distributors-as well as photographers and models-are benefiting from the results. Distributor Mike Rick of Cyber Synergism saw his monthly revenue rocket from $ 10,000 to $ 60,000 in a single month after APIC began its activities.

How Free Sites Get Their Material

Some photographers sell their own material directly to free sites, but usually it's a two-part process a distributor buys photography from a number of original sources, then resells the pictures to site owners.

The vast majority of X-rated pics are either taken digitally or scanned from prints, then stored on CD-ROMs. Each disc contains up to 600 photographs and sells for anywhere from $ 100 for oft-used material to several thousand dollars for exclusives.

A few content sellers, realizing how easy it is for unscrupulous Webmasters to burn duplicate CD-ROMs, don't share their image files with the Webmasters. Instead, they force sites to link directly to files on secure FTP servers-viewers think they're looking at porn on the reed site, but they're actually accessing it directly from the distributor. In order to maintain a successful business, distributors often work with 1,000 or more Webmasters, mostly small-time proprietors who post the material for free. But, recently, there's been a shakeout among these free sites, and distributors are cutting into a steadily shrinking pie.

Worth Paying For

With so much free porn available, pay sites must feature something other than simple pictures. Interactive video, celebrity shots, and images of well-known adult stars are expensive to produce and can also command a lot of money from viewers. So the same distributes lots of pay content companies that create it-they'd be crazy to lose money to a middleman.

One company, the Internet Entertainment Group (IEG) has built annual revenues to about $ 50 million by controlling most of its content from start to finish. Not only does the company charge individual Web surfers to access material (including its notorious shots of celebrities like Dr. Laura Schlessinger), but it also sells its material to magazine and video distributors, becoming one of the first Net-based companies to expand horizontally into other adult markets.

Adult Webmasters

A young entrepreneur flips through erotic pictures on a CD-ROM, picking candidates for her upcoming Web site. She has no experience with pornography, but she knows computers, and she's heard the same success stories as everybody else 25 year old Seth Warshavsky turned a bankrupt phone-sex business into the enormous Internet Entertainment Group; former accountant Beth Mansfield grosses nearly a million dollar a year from Persain Kitty's Adult Links. She's in for a surprise. The easy money days are over.

Mandair, (1995) 1 AC 208, 229. Who stated that "inflict conveys the idea of a direct and immediate doing of harm."

The High Cost of Hosting

Unlike mainstream sites, Web porn deals almost exclusively in bandwidth hogging pictures. Bonus items like animated clips live video and interactive chat suck up even more space.

Adult Webmasters can't get bandwidth the same way as anybody else. Getting axed by an angry ISP or sneaking onto a free mainstream service like GeoCities are the quickest ways to get blacklisted throughout the industry. These unfortunates lose their entire ad banners and link-exchange partners forever. So most adult sites use an adult-oriented hosting service and pay by the amount of material served per month.

A couple thousand users grabbing one or two high-quality images add up to at least two gigabytes per month the usual amount allocated in cheap starter packages. Break the limit, and the bills can multiply five or ten times beyond expectations.

New customers with big money behind them are driving up cost is as well. Paul Hawser, who co-owns South Beach Hosting, notes that "the client who used to balk at $ 2,000 doesn't exit compared with the client who now says 'Great!' when we say '$ 25,000'. Free adult hosting, a new trend is fine for small-scale labours of love, but unworkable for porn proprietors who want to make money-Webmasters must give their banner ad spots away to the hosting company, criminating their main source of potential revenue.

Free Sites Set the Bait

Up to 30 million individuals a day log on to adult Web sites. After running a search at a portal site or adult index, the next stop is probably a sit with free images.

According to Rick Muenyong of the YNOT Adult Network, free sites comprise between 70 and 180 per cent of the adult material out there. These sites are used as "bait" for pay sites and make their money by successfully guiding viewers to premium services on other sites.

Click through and Conversion

Conventional online companies can still get away with charging advertisers for the number of banner ads shown to viewers. In sharp contrast, free porn sites make money only when a user visits an advertiser's site and make a purchase. Typically, a premium site shares between 30 and 60 per cent of each sale with the referring site. This may seem generous, but its actually very difficult for free sites to capitalize on these arrangements. Although 5 or 10 per cent of visitors might click on an ad (known as click through), only one or two out of every thousand will actually purchase the services advertised (known as conversion).

In order to survive, free sites will use almost any trick to raise click through rates false promises of more free content and multiple pop-up ads that appear when a viewer tries to leave are the most annoying recent trends. By and large, viewers don't seem to mind the tricks, as long as there's enough free content to satisfy them. As mainstream advertisers begin to change by click through and conversion, look for these tactics to make their way over to the mainstream Web.

Grabbing Eyeballs

In order to make any money referring customers to pay sites, free sites themselves must attract thousands of users. So far, index sites with thousands of links, such as Persian Kitty's Adult Links, have had the best luck grabbing traffic and making money.

With this lesson in mind, Webmasters aggressively pursue cross-linking agreements. Top ten (or fifty, or three hundred) lists, which rank "partner" sites based on overall traffic, were trendy in 1997, but partners often artificially inflated hit counts through endless circles of links within their sites. Sex Tracker, a more sophisticated service that tracks traffic throughout the entire adult industry, is perhaps the ultimate outgrowth of the list trend: it's 12,000 adult-site. Rankings are a frequent starting point for porn-hungry surfers.

Now free sites are consolidating their material in other ways in order to attract users. In a picture post, for instance, a group of free sites puts text links to individual images on a single, free clearinghouse page.

When users click to each picture, they see a banner advertising the sit it came from and will (hopefully) find the material enticing enough to click through. Free adult hosting services, which make money by selling ads on their customer's sites, are also popular. Neither of these models has yet demonstrated financial success, but they currently rank near the top of Sex Tracker's traffic lists.

Premium Sites Cash In

At some point, a viewer decides that the free material simply isn't enough. One day, he (yes, the vast majority of online porn viewers are still male) clicks on an appealing banner ad, pulls out his credit card and signs on to a pay site.

Attracting Business

Premium adult content, particularly live video and interactive chart, is extremely expensive to produce, and most pay sites buy their material from one of several hundred providers at the very top of the food chain. In order to pay these content providers, the sites need to attract thousands of paying customers and keep them around.

Advertising on other adult sites is the primary way to attract customers. Indeed, pay sites drive the porn industry, sharing revenues with the tens of thousands of free sites that refer customers to them. Premium sites also advertise on mainstream Web sites run a search for the word sex on almost any major portal and notice the banner ad that pops up. But these banners are expensive, as most mainstream sites require payment up front based on impressions, rather than based on the number of customers who actually buy something.

The Porn Presenters

Of course, adult images will never reach some viewers at all. There are plenty of people working to protect children, communities, and society at large from the perceived threat of pornography.

Pornography

The term "pornography' is a generic not a legal term. It relates to a broad range of sexual materials. As noted by the Supreme Court in its Miller V. California Obscenity case, 413 U.S. 15 (1973).

"Pornography" derives from the Greek, the word means: '1(a) description of prostitutes or prostitution; (2)(a) depiction (as in a writing or painting) of licentiousness or lewdness: a portrayal of erotic behaviour designed to cause sexual excitement. The 1986 Attorney General's Commission on Pornography defined pornography as "material that is predominantly sexually explicit and intended primarily for the purpose of sexual arousal".

Indecency

In its only decision involving broadcast indecency FCC v. Pacifica. The U.S. Supreme Court noted in 1978 that the "normal definition of indecent merely refers to non conformance with accepted standards of morality". The FCC presently defines "indecent" for the broadcast media as:

"Language or material that, in context, depicts or describes, in terms patently offensive as measured by contemporary community standards in the broadcast medium sexual or excretory activities or organs."

The definition of "Indecent" is similar to part two of the Miller obscenity definition, but in determining whether a particular TV ad or program, or part thereof, "indecent" it is not necessary to also determine parts one and three of the obscenity test. A single depiction or description on TV of sexual or excretory activities or organs could be a part when taken as a whole did not appeal to the prurient interest or had serious value and was therefore not obscene.

Federal law has prohibited the broadcast of indecent material since 1927. In FCC V. Pacifica, the U.S. Supreme Court upheld the present law (18 USC 1464) as applied to an afternoon broadcast of indecent material. In so doing the Court stated that two attributes of the broadcast media justified special treatment of indecent material.

First, the broadcast media have established a pervasive presence in the lives of "all Americans" and indecent material confronts "the citizen" not only in public but also in the privacy of the home "where the individual's right to be left alone plainly outweighs the First Amendment rights of an intruder". Second, said "the Supreme Court, "Broadcasting is uniquely accessible to children even those too young to read".

Obscenity and Pornography Situation in India

The word "Obscene" has not been defined in the Indian Penal Code. According to the Dictionary meaning it may mean offensively or repulsively indecent especially by offending accepted sexual morality. "Obscenity" is the state or quality of being obscene.

In Ranjit D. Udeshi, (AIR 1965 SC 881) the Supreme Court stated-"The word as the dictionaries tell us denotes the quality of being obscene, which means offensive to modesty or decency lewd, filthy and repulsive. It cannot be denied that it is an important interest of society to supper's obscenity. There is, of course, some difference between obscenity and pornography is that the latter denotes writings, pictures etc., Intended to arouse sexual desire while the former may include writing, etc. not intended to do so but, which gave that tendency both of course offend against public decency and morals but pornography is obscenity in a more aggravated form.

The concept of obscenity would differ from country to country depending on the standard of morals of contemporary society. The standards of contemporary society in India are also fast changing. If a reference to sex by itself is considered obscene, no books can be sold except those, which are purely religious, what one has to see is whether a class, not an isolated case, into whose hands the books, article or story falls suffer in their moral outlook or become depraved by reading it or might have impure and lecherous thoughts aroused in their minds. The change of obscenity must, therefore, be judged from this aspect. (Chandrakant Kakodkar, AIR 1970 SC 1390).

So, the idea as to what is deemed to be obscene varies from age, to age from region to region and even from person to person. The Supreme Court has observed that if a narration or description of a sinful situation is given in a setting emphasizing a strong moral to be drawn from it and condemns the conduct of the erring party as wrong and loathsome, it cannot be said that it has a likelihood of corrupting of morals of those in whose hands it is likely to fall particularly, the adolescent. (Chandrakant Kalyandas Kakodkar), (AIR 1970 SC 1390). It is no justification that the matter published is written by an eminent writer or is composed in a style not easily understood by all or that the publication is a medical one and sold only to registered subscribers. Where obscenity and art are mixed, art must be go preponderating as to throw the obscenity into a shadow or the obscenity so trivial and insignificant that it can have no effect and may be overlooked. In other words, treating with sex in a manner offensive to public decency and morality judged of by the national standards and considered likely to pander to lascivious prurient or sexually precocious minds must determine the result. A balance should be maintained between freedom of speech and expression and public decency and morality but when the latter is substantially transgressed, the former must give way (AIR 1965 SC 881).

The Case of Pornography in India

MUMBAI, India-In a court order that could have serious legal ramifications in India, a judge in Pune has put six directors of a premier portal called Rediff.com on trial for "giving access to pornographic material."

If convicted, the directors face up to two years imprisonment. The Chairman of the portal, Ajit Balakrishnan-a high profile business figure in India-is among those summoned for a Dec.30 hearing. A high-level Intel executive, Tony Janz, was also summoned.

When attorney Rohan Nagpal filed the pornography complaint against Rediff two months ago-on behalf of a law student Ahhinav Bhatt-the general opinion was that the judge would throw the case out. Nagpal's complaint said that Rediff's search engine gave free and easy access to pornographic material. Following the complaint, Judge S. Bhosle ordered a police inquiry.

The police report stated that the portal's search engine didn't create any objectionable material, and that it was in the character of a search engine to give access to everything on the Web. But the judge didn't think that was enough, at this point, to absolve Rediff of blame.

"Considering the allegation that the accused company is advertising their search engine facility and thereby provoking the citizen to view their website, I am of the opinion that enough material is available on, which the accused can he put up for trial", Bhosle said.

To this, Rohan Nagpal said, "Rediff claimed that l23india.com was a directory and that Rediff used a search engine." But their contention was weakened when he showed precedence over the same issue.

The precedence was that in 1998, CompuServe's managing director was sentenced to two years imprisonment for giving access to sites that dealt with child pornography.

He went on appeal, but the point is that after the suit was filed, CompuServe's search engine effectively blocked out all objectionable sites. So he proved to the court that Rediff's claiming, that filtering a search engine is technically not feasible, is not true.

The Rediff chief of corporate communications, Debashish Gosh, said, "We are looking at the relevant documents right now and have not yet decided on the future course of action."

On this Nagpal replied that how carefully Rediff's legal department may read the documents, it is binding under the Indian law for the accused directors to appear in court for the hearing. On this an employee of Rediff at high level commented and claimed that Rediff is been built on long term investors and is in the state of hyper growth, and such cases only have irritation value.

He further added that even God cannot alter the way a search engine work and said "either you ban Indian sites from using search engine, which is a ridiculous idea, or you live with the fact that any Indian user will be able to access porn sites."

He further added "Even if you employ a severe, drastic filter in your search engine it will be a useless tool in three months because new porn sites will come up and your filter will not detect them."

RIGINA v. HICKLIN, 3L R. Q.B. 360, 371.

Cockburn C.J. propounded, that this standard is whether the tendency of the matter charged as obscenity as to deprave and corrupt those whose minds are open to such immoral influences, and into whose hands a publication of this sort may fall.

7

Obscenity and Vulgarity

Introduction

A vulgar writing is not necessarily obscene. Vulgarity arouses a feeling of disgust and revulsion and also boredom but does not have the effect of depraving debauging and corrupting the morals of any reader of the novel or viewer of a film whose minds are open to such immoral influences. (Samaresh Bose v. Amal Mitra, AIR 1986 SC 967).

Obscenity

The 1973 United States Supreme Court landmark case, Miller v. California, established a three-pronged test for determining whether a "work" (i.e., material or performance) is obscene and, therefore, unprotected by the first Amendment. To be obscene, a judge and/or a jury must determine:

1. The average person applying contemporary community standards, would find that the work, taken as a whole, appeals to the prurient interest, and
2. That the work depicts or describes in a patently offensive way as measured by contemporary community standards sexual conduct specifically defined by the Applicable law; and
3. That a reasonable person would find that the work taken as a whole lacks serious literary, artistic, political and scientific value,

Examples of "hard-core sexual conduct", that an obscenity law could include for regulation under the second prong of the test are patently offensive representations or descriptions of

Ultimate sexual acts, normal or perverted, actual or simulated: Masturbation excretory functions and lewd exhibition of the genitals and Sadism and masochism.

[Khorasandijan v. Bush, (1993) 3 WLR 476].

The Court of Appeal granted an injunction prohibiting the interfering with her by acts calculated to impair her health.

The Internet Acts as Biggest Showcase

Sex on the net is the quietest big business in the world. It attracts tens of millions of users. "Respectable" Web businesses rely on it for ad dollars. Online pornography was the first consistently successful e-commerce product and played a major part in the Internet's explosive growth. And adult sites gave us technological advances in advertising user tracking, and e-commerce that have now spread throughout the Web.

But thanks to societal disapproval and fear of legal prosecution, the porn industry on the Intérnet remains largely underground. Most mainstream analysts don't comment on it, and accurate statistics are extremely hard to come by (for instance, estimates range from 20,000 to 7 million active Z-rated sites on the Net).

In 1998, pornography made up 11 per cent of the $ 9 billion consumer c-commerce pie. In 1998, p$_9$rnography made of 11 per cent of the $ 9 billion consumer e-commerce pie. In 1999, porn will make up 8 per cent of the total $ 18 billion in consumer c-commerce. (Estimates from Forrester Research).

In an attempt to understand this cryptic segment of the Internet, decide to follow the money from start (the photographer) to finish (the viewer). It was talked to content providers, entrepreneurs from all parts of the adult industry, analysts, and even programmers taking a stance against filtering software.

Sex on the Web is still a very big business indeed, but as mainstream e-commerce grows, pornography is no longer the major player. We also discovered that the Wild West days when anybody could create an adult site and make a lot of money is increasingly in the hands of a few big players. And nearly everybody is bracing for a crackdown.

MILLER v. CALIFORNIA, 413 U.S. 15 (1973).

Held that material obscenity if the average person, applying contemporary community standards, would find that the work, taken as a whole, appeals to the prurient interest.

Test

The test of obscenity is this whether the tendency of the matter charged as obscenity is to depilate and corrupt those minds are open to such immoral influences and into whose hands a publication of this sort may fall.

[Riggin v. Hickin, (1868 LR 3 Q.B. 360)].

The Supreme Court has observed that this list of obscenity laid down by Cockburn CJ should not be discarded. It makes the Court the judge of obscenity in relation to an impugned book, etc. and lays emphasis on the potentiality of the impugned object to deprave and corrupt by immoral influences.

In Samaresh Nose v. Amal Mitra, AIR. 1986 SC 967, it was observed by the Supreme Court as under

"The concept of obscenity is mould to a very great extent by the social outlook of the people who are generally expected to read the book. It is beyond dispute that the concept of obscenity usually differs from country to country depending on the standards of morality of contemporary society in different countries. In our opinion, in judging the question of obscenity the judge in the first place should try to place himself in the position of the author and from the view of the author the judge should try to understand what is it that the author seeks to convey and what the author conveys has any literary and artistic value.

The judge should thereafter place himself in the position of a reader of every age group in whose hands the book is likely to fall and should try to appreciate what kind of possible influence the book is likely to have in the minds of the readers. A judge should thereafter apply his judicial mind dispassionately to decide whether the book in question can be said to be obscene within the meaning of section 292, Indian Penal Code by an objective assessment of the obscene separately.

In appropriate cases, the courts for eliminating any subjective element or personal preference, which may remain hidden in the sub-conscious mind and may unconsciously, affect a proper objective assessment. My draw upon the evidence on record and also consider the views expressed by reputed or recognized authors of literature on such questions if thereby any for his own consideration and satisfaction to enable the court to discard the duty of making a proper assessment".

The correct test of obscenity, which has been accepted is whether the publications is detrimental to public morals and calculated to produce pernicious effect in depraving and debauching the minds of the persons into whose hands it may come.

A stray passage or a stray story occasionally thrown into a magazine might escape the attention of the readers but to collect such Stories together and to publish them in a book is bound to excite particular feelings in the minds of the readers. A compiler of such a book could not have had any other object in his mind than the one, which is punishable under the law,

SMITH v. CALIFORNIA, 361 U.S. 147 (1959)

Held that strict liability in these cases would seriously restrict the dissemination of books that are not obscene by penalizing booksellers even though they had no notice of book's character. Every bookseller is under the obligation to be aware of the contents of every book in the store.

In a decision of Supreme Court Bobby Art International v. Ompal Singh, AIR 1996 SC 1846, popularly known as "Bandit Queen" case, the fact was this that a film was prepared on the true story of Phoolan Devi who was exposed from her childhood to the brutality and lust of men. She was beaten and raped on a number of occasions.

She was humiliated-stripped nuked, paraded and made to draw water from the well within the circle of a hundred men. The film was presented for certification to the Censor Board and the film was cleared by granting "A" certificate but, in the meantime, the Delhi High Court' on a writ petition restrained the exhibition of the film in India.

Allowing the appeal the Supreme Court observed as under:

> "Bandit Queen", is the story of a village child exposed from an early age to the brutality and lust of men married off to a man old enough to be her father. She is beaten and raped. The village boys make advances, which she repulses, but the village panchayat finds her guilty of the enticement of a village boy because he is of high caste and she has to leave the village.
>
> She is arrested and in the police station filthily abused. Those who stand bail for her do so to satisfy their lust. She is kidnapped and raped during an act of brutality, the rapist is shot dead and she finds an ally in her rescuer. With his assistance she beats up her husband violently.
>
> Her rescuer's assailant and his accomplices and they humiliate her in the sight of the village, a hundred men stand in a circle around the village well and watch the humiliation, her being stripped naked and walked around the circle and then made to draw water. And not one of the villagers helps her, she burns with anger and shame and the urge for vengeance. She gets it and she lidded many of the Thakur too.
>
> It is not a petty. There are no syrupy songs or pirouetting round trees. It is the serious and sad story of a worm turning: a village born female child becoming dreaded dacoit. An innocent who turns into a vicious criminal because lust and brutality have affected her psyche so. The film levels an accusing finger at members of society who had tormented Phoolan Devi and driven her to become a dreaded dacoit filled with the desire to revenge.

R. v. Fellows, R. v. Arnold (unreported decisions).

The Court looked into the activity prior to the offence and was satisfied that there was sufficient activity for them to consider it as publication. In Hicklin's test it was said that:

"......I think the test of obscenity is whether the tendency of the matter charged as 'obscene' is sufficient to deprave and corrupt those whose hand a publication of this sort may fall."

(1868) LR 2 QB 360, 371.

Regina v. Martin Secker and Warburg Ltd., (1954) (Martin case). The Hicklin test should be applied keeping in mind present day standards taking into account the prevailing attitude towards sex.

Roth v. United States, 354 U.S. 476, 489-93.

The Roth Court held that obscenity falls outside constitutional protection and should be judged by the average person applying contemporary community standards and to by the most vulnerable members of the society as propounded by the Hicklin Court.

A Reputation for Fraud

Once the customer has signed up, it's vital to have him stick around for a few months, Premium porn sites offer the same kind of incentives-cheaper prices over the long term, special deals, discounts for signing friends up, and so on-as any other subscription-oriented business. Many believe that the uniqueness or quality of their content will encourage long-term membership as well.

But, despite all this, the average customer stays on a specific pay service for only three and a half months. With such financial pressure to keep customers, some pay sites have stooped to shady business practices. Many services make it difficult to cancel memberships, hiding "cancel" buttons or changing phone numbers without warning. Some promise one free month of access but then secretly charge for the first month before allowing customers a free second month.

One insider even told us of a company that shared its credit card database with other Webmasters who fraudulently charged the cardholders for services that were neither ordered nor delivered. When the cardholders began filing fraud claims with their credit card companies, the other sites declared bankruptcy and split with the loot.

Pornography is enough of a loaded issue to attract government attention on its own, but widespread allegations of fraud makes a crackdown even more likely. Rick Muenyong of the YNOT Adult Network worries that a few bad apples will spoil the entire industry. "Either the Better Business Bureau or the FTC is going to come in, and we're all going to pay for it." This fear of government intervention pervades the industry and is one reason why many Net porn insiders are looking to get out of the business.

DOE v. AMERICA ON LINE, INC., 718 So. 2d 385.

It was held that AOL enjoyed complete immunity against any action of obscenity by virtue of section 230, this section states that no provider or user of an interactive computer service shall be treated as the publisher or speaker of any information provided by another.

Internetiquette: Fact or Fiction?

The media is buzzing with discussions of ethics and propriety on the Internet. On a daily basis one may find an item somewhere discussing instances of Internet communications that may constitute sexual harassment, pornography, hate mail, vulgarity, obscenity, profanity, threats, torts such as defamation and the invasion of privacy, crime schemes, infringements of intellectual property, rudeness, or bad taste.

Examples of such messages motivate state and federal legislators in the U~S. to propose measures prescribing categories of speech on the Internet and defining new contexts for electronic crime. Indeed, as this article is being written, Congress is hurrying to pass a bill that will criminalize the sending of "indecent" messages to minors. Various groups, professional and otherwise, discuss the establishment of standards for network communications while others protest against any regulation of the Internet so that it remains subject only to "self-regulation" by its users.

Those who urge standards and protocols maintain the "self-regulation" won't work because the tolerant will be victimized by the intolerant and the "bad" will drive the "good" off the national and international information highways. This is denied by those who say that the First Amendment requires electronic speech to be free of regulation and that Internet "community" standards are developing a workable "netiquette" of propriety. Some pros and cons of internet regulation, the application of Constitutional and common law to the environment of electronic digital technology, and some premises for a framework for network regulation.

In spite of the First Amendment's prohibition of the government regulation of speech, we all have heard that one can't yell "fire" in a crowded theatre, we don't think users should be allowed to yell "fire" on the Internet, either, because it is believed that the Internet-a global information network-will not achieve its vaunted potential unless it is a truly "users friendly" environment.

Individuals should be able to enter cyberspace reasonably free from harassment or abuse and with confidence that the integrity of their communication will be respected and adequately protected. Of course, when one goes out into the world there are risks of being offended, exploited or victimized. Society reacts to its environment with varying levels of tolerance or control; if crime appears to be rampant then freedoms become restricted as society responds with defensive measures to control anti-social behaviour.

We witness that phenomenon regarding cyberspace today in the form of the legislative proposals mentioned earlier. Surely cyberspace cannot be an Eden absolutely free of offensiveness; neither should it be a sanctuary for those who would prey on others. "Rules of the road" are necessary whether the highway is an Interstate or on the Internet.

Indeed, even those who argue against government regulation of the Internet generally agree that some speech is inappropriate and should be banned, the best example being commercial advertising. Probably the best known incident involved the law firm and Canter and Siegel (C and S), which posted widely on Usenet newsgroups advertisements for their services in connection with entering the U.S. green card lottery.

Commercial ads looked upon as "junk e-mail", are frequently prohibited by "netiquette" from being posted to newsgroups or "chat rooms". The C and S postings were sent to newsgroups irrelevant to immigration matters and the ads were sent to literally thousands of forums and displayed repeatedly, conduct especially abhorred by Internet enthusiasts.

As a result, "self-help" measures were employed by system users to "bomb" the C and S account-send them a torrent of complaint messages that overloaded the C and S service-provider and led to the termination of the C and S account, which nevertheless was then established with another provider.

The point here is that "self-regulation" is considered by the Internet "freedom writers" to be O.K. For instance, the Internet Advertisers Blacklist has been established on, which is posted the names and addresses of those who are considered by the list operator to have advertised improperly. Users are invited to punish the violator in a variety of ways, from product/service boycotts to deluging the offender with all sorts of creative communications. The operator of the Blacklist says:

"The Internet is probably as close to an anarchy as we can get. This is good. Therefore, punishing of unwelcome behaviour should be done by private individuals, following the same grass roots philosophy that governs the rest of the net."

Though self-help may be an appropriate remedy in limited instances, it is doubtful that rule by "vigilante justice" in cyberspace will be better than it is in any other place. In examining the colourful vocabulary in connection with prohibited behaviour and self-help procedures we find such words as "spamming, velveeta and jello", which do not refer to those products, and others such as cancelbot, cancelmoose, flaming, bombs, traps, killfiles, and more.

Obviously, there is enough objectionable on the Internet to warrant a special vocabulary for wrongs and remedies. Regarding the latter, the words are suggestive of electronic warfare, which, in microcosm, may be what takes place with some frequency in cyberspace.

Abbas v. Union of India, (AIR 1971 SC 481).

The problem is multiplied manifold in an area like pornography, which has as its basis certain 'moral' standards and uses controversial parameters like 'indecency' and 'obscenity'.

State of Karnataka v. Baseer, 1979 Cri. L.J. 1183 (Kar.).

To escape liability, the onus is on the accused to prove lack of knowledge about the obscene or indecent contents of the material in question.

Smith v. California, 361 U.S. 147 (1959).

Held, that strict liability in these cases would seriously restrict the dissemination of books that are not obscene by penalizing booksellers even though they had no notice of books' character. Every bookseller is under the obligation to be aware of the contents of every book in the store.

Ranjit Udeshi v. State of Maharashtra, AIR 1973 SC 1230.

Held, that if knowledge were made a part of the guilty act and if the prosecution were required to prove it, an almost impenetrable defense would be placed in the hands of the offenders. In India, the courts would presume that the accused is guilty unless he proves lack of knowledge on his part.

8

Spam

Introduction

When the postman delivers your mail, you are quiet often greeted with several ads sent by various companies from the sleazy operators who send "Fill in this puzzle and get a camera", etc. There's also the chain mail stuff like "Chant Sai Baba's name twenty times and send 20 copies of this letter to your friends." Fair enough-this direct marketing is just a mild annoyance, and besides, they are paying the postal department, not you. All you have to do is to throw it into the dustbin, tearing it into little bits if you are sufficiently irritated.

In the cyber world any such unwanted mail is called junk mail or Spam. Now suppose you got all this junk mail postage due and were forced to pay the postman out of your own pocket for the privilege of receiving this junk. Or you got 5 page ads on your office fax, or their telemarketers called you up on your cell phone? Right-You wouldn't be all that amused. Now that almost everyone has at least a Hot-mail account, the same problem has moved to e-mail-but magnified several times. Junk e-mail (or Spain) is a huge problem throughout the Internet.

According to an informal survey of several major ISPs, most said that over 30% of the e-mail reaching their users were Spam. Thus, they had to invest thousands of dollars in more powerful hardware and extra handwidth, and had to take on additional staff to deal with Spam complaints. All these extra costs were ultimately passed on to the customers, none of whom had asked to receive the Spam in the first place. Besides this hidden cost, there is a direct cost. People have to pay money for the dubious privilege for receiving all this Spam.

For example, my friend X was in a small town and decided to check his Hot-mail. So, he went to the only cyber cafe in town. When he logged in, the inbox took long to load on an ultra slow connection. All the while, X moodily glared at the clock and thought of all the cash, which was flying away-from his slim wallet into the bulging money bags of the cyber cafe owner, who charged Rs. 90 per hour. At last, the inbox opened up-showing ten new waiting for him. These were-

Pornographic Spam (Click here for XXX)	4
Buy now!!! Better than Viagra, Limited stock available	2

The Internet Spy-Find out about everyone	2
Hot new Internet stocks-But now and become a millionaire	1
Chain Mail (Chant this mantra 20 times and forward it to 20 people)	1
Legitimate e-mails	0

His bill came to Rs. 50-all for the privilege of downloading this junk. You should have heard him cursing. On the other hand, he became quite happy when I showed him how to complain to all the spammer's ISPs-and he started getting several mails saying "This user's mail id/ website has been deleted for spamming. Sorry for the inconvenience."

It's the skewed economics of the Internet that created and blew up this problem. Unlike postal mail, where the entire cost is borne by the marketer, there is no per-message charge to send e-mail. It's included in your ISP's bill. This is excellent for people who want to keep in touch with friends and relatives, but the economic naturally lend them to abuse. All a spammer needs to send out a million messages is, an Internet account, a list of e-mail addresses of various people (none of whom asked for his junk in the first place), and a computer.

According to a survey conducted earlier this year by the antispam website, namely, choose your mail estimated that pornographers are responsible for 30.2% of the Spam on the Net today. Just behind them, are the "Get Rich Quick" and "Make Money Fast" scam artists, who send about 29.6% of the Spam. The remainder advertises assorted products and services.

Most ISPs forbid spamming and disconnect the Internet accounts and websites of any spammer. So, spammers often attempt to cover their tracks by sending mail through insecure servers around the world instead of their ISP's mail servers. This passes on most of the cost to the insecure server's owner, who has to clear up the mess caused by the spammer-while legitimate e-mail reaching his users is blocked in a mammoth traffic jam.

Recently, a disturbing trend has cropped up. Even legitimate, reputed companies have started sending Spam mails. The real problem in the coming year won't be from fly-by-night crooks and scam artists; it will be from legitimate companies that view Spam (or unsolicited bulk e-mail) as a way to market themselves more effectively. How much mail would you get if every company you have done business with, every supermarket you bought from, sent you an e-mail once a week telling you about their latest "special offer". And suppose their competitors at once got hold of your e-mail address and sent you another mail trying to convince you to buy from them.

Other companies get hold of a corporate directory (like the local chamber of commerce directory, or the yellow pages) and send ads to each e-mail address they see in the list. Some others know that sending e-mail to allusers@de13.vsnl.net.in will send a copy of the e-mail to all users on the De13 VSNL server.

The reasoning behind this is, "You are receiving this mail because you happen to be in the industry and we view you as a very important and focused client, or you chose to subscribe to our mailing list, or were added by a friend."

Exactly, what is being meant hereby is that one is forced to receive a Spain just because he has an e-mail address, though he has never asked for this mail, and don't want it at all? As for the last excuse, all responsible marketers are supposed to send a confirmation mail to the address from, which a "subscription request" was received.

An ethical marketer must only send his sales promotions to people who have specifically requested such promotions, and subsequently confirmed that they really do want to receive such material. Any mailing list software (such as Listserv and Majordomo, or the web-based e-Groups and Topica) does this automatically.

If you have a website and someone sends you feedback or signs up for something on your site (say a free e-mail account), then specifically mention that you are going to send promotional material to the customer if he signs up for this service. Also consider including a check box on the sign-up form, by clicking, which the customer can indicate that he does not want to receive any ads from you. Respect the customer's sentiments by not sending him e-mail unless he requests it.

Netizens, who realized that technology alone couldn't stop junk e-mail, and a concerted effort from the online community, as a whole is necessary, founded CAUCE.

As long as there is an economic incentive to send junk e-mail, users and Internet Service Providers will need some legal recourse to stop the growing flood. Therefore, CAUCE has consistently proposed various new laws and amendments in various countries.

Spammers have now discovered India it appears. The anti Spam community around the world has noticed a steady increase in the amount of Spain originating from Indian open relay SMTP servers.

The problem is compounded by the fact that several of these servers are running old Mail Transport Agents (mostly outdated versions of Send mail), which are anonymous open relays. That is, they allow spammers to relay mails without the sender's IP address being stamped in the headers, as is the case with most modern MTAs.

Here is a partial list of the Indian servers, which have been abused, in the past few days. All these are running outdated send mail versions.

(1) National Informatics Centre, Karnataka (kar.kar.nic.in)- They were running an insecure, outdated version of send mail on a Sun Unix Platform (SMI/SVR4), and were listed in the MAPS RBL list. After I mailed them with the facts, the systems administrator Mr. D.K. Krishna Rao took prompt action to upgrade to send mail 8.9.1 and secure their server (which was, therefore, removed from the RBL list).

(2) VSNL-Several VSNL servers in India (Calcutta, Delhi, Bombay, and Bangalore) were open relays running outdated versions of send mail, and were frequent targets of abuse by spammers. Most of them have been closed and their MTAs upgraded, thanks to the initiative taken by CAUSE members who convinced VSNL in their local cities to upgrade. Also there is an implemented port 119 (NNTP) router blocks on VSNL servers throughout India. This lifted a recent UDP (Usenet Death Penalty) imposed on VSNL to protect newsgroups from frequent attacks by a notorious Usenet spammer called hip crime.

(3) Tata institute of fundamental research-tifr.res.in.

Again an SMI-SVR4 box. Based on a phone number mentioned in the Spam, the spammer has been traced down and the details mailed to the TIFR sysadmin. The server has since been upgraded.

There are more such servers, mostly in the. Ernet.in and. nic.in domains. Spammers routinely carry out port scans, hoping to find open relays or other security vulnerabilities. These are promptly exploited, bringing the server to its knees with the extra mail load, and perhaps getting it listed in various anti Spam blacklists such as the MAPS RBL and RSS, and ORBS.

ADM JABALPUR'S CASE, (1973) 4 SCC 225

"In view of the fact that an established principle of law postulates that if there are two possible interpretations of a municipal law, the one favouring international law is to be taken".

To prevent this abuse of your server, and stop spammers in their tracks, please ensure that you are not running servers with open relays or other security holes.

Stanley v. Georgia, 394 U.S. 557

"The Court held that an individual has the right to read or view obscenity at his home but that right does not include a right to distribute it, transport it."

Zippo Mfg. Co. V. Zippo Dot Com.inc., 952 fsupp. 1119, 1123.

Purposeful availment was found based on the defendant's interactive web site and contracts with 3000 individuals and seven internet access providers in Pennsylvania in a trade mark infringement suit.

9

Computer Viruses on the Internet

History, Evolution and Reality

Computer viruses are called viruses because they share some of the train of biological viruses. A computer virus passes from computer to computer like a biological virus passes from person to person.

Traditional computer viruses were first widely seen in the late 1980s, and they came about because of several factors. The first factor was the spread personal computer (PCs). Prior to the 1980s, home computers were locked away for they were toys. Real computers were rare and they were locked to spread to business and homes because of popularity of the IBM PC (released in 1980) and the Apple Macintosh (released in 1984). By the late 1980s, PCs were widespread in business, homes and campuses.

The second factor was the use of computer 'bulletin boards". People could dial up a bulletin board with a modern and download programs of all types. Games were extremely popular; and so were simple word processors, spreadsheets, etc. Bulletin boards led to the precursor of the virus known as the Trojan horse. A Trojan horse is a program that sounds really cool when you read about it so you download it. When you run the program, however, it does something uncoil like erasing your disk. So you think you are getting a neat game but it wipes out your system. Trojan horse only hit a small number of people because they are discovered quickly. Either the bulletin board owner would erase the file from the system or would send out messages to warn one another.

The third factor that led the creation of viruses was the floppy disk. In memory immediately and it is able to run whenever the computer is on. Boot sector viruses can infect the boot sector of any floppy disk inserted in the machine, and on college campuses where lots of people share machine they spread likes wildfire.

E-mail viruses

The latest things are the e-mail viruses and the Melissa virus in March of 1999 was spectacular. Melissa spread in Microsoft Word document sent via e-mail and it worked like someone created the virus as a word document.

Uploaded to an Internet Newsgroup. Anyone who downloaded the document and opened it would trigger the virus. The virus would then send the document (and therefore itself) in an e-mail message to the first 50 people in the person's address book. The e-mail message contained a friendly note that included the person's name, so the recipient would open the document thinking it was harmless. The virus would then create 50 new messages from the recipient's machine. As a result, the Melissa virus was the fastest spreading virus ever seen! As mentioned earlier, it forced a number of large companies to shut down their e-mail system.

The ILOVEYOU virus, which appeared on May 4, 2000, was even simpler. It contained a piece of code and attachment. People who double clicked on the attachment allowed a piece of code to execute. The code sent copies of itself to everyone in the victim's address book and then started corrupting files on the victim's machine. This is as simple as a VIRUS CAN GET; it is really more of a Trojan horse disputed by e-mail then it is virus. Virus that spreads quickly is a little lie that-it creates a bomb inside a computer, and the more computers that get infected, the more "fun" the explosion.

The third reason probably involves bragging right, or the thrill of doing it Sort of like Mt. Everest. The mountain is there and no one has climbed it, so someone is compelled to it. If you are a certain type of programmer and you see a security hole that could be exploited, you might simply be compelled to exploit the yourself before someone else beats your to it "Sure, I could TELL someone about the hole. But wouldn't it be better to SHOW them the hole?" That sort of logic leads to many viruses.

Of course, all of the virus creators miss the point that they cause real damage too real people with their creations. Destroying everything on a person's hard disk is real damage. Foreign the people inside a large company to waste thousands of hours cleaning up after a virus is real damage. Even a silly message is real damage because a person then has to waste the time getting rid of it, For this reason, the legal system is getting much harsher in punishing the people who create viruses.

Computer Viruses by Biological Analogy

We and our colleagues at the IBM Thomas J. Weston Research center have found the biological analogy you be helpful in understanding the propagation of computer viruses on a global scale and inspirational in our development of defense against them. Building on decades of research by mathematical epidemiologists, we have obtained some understanding of the factors that govern how quickly viruses spread. Our efforts to find efficient methods of detecting viruses and the relations among them owe much to pattern-matching techniques developed by computational biogases. Furthermore, we have also drawn inspiration for defense against pathological software from the vertebrate immune system and its astounding ability to repel or destroy pathogens.

Computer viruses can trace their pedigree to John Von Neumann's studies of self-replicating mathematical automata in the 1940s. Although the idea of programs that could infect computer dates to the 1970s, the first well document case of a computer virus spreading "in the wild" occurred in October, 1987, when a code snippet known as the "Brain" Virus appeared on several dozen diskettes at the University of Delaware. Today viruses afflict at least a million computers every year. User spends several hundred million dollars annually on antiviral products and services, and this figure is growing rapidly.

CLASSIFYING VIRUS BY PREVENTION METHODS

Macro Viruses

A macro is an instruction that carries out program commands automatically; many common applications (e.g. word processing, spreadsheet, and slide presentation application) make use of macro. Macro viruses are macro and unwittingly execute this macro virus it can then copy itself into that application's start up files. The computer is now infected-a copy of the macro resides on the machine.

Any document on that machine that eases the same application can then become infected. If the infected computer is on a network, the infection is likely to spread rapidly to other machines on the network. Moreover, if a copy of an infected file is passed to anyone else (for example, by e-mail or floppy disk), the virus can spread to the recipient's computer. This process of infection will end only the virus is noticed and all viral macros are eradicated. Macro viruses are the most common types of viruses.

Boot Sector Viruses

The boot sector is the first software loaded into our computer. This program resides on a disk, and disk can be either the hard disk inside the computer, a floppy disk or a CD, when a computer is switched on, the hardware automatically locates and runs the boot sector program. This program then loads that rest of operating system into memory. Without a boot sector, a computer cannot runs software.

Viruses today

The number of known viruses surpassed 50,000 in August 2000. A large majority of those (74%) are parasite viruses (attacking executables), second are macro viruses (19%) and 7% are boot sector viruses. In May, 2000 88% of infection reported to siphons were due to macro viruses, 9% due to parasitic viruses and only 3% due to boot sector viruses. Note that a reported infection is counted as a single unit regardless of whether the virus infected one machine or 10,000 machines; the statistics quoted are not 'bomb-proof' but simply an indication of what is out there.

The number of new viruses discovered every month continued to increase in the second quarter of 2000; the Sophist virus lab was processing 800 new viruses every month.

Anti-virus companies are all faced with the dilemma of how to priorities detection of viruses researching their virus laboratory, it is impossible to predict, which (if any) of the new viruses must simply be analyzed and the detection/disinfecting for them included in the anti virus software. However, there is a group of viruses, which have a greater potential to spread rapidly. Viruses, which are 'internet-enabled' and, which exploit some form of common social engineering factor (such as the Love Letter virus) obviously fall into this category.

Virus Entry Point

In order to establish where anti-virus software should be delayed in an organization, it is important to establish what are the common virus entry points.

E-MAIL

An overwhelmingly large proportion of infections today is caused by infected e-mail attachment. The ease with, which a user can click on an attachment and launch an application is a significantly inviting (e.g., 'kindly check the itched LOVELETTER coming from me.') and the visible attachment extension sufficiently innocent in the eyes of an average user (e.g., LOVELETTER-FOR-YOU TXT.vbs-text files cannot carry an infection, can they?), the temptation for a user can become overwhelming.

ACLU v. RENO, 217 F.3d 162

"An e-mail address provides no authoritative information about the addressee, who may use an e-mail "alias" or an anonymous re-mailer". "With the possible exception of an e-mail to a known recipient, most content providers cannot determine the identity and age of every user accessing their material."

World Wide Web

The web crawling with sites carrying virus-infected material. Desktop access to the web is technologically possible but also viewed as and expected in today's workplace. Downloading potentially infected files is too easy.

Floppy Disk and CDs

The use of disks has decreased radically with the advent of networks, but most PCs still come with a floppy drive fitted as stranded 3% of all infection are due to boot sector viruses, which shows that floppy disks are not dead (yet). CDs (especially magazine cover CDs) have also been shown to be restively frequent virus carries.

Anti Virus Software Administration

Since the effectiveness of ant-virus in use today depends on frequent update, it is very important that effective tools are available to deploy upgrade and administration anti-virus software throughout the organization.

Updates over the Internet

Automatically updating anti-virus software over the Internet is an attractive (zero workload concept) concept for system administrations.

It does however have deep implication for the overall security of the organization since it effectively out sources the control and the decision-making process over what software gets installed in the company network to the anti-viral software supplier. Few organizations are happy with this proffering to place a human specialist in the loop. The specialist can then decide what, how and when to specialist in the deploy the updates. Any such new software con also is treated before being deployed company-wide.

Administration

The administrator of a large anti-virus software installation needs the tools to communicate with the anti-virus software effectively (admin-software) administrator needs regular feedback; both virus and non-virus related (software-admin).

Three main techniques are used to distribute e updates over the company network push, pull and combined push/pull. Each has its advantages and disadvantages and the decision on, which is best suited will depend heavily on the network structure, sped of connections, network usage patterns, etc.

Recovery from Virus Attack

Should the unthinkable happen and a virus manages to penetrate all the defenses put in its path, the company must have effective procedures in place to be able to contain the infection on as few PCs as possible as well as restoring these PCs to their pre-infection state. This is a relatively complex subject with no easy solutions.

Viruses

When a healthy man gets ill with some disease or the other, it is said in the scientific language that he probably may have infected by some virus in his body, which have got transferred from either of the outer sources, which effect the body of that particular person and that effect can lead to any extent.

Likewise in the Internet or so called Cyber World, the people, i.e., the computers and the data inside them can also be affected by so-called viruses, which has the power to' destroy the computer as whole. They are so made as to either create a very little damage to computer or destroy all the computers on one line, one server, or on the same network. They can do what one can't even think of, and that is the main reason why they are the biggest threat on the net today.

Among thousands of viruses on the net today they are some of the viruses whose origin is in India, and like other viruses they are also dangerous enough to affect the computer system in, which they get transferred from a source like: -

DIE HARD

Die-Hard is a resident fast infector, which targets COM and EXE files. It is known to be in the wild especially in India, where it was found in September 1994. Die-Hard has also been sighted in Singapore, Indonesia and USA and in many parts of Europe.

When the virus is executed, it goes resident in memory, decreasing the available DOS memory by 9232 bytes. Die-Hard infects all executed or opened COM and EXE files. The infected files grow by exactly 4000 bytes.

Die-Hard activates on the 3rd, 11th, 15th, or 28th of any month, provided the day is Tuesday and the virus has already infected at least 13 files. The virus will then wait until some program changes the screen to graphics mode. At this time the virus will display an animation of large 'S' and 'W' characters on the screen. It will also deny write access to files, displaying text 'SW Error".

JOSHI-Joshi is reported to have originated in India. It infects the partition boot sector of hard disks: storing the original, as well as the rest of the virus code elsewhere on tract 0, heads 0. Just like the brain virus, Joshi redirects attempts to read the virus code while it is active in memory.

The virus activates on January 5th of any year and displays the message:

Happy Birthday Joshi

V-SIGN-V-Sign is a typical boot sector virus, except that it uses slightly polymorphic encryption. V-Sign infects DOS boot sectors on diskettes and Master Boot Records on hard disks. It is only able to infect a hard disk when you boot a machine with an infected diskette in drive. A, at this the virus infects the Master Boot Record, and after that it will go resident to high DOS memory during every boot-up from the hard disk. Once V.Sign gets resident to memory, it will infect practically all non-write-protected diskettes used in the machine.

WOLLEH-Wolleh is a simple hoot virus, which infects DOS boot sectors on hard drives and floppies.

Wolleh contains the text "wolleH".

Wolleh was found in the wild in India in March 1997.

10

Conclusion

Introduction

Given the unrestricted number of free Web sites, the Internet is undeniably open to exploitation. Known as cyber crimes, these activities involve the use of computers, the Internet, cyberspace and the World Wide Web. "Any criminal activity that uses a computer either as an instrumentality, target or a means for perpetuating further crimes comes within the ambit of cyber crime", says Supreme Court advocate and cyber law expert.

The 5P mantra for online security Precaution, Prevention, Protection, Preservation and Perseverance, "Take security seriously", he says "If you protect your customer's data, your employee's privacy and your own company, then you are doing your job in the grander scheme of things to regulate and enforce rules on the Net through our community".

Awareness is important, and any matter should be reported at once. More importantly, users must try and save any electronic information trial on their computers. That's all one can do, then, until laws become more stringent or technology more advanced.

Cyber Crime—Hardships to Curb It

Crime is an act or omission, which is prohibited by the law particularly criminal. Cyber-Crime is the latest and perhaps the most specialized and dynamic field in cyber-laws. One of the greatest lacunae of this field is the absence of a set of comprehensive law anywhere in the world. Further, the growth ratio of Internet and cyber-law is not proportional too.

The era of nuclear warfare conceived the idea of a system, which could even survive the devastation of nuclear weapons. "A post-apocalypse command grid" was the original idea for Internet-'Bruce Sterling' has stated. The idea of 'Internet' was conceived in the early 60's while a code for its regulation was mooted in late 90's.

This clearly brings about the reason for the complication of cyber-crime. Cyber-Crime may be said to be an act, which violates netesthetics.

India has enacted the first I.T. Act, 2000 based on the UNCITRAL model recommended by the general assembly of the United Nations by a resolution dated 30th January 1997. The preamble to this Act gives a very clean picture in this regard.

Chapter XI of this Act deals with offences/crimes along with certain other provisions scattered in this Act. The various offences, which are provided under this chapter, are: -

- Tampering with Computer source documents S. 65:
- Hacking with Computer systems S. 66:
- Publishing of material obscene in electronic form S. 67
- Access to protected system 5. 70;
- Misrepresentation S 71,
- Breach of Confidentiality and Privacy 5. 72;
- Fraud S. 74;

Further Chapter IX under provision of S. 43 refers to the damage to Computer, Computer system, etc.

Commission of Cyber-Crime may be broadly divided against three basic groups: -

1. Individual (a) Person and (b) Property of an individual.
2. Organization (a) Government and (b) Firm, Company, Group of Individuals.
3. The following are the crimes, which can be committed against the followings groups against individuals: -

   (i) Harassment via e-mails

   (ii) Cyber-Stalking.

   (iii) Dissemination of obscene material

   (iv) Defamation

   (v) Hacking/cracking

   (vi) Indecent exposure

   Individual Property: -

   (a) Computer vandalism

   (b) Transmitting virus.

   (c) Netrespass

   (d) Unauthorized control over computer system

(e) Hacking/cracking

Against Organization: -

- Hacking and Cracking.
- Possession of unauthorized information,
- Cyber terrorism against the government organization.

Distribution of pirated software, etc.

Against Society at large: -

1. Pornography (basically child pornography)
2. Polluting the youth through indecent exposure
3. Trafficking

The elementary problems, which are associated with Cyber-Crimes, are: -

(i) Jurisdiction is the highly debatable issue as to the maintainability of any suits, which has been filed. Today with the growing arms of cyberspace the territorial boundaries seems to vanish. Thus the concept of territorial jurisdiction as envisaged under Section 16 of C.P.C. and Section 2 of the I.P.C. will have to give way to alternative method of dispute resolution.

(ii) Loss of evidence is a very common and expected problem as all the data are routinely destroyed. Further, collection of data outside the territorial extent also paralyzes this system of crime investigation.

(iii) Cyber Army-There is also an imperative need to build a high technology crime and investigation infrastructure, with highly technical staff at the other end.

(iv) A law regulating the cyber-space, which India has done?

(v) Though Section 75 provides for extra-territorial operations of this law, but they could be meaningful only when backed with provision recognizing orders and warrants for information issued by competent authorities outside their jurisdiction and measure for cooperation for exchange of material and evidence of computer crimes between law enforcement agencies.

(vi) Use of encryption of messages, virtually private networks, etc. also creates a big problem to trace the activities of cyber criminals.

(vii) Cyber savvy judges are the need of the day. Judiciary plays a vital role in shaping the enactment according to the order of the day. One such stage, which needs appreciation, is the P.I.L., which the Kerala High Court has accepted through e-mail.

(viii) The procedural obligation, which has to be, fulfilled such as letters rogatery U/s 166A and 166B of the Cr.P.C. and bar in case of crimes committed outside India. (i.e., prior approval of the Central Government).

Perfect is a relative term. Nothing in this world is perfect. The persons who legislate the laws and by-laws also are neither perfect. The laws therefore enacted by them nor can be perfect. This law has emerged from the womb of globalization. It is at the threshold of development. In due course of exposure through varied and complicated issues it will grow to be a piece of its time!

Resons for Commission of Cyber Crimes

1. Reliance on terrestrial laws is an untested approach- despite the progress made in many countries; most countries still rely on standard terrestrial law to prosecute cyber crimes. The majority of countries are relying on archaic that predate the birth of cyberspace and have not yet been tested in Court.

2. Weak penalties limit deterrence- The weak penalties in most updated criminal statutes provide limited deterrence for crimes that can have large-scale economic and social effects.

3. Self-protection remains the first line of defense- the general weakness of statute increases the importance of private sector efforts to develop and adopt strong and efficient technical solutions and management practices for information security.

4. A global patchwork of laws creates little certainty- Little consensus exists among countries regarding exactly, which crimes need to be legislated against. Unless crimes are defined in a similar manner across jurisdictions, co-ordinate efforts by law enforcement officials to combat cyber crime will be complicated.

5. A model approach is needed- Most countries, particularly those in the developing world, are seeking a model to follow. These countries recognize the importance of outlawing malicious computer-related acts in a timely manner in order to promote a secure environment for e-commerce. But few have the legal and technical resources necessary to address the complexities of adapting terrestrial criminal statutes to cyberspace. A co-ordinate, public-private partnership to produce a model approach can help eliminate the potential danger from the inadvertent creation of cyber crime havens.

Recommendations

The weak state of global legal protections against cyber crime suggests three kinds of actions:

Firms should secure their networked information.

Laws to enforce property rights work only when property owners take reasonable steps to protect their property in the first place. As one observer has noted, if homeowners failed to buy locks for their front doors, should towns solve the problem by passing more laws or hiring more police? Even where laws are adequate, firms dependent on the network must make their own information and systems secure. And where enforceable laws are months or years away, as in most countries, this responsibility is even more significant.

Government should assure that their laws apply to cyber crimes

National governments remain the dominant authority for regulating criminal behaviour in most places in the world. One nation already has struggled from and ultimately improved, its legal authority after a confrontation with the unique challenges presented by cyber crime. It is crucial that other nations profit from this lesson, and examine their current laws to discern whether they are composed in a technologically neutral manner that would not exclude the prosecution of cyber criminals. In many cases, nations will find that current laws ought to be updated. Enactment, of enforceable computer crime laws that also respect the rights of individuals are an essential next step in the battle against this emerging threat.

Firms, governments and civil society should work co-operatively to strengthen legal frameworks for cyber security

To be prosecuted across a border, an act must be a crime in each jurisdiction. Thus, while local legal traditions must be respected, nations must define cyber crimes in a similar manner. An important effort to craft a model approach is underway in the Council of Europe comprising 41 countries.

The Council is crafting an international Convention on Cyber Crimes. The Convention addresses illegal access, illegal interception, data interference, system interference, computer-related forgery, computer-related fraud, and the aiding and abetting of these crimes. It also addresses investigations matters related to jurisdiction, extradition, the interception of communications, and the production and preservation of data. Finally, it promotes co-operation among law enforcement officials across national borders.

Late in its process, the Council began to consider the views of affected industry and civil society. This process is making the Council's product more realistic, practical, efficient, balanced, and respectful of due process that protects individual rights. At this point, most observers support provisions to improve law enforcement co-operation across borders. However, industry, through the World Information Technology and Services. Alliance (see www.sitsa.org/press) argues that the requirements on service providers to monitor communications and to provide assistance to investigators, as outlined in the Draft Convention, would be unduly burdensome and expensive.

Another provision considered objectionable could criminals the creation and use of intrusive software, or hacking programs, which are designed for legitimate security-testing purposes. This action could stifle the advances in technology vital to deep up with evolving cyber threats. Privacy and human rights advocates (see www.gik.org) object to the Draft Convention's lack of procedural safeguards and due process to protect the rights of individuals, and to the possibility that the ensuing national laws would effectively place restrictions on privacy, anonymity, and encryption.

The Council plans to release a final draft of the Convention in December 2000. In 2001, a political process involving national governments will determine the scope and coverage of the final Convention.

Because of cyber crimes' international potential, all countries, and all companies, are affected. Interested parties, including national governments from outside Europe, and businesses and non-governmental organizations from around the world, should participate vigorously in a consensus process to develop measures that support effective international law enforcement and foster continued growth and innovation.

Cyber Laws in India

In May 2000, both the Houses of the Indian Parliament passed the Information Technology Bill. The Bill received the assent of the President in August 2000 and came to be known as the Information Technology Act, 2000. Cyber laws are contained in the IT Act, 2000.

This Act aims to provide the legal infrastructure for e-commerce in India. And the cyber laws have a major impact for e-businesses and the new economy in India. So, it is important to understand what are the various perspectives of the IT Act, 2000 and what it offers.

The Information Technology Act, 2000 also aims to provide for the legal framework so that legal sanctity is accorded to all electronic records and other activities carried out by electronic means. The Act states that unless otherwise agreed, an acceptance of contract may be expressed by electronic means of communication and the same shall have legal validity and enforceability. Some highlights of the Act are listed below

Chapter II of the Act specifically stipulates that any subscriber may authenticate an electronic record by affixing his digital signature. It further states that any person can verify an electronic record by use of a public key of the subscriber.

Chapter III of the Act details about Electronic Governance and provides inter alia amongst others that where any law provides that information or any other matter shall be in writing or in the typewritten or printed form, then, notwithstanding anything contained in such law, such requirement shall be deemed to have been satisfied if such information or matter is-rendered or made available in an electronic form; and accessible so as to be usable for a subsequent reference.

The said chapter also details the legal recognition of Digital Signatures.

Chapter IV of the said Act gives a scheme for Regulation of Certifying Authorities. The Act envisages a Controller of Certifying Authorities who shall perform the function of exercising supervision over the activities of the Certifying Authorities as also laying down standards and conditions governing the Certifying Authorities as also specifying the various forms and content of Digital Signature Certificates. The Act recognizes the need for recognizing foreign Certifying Authorities and it further details the various provisions for the issue of license to issue Digital Signature Certificates.

Chapter VII of the Act details about the scheme of things relating to Digital Signature Certificates. The duties of subscribers are also enshrined in the said Act.

Chapter IX of the said Act talks about penalties and adjudication for various offences. The penalties for damage to computer, computer systems, etc. has been fixed as damages by way of compensation not exceeding Rs. 1,00,00,000 to affected persons. The Act talks of appointment of any officers not below the rank of a Director to the Government of India or an equivalent officer of State Government as an Adjudicating Officer who shall adjudicate whether any person has made a contravention of any of the provisions of the said Act or rules framed thereunder. The said Adjudicating Officer has been given the powers of a Civil Court.

Chapter X of the Act talks of the establishment of the Cyber Regulations Appellate Tribunal, which shall be an appellate body where appeals against the orders passed by the Adjudicating Officers, shall be preferred.

Chapter XI of the Act talks about various offences and the said offences shall be investigated only by a Police Officer not below the rank of the Deputy Superintendent of Police. These offences include tampering with computer source documents, publishing of information, which is obscene in electronic form, and hacking.

The Act also provides for the constitution of the Cyber Regulations Advisory Committee, which shall advice the government as regards any rules, or for any other purpose connected with the said Act. The said, Act also proposes to amend the Indian Penal Code, 1860, the Indian Evidence Act, 1872, the Bankers' Books Evidence Act, 1891, the Reserve Bank of India Act, 1934 to make them in tune with the provisions of the IT Act.

Advantages of Cyber Law

The IT Act, 2000 attempts to change outdated laws and provides ways to deal with cyber crimes. We need such laws so that people can perform purchase transactions over the Net through credit cards without fear of misuse. The Act offers the much, needed legal framework so that information is not denied legal effect, validity or enforceability, solely on the ground that it is in the form of electronic records.

In view of the growth in transactions and communications carried out through electronic records, the Act seeks to empower government departments to accept filing, creating and retention of official documents in the digital format. The Act has also proposed a legal framework for the authentication and origin of electronic records/communications through digital signature.

From the perspective of e-commerce in India, the IT Act, 2000 and its provisions contain many positive aspects. Firstly, the implications of these provisions for the e-businesses would be that e-mail would now be a valid and legal form of communication in our country that can be duly produced and approved in a court of law.

Companies shall now be able to carry out electronic commerce using legal infrastructure provided by the Act.

Digital signatures have been given legal validity and sanction in the Act.

The Act throws open the doors for the entry of corporate companies in the business of being Certifying Authorities for issuing Digital Signatures Certificates.

The Act now allows Government to issue notification on the web thus heralding e-governance.

The Act enables the companies to file any form, application or any other document with any office, authority; the appropriate Government may prescribe body or agency owned or controlled by the appropriate Government in electronic form by means of such electronic form as.

The IT also addresses the important issues of security, which are so critical to the success of electronic transactions. The Act has given a legal definition to the concept of secure digital signatures that would be required to have been passed through a system of a security procedure, as stipulated by the Government at a later date.

Under the IT Act, 2000, it shall now be possible for corporate to have a statutory remedy in case if anyone breaks into their computer systems or network and causes damages or copies data. The remedy provided by the Act is in the form of monetary damages, not exceeding Rs. 1 crore.

Salient Features of the IT ACT, 2000

The Act has defined cyber crime for the first time and provided for penalties, punishment and compensation for hacking unauthorized access to computer networks altering data base, introducing computer viruses, disruption of services, copying of Intellectual Property Rights (IPR) protected software tampering with electronic documents and committing electronic forgery.

The new cyber laws have a provision of penalties up to Rs. 1 crore for damaging computer systems and three year jail term with a fine of Rs. 2 lakh for hackers. But these penalties don't mean much if the existing police investigating officers, forensic scientists, and the judiciary are not familiar with the intricacies of the Internet.

The already over-loaded and under-manner judiciary cannot cope with an entirely new dimension of law breaking. However, the police, the judiciary and the forensic scientists will have to be trained for making them computer savvy for handling cyber crimes.

For successful prosecution of the computer crime cases, it is essential that the judiciary is made aware of the associated technological aspects to enable them to appreciate the evidence placed before them and to understand various hurdles in the path of the investigators. The salient features of the fl' Act, 2000 are as follows:

Provides legal recognition to e-commerce, which means that contracts can be enforced.

Records can be kept in an electronic form. Written records also mean electronic records for the purpose of law provide legal recognition for digital signatures. Digital signatures of the authenticated by Certifying Authorities.

Certifying Authorities to be overseen by a Controller of Certifying Authorities.

Cyber crimes defined for the first time.

Adjudicating authorities to decide if cyber crimes have been committed.

Cyber Law Appellate Tribunal to be set up to hear appeals against adjudicating authorities.

Amendment of Indian Penal Code (1860), Indian Evidence Act (1872), Bankers Book Evidence Act (1891) and the Reserve Bank of India Act (1934) to bring them in tune with the information technology regime.

The provisions of the Act do not apply to a negotiable instrument, a power of attorney, a trust, a will and any contract for the sake or conveyance of immovable property or any interest in such property. It is significant that it applies to any offence or contravention committed outside India by any person (irrespective of his nationality), if it involves a computer, computer system, or computer network located in India.

It excludes network service providers from its ambit for any third party information (that is, any information dealt with by them in their capacity as intermediaries) or data made available by them, if they prove that the offence was committed without their knowledge, and they had taken all precautions to prevent such commission. However, more explicitly, various computer crimes that are not yet defined in the Act may be taken up to deal with the rapid technological changes that would he taking place in future.

The Information Technology Act, 2000 being India's first cyber law is the central legislation, which has been created by the Parliament of India, interestingly it applies not only to the whole of India including the State of Jammu and Kashmir but also to any contravention or violation committed thereunder by any person anywhere in the world State Governments have also been given the power to enact appropriate rules in the field of Information Technology.

In fact, Section 90 of the IT Act categorically states that the State Government may, by notification in the official Gazette, make rules to carry out the provisions of the Information Technology Act. The rules to be made by the State Governments may include the electronic forms through, which common man communicates with the Government Departments or the format in, which electronic record.

The State Governments have appropriate power to legislate rules thereunder apart from List, which is detailed in the Constitution of India. Of course, it is under Section 90 of the IT Act shall immediately be laid before each House of the State Legislature for approval.

11

The Information Technology Act, 2000

General Definitions

1. **Computer**- Means any electronic, magnetic optical or other high speed data processing device or system, which performs logical arithmetic and memory functions by manipulations of electronic magnetic or optical impulses, and includes all input, output, processing storage computer software or communication facilities, which are connected or related to a computer in a computer system or computer network. [Sec. 2(1)(I)]

2. **Computer network**- Means the interconnection of one or more computer through- (i) the use of satellite microwave, terrestrial line or other communication media, (ii) terminal or a complex consisting of two or more interconnected computers whether or not the interconnection is continuously maintained. Sec. 2(1)(I)

3. **Data**- Means a representation of information, knowledge, facts, concepts or instructions, which are being prepared or have been prepared in a formalized manner, and is intended to be processed, is being processed or has been processed in a computer system or computer or computer network and may be in any form or internally stored in the memory of the computer. Sec. 2(1)(O)

4. **Electronic form**- With reference to information, means any information generated, sent, received or stored in media, magnetic, optical, computer memory, micro-film, computer generated micro fiche or similar device. Sec. 2(1) R

5. **Information**- Includes data, text, images, sounds, voice, codes, computer programmes, software and data bases or micro films or computer generated micro fiche. Sec. 2(1)(v)

6. **Digital signature**- Means authentication of any electronic record by a subscriber by means of electronic method or procedure in accordance with the provision of Section 3. Sec 2(1)(p)

   a. **Affixing digital signature**- Means adoption of any methodology or procedure by a person for the purpose of authenticating an electronic record by means of digital signature.

   b. **Authentication of electronic records**- Any subscriber may authenticate an electronic record by affixing his digital signature, the authentication of the electronic record shall be effected by the use of asymmetric crypto system and hash function, which envelop and transform the initial electronic record into another electronic record. Hash function means an algorithm mapping or translation of one sequence of bits into another. Electronic record can be verified by using the public keys of the subscriber. Two keys available (a) private key pair used to create a digital signature, (b) public key used to verify the digital signature. Sec. 3

Attribution, Acknowlegement, and Despatch of Electronic Records

1. **Attribution to the originator**- If any electronic record was sent by the originator himself or by a person who had authority to act on behalf of the originator or by an information system programmed by or on behalf of the organizer to operate automatically Sec. 11.
2. **Acknowledgement of receipt**- An acknowledgement of receipt of an electronic record may be given by the addressee either by an communication, automated or otherwise or by any conduct sufficient to indicate that the record has been agreed by the originator. Where the acknowledgement has been prescribed than accordingly, if the originator does not receive the acknowledgement within a prescribed period have where no acknowledgement was prescribed. Within a reasonable time, then after a notice to this effect has been given and no response received the record shall be treated as if it was never sent (Sec. 12).
3. **Despatch and Receipt** (Sec. 13)- Save as agreed to between the originator and addressee, the despatch of an electronic record occurs when it enters a computer resource outside the control of the originator and the receipt of the record occurs otherwise than as agreed between the parties as follows: -

   (1) If the addressee as designated a computer for the purpose of receiving electronic records: -

   (a) Receipt occurs at the time when the record enters the designated computer rccord.

   (b) When the record is sent to the computer record not designated by the addressee receipt occurs at the time when the addressee retrieves the record.

   (2) If the addressee has not désignated the resource along with the timings, the receipt occurs when the electronic record enters the computer resource of the addressee.

The place of despatch is deemed to be at the place where the originator has his place of business and the place of receipt where the addressee has his place of business. (Usual place of business means the place where it is registered).

What is a secure digital signature?

If it can be verified that a digital signature at the time it was affixed was: -

(1) Unique to the subscriber affixing if,

(2) Capable of identifying the subscriber,

(3) Created in a manner or means under the exclusive control of the subscriber related to the electronic record to, which it relates in such a manner that if the record was altered the digital signature would be invalid.

Regulation of Certifying Authorities

(1) The Central Government may appoint a Controller of Certifying Authority and may also appoint such number of Deputy Controllers and Assistant Controllers as it deems fit. Sec. 17

(2) Functions of Controller- [Sec. 18]

(a) Exercising supervision over the activities, laying down the standard and certifying authorities.

(b) Specifying the qualifications and experiences of the employees and the conditions subject to, which the certifying authorities shall conduct business.

(c) Specifying the form and content of a digital signature certificate and the key and the manner in, which the accounts are to be maintained.

(d) Specifying the conduct, resolving the conflict of interest bit authorities and subscribers, laying down duties and maintaining the database and facilitating the establishment of any electronic system, etc.

(3) Controller shall be the repository of all the digital signature certificates. [Sec. 20]

(4) Any person may make the application to the Controller for a license to issue digital signature certificate provided he fulfils the requirement as may be prescribed by the Central Government. The license granted under this section shall-

(a) be valid for a period as prescribed by the Central Government;

(b) Not be transferable or heritable;

(c) be subject to Government. [Sec. 21]

(5) Every application for issue of license shall be accompanied by- [Sec. 22]

(a) A certification practice statement.

(b) A statement including the procedures with respect to identification of the applicant.

(c) Payment of fees not exceeding 25000 rupees.

(d) Such other document, as may be prescribed by the Government.

(6) An application for renewal shall be made not less than 45 days before the expiry of the period of the validity of license. [Sec. 23]

(7) Suspension of license- The Controller may, if he thinks that a Certifying Authority has-

(a) Made a statement in or in relation to, the application for the issue or renewal of the license, which is incorrect or false in material particulars.

(b) Failed to comply with the terms and conditions subject to, which the license was granted.

(c) Failed to maintain the standards specified under section 20(2)(b)(b).

(d) Contravened any provision of this act, rule, regulation or order made thereunder.

No license shall be revoked unless the certifying authority has been proposed revocation.

No license shall be suspended for a period exceeding ten days opportunity of showing cause against proposed suspension. Once the license has been suspended the certifying authority shall not issue any digital signature certificate. [Sec. 25]

(8) The Controller or any officer authorized by him shall take up investigation of any contravention of the provision, rule or regulation made under this act. [Sec. 28]

(9) Controller if he had reasonable cause to suspect that any contravention of the provision of this act has been committed. Have access to any computer system, any apparatus, data or any other material connected with such system any apparatus data or any other material connected with such system for the purpose of searching or causing a search to be made for obtaining any information or data contained in or available to such computer system. [Sec. 29]

Procedures to be followed by Certifying Authority [Sec. 30]

(a) Make use of hardware, Software and procedure that are secure from intrusion and misuse.

(b) Provide a reasonable level of reliability in its service, which are reasonably suited to the performance of intended function.

(c) Adhere to security procedure to ensure thatsecrecy and privacy of the digital signature are assured.

(d) Observe such other standards as may be specified by regulations.

Disclosures: [Sec. 34]

Every certifying authority shall disclose

(a) Its digital signature certificate, which contains the public key corresponding to the private key, used by that certifying authority to digitally sign another digital signature certificate.

(b) Any certification practise statement relevant thereto.

(c) Notice of revocation or suspension of its certifying authority certificate.

(d) Any other fact that materially and adversely affects either the reliability of a digital signature certificate, or authorities ability to perform its services.

Issue of Digital Signature Certificate: [Sec. 36]

A certifying authority shall certify that

(a) It has complied with the provision of this act and the rules in regulation.

(b) It has published the digital signature certificate or otherwise made it available to such person relying on it and the subscriber has accepted it.

(c) The subscriber holder the private key corresponding to the public key listed in the digital signature certificate.

(d) The subscriber's public key and private key constitute a functioning key pair.

(e) The information contain in the digital signature certificate is accurate.

(f) It has no knowledge of any material fact, which if had been included in the digital signature certificate would adversely affect the reliability of the representations in clauses (a) to (d).

Suspension of Digital Signature Certificate: [Sec. 37]

The certifying authority

(a) On receipt of a request from:

  (1) The subscriber listed in the digital signature certificate,

  (2) Any person duly authorized to act on behalf of the subscriber.

(b) Is of opinion that the digital signature certificate should be suspended in public interest. May suspend such digital signature certificate.

Suspensions shall not exceed the period of fifteen days unless the subscriber has been given an opportunity of being heard in the matter.

Revocation: [Sec. 38]

A certifying authority may:

(a) Where the subscriber or any other person authorized him makes a request to that effect.

(b) Upon the death of subscriber.

(c) Upon the dissolution of the firm or winding up of the company where the subscriber is a firm or a company.

(d) Where as material fact represented in the digital signature certificate is false or has been concealed.

(e) Where a requirement for issuance of the digital signature certificates was not satisfied.

(f) Where the certifying authorities private key or security system was materially affecting the digital signature certificate reliability.

(g) Where the subscriber has been declared insolvent.

Maybe revoke the digital signature certificate issued after giving an opportunity of being heard to the subscriber and on revocation ought to communicate the same to the subscriber.

Duties of Subscribers

(1) Generation of key pair by applying the security procedure. [Sec. 40]

(2) Acceptance of digital signature certificate, when the subscriber publishes or authorizes the publication- (a) to one or more persons; (b) in a repository; (c) demonstrates the approval in any other manner. [Sec. 41 (1)]

(3) Every subscriber shall exercise reasonable care to retain control of the private key corresponding to the public key listed in the digital signature certificate and takes all steps to prevent its disclosure to a person not authorized to affix the digital signature of the subscriber. The subscriber shall communicate any compromise to the private key, without any delay to the certifying authority; it is further declared that the subscriber shall be liable till he has informed the certifying authority of the compromise. [Sec. 42]

(4) All representation and information contained in the digital signature certificate after acceptance by the subscriber shall be held to be true for the purpose of persons relying on the information available in the digital signature certificate. [Sec. 41(2)]

Penalties and Adjudication

(1) If any person without permission of the owner or any other person who is incharge of a computer, computer system or computer network-

(a) Accesses such computer, computer system or network.

(b) Downloads, copies or extracts any data, computer database or information.

(c) Damages or causes to be damaged any computer, computer system or network data computer database or any other programmes.

(d) Disrupts or causes disruption.

(e) Denies or causes the denial of access to any persons authorized to access.

(f) Provides any assistance to any person to facilitate access in contravention of the provisions of this act.

(g) Charges the services availed of by a person to the account of another person by tempering with or manipulating any computer, computer system or network.

He shall be liable to pay damages up to ten lakhs to the person so affected. [Sec. 43]

General definitions [Sec. 43]

(1) "Computer contaminant means any set of computer instructions that are designed:

(a) To modify, destroy, record, transfer data or programme residing within a computer system or network

(b) By any means to usurp the normal operation of the computer, computer system or network.

(2) "Computer database" means representation of information knowledge affects concepts or instructions in text, image, audio, video that are being prepared or have being prepared in a formalized manner or have been produced by a computer, computer system or network,

(3) "Computer virus" means any computer instruction, information data or programmer that destroys, damages, degrades or adversely affects the performance of a computer resource or attaches itself to another computer resource and operates when a programme data or instruction is executed or some other event takes place in that computer resource.

(4) "Damages" means to destroy, alter, delete, add, modify or rearrange any computer resource by any means.

If any person who is required under this act to- (Section 44]

(a) Furnish any document, return or that report to the controller or the certifying authority fails to furnish the same shall be liable to a penalty not exceeding 150000 for each such failure

(b) File any return or furnish any information books or other documents within the time specified, shall liable to penalty not exceeding 50000 for everyday during, which such failure continues

(c) Maintain books of accounts or records, fails to maintain the same, shall be liable to a penalty not exceeding 10000 rupees for every- day during, which the failure continues.

Residuary Penalty- [Section 45]

If any person contravenes any rules or regulations made under this act, he is liable to compensation up to 25000 rupees to the person affected by such contravention.

Power to Adjudicate- [Sec. 46]

(1) The Central Government shall appoint any officer not below the rank of a Director to the Government to be an adjudicating officer for holding an enquiry for any contravention of any of the provision of this act or any rule, regulation, direction, or any order made by the Central Government.

(2) A reasonable opportunity for making a representation shall be given to the person against whom the enquiry was made by the adjudicating officer, and on his satisfaction he may impose such penalty or award such compensation as he deems fit. The jurisdiction of the adjudicating officer shall be specified by the Central Government.

(3) Factors to be taken into account by the adjudicating officer- [Sec. 47]

(a) The amount of gain of unfair advantage wherever quantifiable made as a result of the default.

(b) The amount of loss caused to any person as a result of the default.

(c) The repetitive nature of the default.

Cyber Regulation Appellate Tribunal

(1) Central Government shall establish one or more appellate tribunals to be known and places Regulation Appellate Tribunal and shall specify the matters and places in relation to, which the tribunal may exercise jurisdiction. [Sec. 48]

(2) The tribunal shall consist of one person only to be appointed by the Central Govt. referred to as Presiding Officer in this act. [Sec. 49]

(3) A person shall not be qualified for appointment as a presiding officer unless: (a) he is or has been or is qualified to be a judge of the High Court, (b) is or has been a member of Indian Legal Services and is holding or has held a post in Grade I of that service for a term of five years.

(4) The presiding officer shall not be removed from the office except by an order by the Central Govt. on the ground of proved misbehaviour court.

(5) CAT shall not be bound be the procedure laid down be the CPC, but shall be guided by the principles of natural justice and subject to other provisions of this act. The CAT shall have the same powers as are vested in the civil courts, for the purpose of discharging its functions under this act the CAT shall have the same powers as are vested in the civil courts, for the purpose of discharging its functions under this act namely- [Sec. 58]

(a) Summoning and enforcing the attendance of any person and examining him on oath.

(b) Requiring the discovery and production of documents of other electronic records.

(c) Receiving evidence on affidavits.

(d) Issuing commissions for the examination of witnesses or documents.

(e) Reviewing its decisions.

(f) Dismissing an application for default or deciding it exparte.

(g) Any other matter, which may be prescribed.

(6) The provisions of Limitation Act shall apply as far as to an appeal made to the CAT. Civil courts shall not have jurisdictions to entertain any suit or proceeding in respect of any matter constituted under this act and no injunction shall be granted by any court or other authority in respect of any action taken or to be taken or to be taken in pursuance of any power conferred by or under this Act. Further, any person aggrieved by any decision or order of CAT may file any appeal to the High Court within 60 days from the date of communication of the decisions or order.

Offences

(1) Whoever knowingly or intentionally conceals destroys, or alters or intentionally or knowingly cause another to conceal. Destroy or alter any computer source code used for computer system or network, shall be punishable with imprisonment up to three years or with fine, which may extend up to 200000 rupees or with both. For the purposes of this section computer source code means the listing of programs computer commands, designs and layout and program analysis of computer resource in any form. [Sec. 65]

(2) Whoever with the intent to cause or knowing that he is likely to cause wrongful loss or damage to the public or any person, destroys or deletes or alters any information. Residing in a computer resource or diminishes its value or its utility or affects it injuriously by any means commits hacking shall be punished with an imprisonment up to three years or with fine, which may extend up to 200000 rupees or with both. [Sec. 66]

(3) Whoever publishes or transmits in the electronic form any material, which is obscene shall be punished conviction with imprisonment of either description for a term, which may extend to five years and with fine, which may extend to one lakh rupees and in case of subsequent conviction imprisonment of a term, which may extend to 10 years with fine- 2 lakhs. [Sec. 67]

(4) For obtaining any license or digital signature certificate if any person makes any misrepresentation or suppresses any material facts shall be punished with imprisonment of two years or with fine- 1 lakh rupees or with both. [Sec. 71]

(5) Penalty for breach of confidentiality and privacy-imprisonment-2 years or with fine- 1 lakh rupees or with both. [Sec. 72]

(6) Publication for fraudulent purposes; imprisonment-2 years or with fine- 1 lakh rupees or with both. [Sec. 74]

(7) If any person publishes a digital signature certificate or otherwise makes it available to any other person with the knowledge that: - (a) the certifying authority listed in the certificate has not issued it; or (b) the subscriber listed in the certificate has not accepted it; (c) the certificate has been revoked or suspended unless such publication is for the purpose of verifying a digital signature created prior to such suspension or revocation, he shall be punished to imprisonment-2 years or fine- 1 lakh rupees or both. [Sec. 73]

(8) Subject to the provisions of sub-section (2), the provisions of this Act shall also apply to any offence or contravention committed outside India by any person irrespective of his nationality. For the purpose of sub-section (1) this Act shall apply to an offence or contravention outside India by any person if the act conduct constituting the offence or contravention involves a computer, computer system or computer Network located in India. [Sec. 75]

(9) Confiscation any computer, computer system, floppies, compact disks tapes provisions of this Act, rules, orders or regulations made thereunder, the court may, instead of making an order for confiscation make such other order authorized by this Act against the person as it may think fit. [Sec. 76]

(10) No penalty imposed or confiscation made under this Act shall prevent the imposition of any other punishment to, which the person affected thereby is liable under any other law for the time being in force. [Sec. 77]

(11) Notwithstanding anything contained in the CPC, a police officer not below the rank of Deputy Superintendent of Police shall investigate any offence under this Act. [Sec. 78]

The Act declares that no person providing any services as a network services provider shall be liable under this act, rules or regulations made for any third party information or data made available by him if he proves that the offence or contravention was committed without his knowledge or that he had exercised due diligence to prevent the commission of such offence or contravention. "Network provider" means an intermediary.

"Third party information" means any information dealt with by a network service provider in his capacity as intermediary. [Sec. 79]

Section 80 empowers police and other officers to enter into any public place and search and arrest without warrant any person found therein who is reasonably suspected of having committed or about to commit any offence under this Act.

12

The IT Act, 2000 : Provision and Related Issues

Introduction

The IT Act, 2000 is the first kind of legislature created in the Indian Legal System that addresses the need of the Information Technology Age. In the past 10 years or so, the revolution in the information Technology world has set new standards for people in society. It has led to a change in the Latently of people, communities and Business.

The role that a computer plays is getting more and more evolved in society and as a result the measures needed from law are also increasing. The needs to have an updated Legal structure in lieu of the changes in Technology was felt especially during the 90's as there was rapid development especially in the post-Internet era.

A computer was now not merely a complicated machine that would perform elusive functions, it now had become a part of everyday life and people were finding the use of the machine in simple forms. The computers were now a medium of communication, a tool for working and a device with multipurpose applications.

The IT Act essentially addresses certain concerns that Law has faced with emergency of Computers. Primarily the issues related to the Internet and Computers are-

1. Recognition of Computer Data, Paper v. Digital Copy, Establishing equality between traditional law and Digital versions.

2. Evidentiary Value of Electronic Data

3. Jurisdiction on the Internet

4. Business Transactions in the Digital Age

5, Governance and Regulation of the Internet including verification on the Internet.

The legal issues relating to Digital Technology, the Internet and also other aspects of the use of computers are mentioned in brief with illustrative examples below.

Jurisdiction on the Internet

Introduction

Computer Technology and E-commerce have grown to become the buzzwords in corporate circles. The lure of conducting global operations through computers and web can reach web sites has become irresistible. Ironically, because a page on the World Wide Web can reach web Surfers every state.

In the nation and perhaps every nation on earth, there arises the issue of where exactly a person who has a cause of action, based upon a web transaction, may sue anywhere on wrath can certainly have a chilling effect on perhaps the most powerful medium in the history of communication. Have heralded the emergence of the Internet as signaling a near-evisceration of traditional choice-of-law analysis. As users and system an operator (sysops) encounter-conflicts and seeks to resolve disputes. They take action to establish rules and decide individual cases.

Moreover, the Internet's doctored nature makes it likely that any given Internet transaction will involve parties from more than one jurisdiction. All this creates a new from of law-a law of cyberspace-based on private contracting on a global basis and introduced by a combination of the sysop's ultimate right to banish unruly users and the user's ultimate right to migrate to other on line service providers. As a consequence of this, analysts have thrown up a number of suggestions. Some suggest that cyberspace requires its own set of jurisdictional rules thus extinguishing geographical borders. Certain aspects of the Internet have been compared to surface mail and telephone systems, as well as advertisements in national publications.

Jurisdiction-the concept

The effectiveness of a judicial system resets on a bedrock of regulations, which define every aspect of a system's functioning-and principally, its jurisdiction. A court must have jurisdiction, venue and appropriate service of process in order to hear a case and render an effective judgment. Jurisdiction is the power of a court to hear and determine a case. Without jurisdiction, a court's judgment is ineffective and important.

Such jurisdiction, is essentially of two types namely subject-matter jurisdiction and personal jurisdiction, and these two must be conjunctively satisfied for a judgment to take effect. It is the presence of jurisdiction that ensures the power of Informant to a court-and in the absence of such power, the verdict of a court is to say the least, of little or no use. Moreover, only generally accepted principals of jurisdiction would ensure that courts aboard also enforce the orders of other judicial bodies.

Internet jurisdiction

The whole trouble with Internet jurisdiction is the presence of multiple parties in various parts of the world who have only a virtual nexus with each other. Then, if one party wants to sue the other where can he sue? Traditional requirement generally en-compass two areas firstly the place where the defendant resides, or secondly where the cause of action arises. However, in the context of the Internet, both theses are difficult to establish with any certainty. Even a childishly simple transaction can give rise to a mind-boggling issue of jurisdiction the Net.

For example, A, in India, decides to download an article from a web site, and pays money for it through a credit card, and then is unable to perform the download. He wants to sue the owner of the site. But the owner is in Thailand. The site itself is based in a server in Brazil. Where does the defendant reside? The Transaction occurred on the net. So was it in India, or in Brazil?

Issues of this nature have contributed to the complete confusion and contradictions that plague judicial decisions in the area of Internet jurisdictions. Considering the lack of physical boundaries on the Internet, is it possible to reach out beyond the court's geographical boundaries to haul a defendant into its court for conduct in "cyberspace"?

It is worth examining the decision in cyber sell, I nc. As a typical example of a fact situation involving a conflict over Jurisdiction. The case involved a service mark dispute between two corporations, one at Orlando and another at Arizona.

The court had to address the issue of weather the mere use of a web-site by the Florida corporation. The court answered the questions in the negative, focusing on traditional analysis established by the US Supreme Court concerning the due process aspects of personal jurisdiction : "it is essential in each case that there be some act by, which the defendant purposefully avails itself of the privilege of conducting activates within the forum state thus invoking the benefits and protections of its laws."

The Court rejected the plaintiffs argument that by employing a web page, without more a web publisher was subject to jurisdiction in the plaintiff's from. The court also rejected the plaintiffs reliance on the "effects-test", holding, that the test does not apply with the same force to a corporation as it does to an individual "because a corporation does not suffer harm in a particular geographic location in the same sense that an individual does".

A similar result was reached in Smith V. Hobby Lobby Stores inc. v. Boto Co. "The court held there were insufficient contacts for personal jurisdiction over the counter defendant, where this company had no real contact with the state aside from a Web page that could be accessed from the state".

However, decision of this nature does not solve the entire issue. Not only are there contradictory judgments, but also more complex fact situations give rise to progressively confusing holdings, with little or no consistency.

For example in Edias Software International L.L.C. v. Basis International Ltd., the contractual relationship between an Arizona limited liability company and a new Mexico corporation combined with be defendant's use of the Internet was used to justify jurisdiction in Arizona not-withstanding that the contract provided that would be governed by the law of the state of New Mexico.

Another illustrative matter is that of United States v. Thomas, which involved a California couple who operated a computer bulletin board that contained various sexually explicit images and also offered sexually explicit videotapes for sale.

A United States postal inspector, surfing the web came across the web site and applied for membership on the bulletin board from his office in Tennessee. He also ordered several videotapes. After the password was issued and the tapes delivered, the couple was arrested. They were indicted in the Western District of Tennessee and charge with various violations of federal obscenity laws. "Obscene" was required to be judged inter alia, by community standards of Memphis, Tennessee, where the allegedly obscene materials were received. The defence, on the other hand, argued that the defendants should be judged by the community standards of Milpitas, California, or, failing that by the standards of cyberspace itself.

The court ruled that "juries are properly instructed to apply the community standards of the geographic area where the materials are sent," and that the community standards of Tennessee should therefore apply. The defendants argued that they did not cause the images to be transported to Tennessee. They merely made the images available online for members of the bulletin board; it was the postal inspector who caused the images to enter Tennessee by downloading them.

While dismissing this argument, the court notes that the defendants were technologically able if they had so chosen to limit user access in jurisdiction with more restrictive obscenity laws than those in California. Because defendants know they had a member in Memphis they could be held to the moral standards of the community. Thus because the defendants entered into a transaction with a member in Memphis, they could be judged by reference to those standards. "Fast situations such as this raise multifarious questions that are difficult, if not impossible to answer with the application of contemporary legal principles. Then to what extent should we force old models and analogies on this new way of communicating and doing business"?

Cases of Cyberspace Jurisdiction

The earliest reported decision is Pres-Kap, Inc' V. System One, Direct Access, Inc., which involved electronic contacts through a computerized airline reservation system. The plaintiff owned and operated a computerized airline reservation system. The computer base for the system, as well as the plain-tiffs main billing office, was in Florida. A branch business office operated out of New York. The defendant, a New York corporation, owned and operated a travel office in New York.

The two parties negotiated a lease contract in New York, the breach of, which was the subject of the lawsuit. The court found only two contacts between the defendant and the forum-state Florida, namely that the defendant forwarded lease payments to a billing office in Miami, and that the defendant's computers made electronic contacts with the plain-tiffs computer base in Florida. Citing Burger King Corp v. Rudzewicz, the court found that a contract with an out-of state party alone could not establish jurisdiction.

That left only the electronic contacts for the court to consider. The Florida Appeals Court held that electronic contacts with a computer database located in the forum-state were insufficient to establish personal jurisdiction. Thus, the defendant did not purposefully avail, himself of Florida's jurisdiction, and the first prong of the test failed. In addition, the court warned about the unfairness of allowing jurisdiction where the only contacts are between computers.

In Panavision v. Toeppen, the plaintiff, a Delaware limited partnership with its principal place of business in Los Angeles, California, succeeded in establishing jurisdiction in California over an individual residing in Illinois by relying chiefly upon the effects test. The case focused on a domain name dispute, involving an alleged "cybersquatter", who occupied Panaviskm's domain name with the intent of extorting money from it.

The court ruled, based on the effects test, that personal jurisdiction was proper because, "Toeppen allegedly registered Panavision's trade marks as domain names with the knowledge that the names belonged to Panavision and with the intent to interfere with Panavision's business Toeppen has harmed Panavision, the brunt of, which Panavision has borne in California, which Toeppen knew would likely happen because Panavision's principal place of business and the heart of the theatrical motion picture and television camera and photographic equipment business are in California."

Advertising on the web

The US courts have issued strongly divergent opinions on whether jurisdiction can be based solely on an Internet presence, without any contractual relationship between plaintiff and defendant. Some cases have held that advertising on the Internet is enough to create jurisdiction, while other cases reach the opposite conclusion.

In Inset Systems, Inc. v. Instruction Set, Inc., 35 the court held that advertising over Internet was purposefully directed toward the forum-state. The plain-tiff Inset System, Ins ("Inset") was a Connecticut corporations with office and principal place of business in Instruction Set did not have employees in Connecticut nor regularly conduct defendant. Instruction Set was a Massachusetts corporations and principal place of business in Massachusetts. Instruction Set did not have employees in Connecticut, nor regularly conduct business there. Inset involved a dispute between one company's trademark and another's Internet domain name.

Since 1986, Inset had owned the federally registered trademark "INSET". Thereafter,

Instruction Set obtained "INSET. COM" as its Internet domain address. Instruction Set also used the telephone number "1-800-US-INSET" to advertise its goods and services. Inset brought this suit for trademark infringement.

In deciding personal jurisdiction, the court looked to the Connecticut long-arm statute and applied the due process, minimum contact's analysis. The court found that Instruction Set had repeatedly solicited business over the Internet, and thus satisfied the long-arm statute. Finding the travel distance between Connecticut and Massachusetts to be "minimal," the court concluded that jurisdiction comported with fair play and substantial justice".

The US District Court for the Eastern District of Missouri reached a similar conclusion in Maritz, Inc. v. Cyber Gold, Inc." finding that it had jurisdiction over a California defendant in a trade mark infringement case where the defendant's only contact with the state was through its California-based web site, which was accessible in Missouri". These cases are analyzed later in the context of active and passive web sites.

On the other hand, in Bensusan Restaurant Corp. V. King, no personal jurisdiction was found where a web publisher in Missouri published a general access web page that contained ticketing and event information about a jazz dub known as "The Blue Note" in Columbia, Missouri. Tickets, however, were not available directly from the web site. The club owner was sued in New York by a New York corporation that owned "The Blue Note," a popular club in Greenwich Village and, which owned the rights to the "The Blue Note" federal mark. The court observed, "Creating a site, like placing a product into the stream of commerce, may be felt nationwide-or even worldwide-but, without more, it is not an act purposefully directed toward the forum-state."

The court also found that the exercise of personal jurisdiction would violate Constitutional due process, stating that "creating a site, like placing a product into the stream of commerce, may be felt nation wide-or even worldwide-but, without more, it is not an purposefully directed toward the forum state." Tl-ie court found that Bensusan's argument that King should have foreseen that New York users would access his site is insufficient to satisfy due process requirements.

Active v. Passive Web Sites

For jurisdiction purposes web-sites are split into two groups passive and interactive. Passive sites provide information in a "read only" format. Passive activity is considered a "posting" of information, lacking interaction and is typically an advertisement on the Web. Interactive sites encourage browser and/or providing background on the browser's interests or buying habits. It is no surprise that courts are more willing to find that a web publisher who solicits information about the forum's residents is purposefully availing itself of the forum's benefits than a publisher who simply provides information about the publisher, its products and services".

Thus, in Zippo Mfg. Co. v. Zippon Dot Corn, Inc", purposeful availment was found based the defendant's interactive web site and contracts with 3000 individuals and seven. Internet access providers in Pennsylvania in a trade mark infringement suit. The web site here allowed browsers to sign up for the defendant's Internet news service. Defendant was a California company, its employees were located in California, and it maintained no offices in Pennsylvania, where the suit was brought.

Out of the defendant's approximately 1,40,000 paying subscribers worldwide, about 3,000 were Pennsylvania residents. Those subscribers contracted to receive the defendant's service by visiting its Web site and filling out an on-line application. The defendant also entered into agreements with seven Internet access providers in Pennsylvania to allow subscribers to access its news service.

The court concluded that because of the 3,000 Pennsylvania subscribers and the agreements with Pennsylvania ISPS, the defendant had purposefully availed itself of Pennsylvania's jurisdiction. The defendant had minimum contacts with the form-state. Zippo provides a good framework for determining what level of Internet contacts warrants an exercise of jurisdiction. The court envisioned a sliding scale based on the nature and quality of commercial activity" conducted over the Internet. At one end of the spectrum is a defendant who enters into continuing contracts with residents of for jurisdictions, where in assertion of jurisdiction would be appropriate.

At the opposite end is a defendant who has simply posted information on a web site accessible by residents of foreign jurisdictions, where an exercise of jurisdiction would clearly not be appropriate. The middle ground consists of web sites where a user can exchange information, and a court must determine whether to assert jurisdiction by "examining the level of interactivity and commercial nature" of the exchange on the web site. No matter where parties may fall on the spectrum, they should recognize that engaging in commercial activity over the Internet might spawn liability in foreign jurisdictions if that activity consists of something more than a simple posting of information".

Electronic Mail Transactions

Sending e-mail to an individual whose location is known to the sender is similar to set regular mail addressed to an individual at a known location. Thus, one could argue that there is little reason not to exercise jurisdiction over the sender in the location to, which the e-mail was sent. Thus, in Resuscitation Technologies Inc. v. Continental Health Care Corp., "the New York defendant had extensive communication with the Indiana plaintiff, including 80 e-mails. The court in Indiana found the level of activity directed to Indian was substantial-thus giving Indiana personal jurisdiction over the defendant."

However, the issue is far from this simple. Technology behind the Internet has introduced a number of complications. Firstly, an e-mail address does not always indicate the geographical address of the sender. For example, sumitis@hotmail.com could be located anywhere in the world. Similarly, even if one has an e-mail address with a geographic such as sumitis@delhimail.com, one can arrange for it to be forwarded to another or one may access die account from a location outside Delhi.

All these factors have fuelled judicial confusion with regard to the effect of e-mail. As the District Court recognized in ACLU v. Reno", "an e-mail address" provides no authoritative information about the addressee who may use an e-mail 'alias' or an anonymous re-mailer." "With the possible exception of an e-mail to A known recipient, most content providers cannot determine identity and age of even user accessing their material."

Thus, except for e-mail sent to a known recipient, it may be difficult to say that e-mail distribution is a method by, which a Company purposefully use it of the privilege of conducting activities within the recipient's forum State.

Analysis

In general, courts applying the rules of personal jurisdiction to cyberspace have required "something more" than mere electronic contacts to support an exercise of jurisdiction. In addition to electronic contacts, there must be some act purposefully directed toward the forum-state. Thus, courts have focused on the purposeful availment prong of the due process, minimum contacts test. "Though, in exceptional cases, courts have conferred jurisdiction in the absence of my connection beyond a web site, this is unlikely to be sustained in the long run.

It is, firstly, impossible to enforce decisions of this nature in every case, considering that often the web site owner may be in a hostile country, or in a jurisdiction that simply refuses to recognize the jurisdiction of the court issuing the original decree."

Secondly, such an approach would cause considerable inconvenience to any large-scale form of e-business, and could contribute to stagnation of the Internet-something that must be avoided at all costs.

As demonstrated by the cases discussed above, the existing body of law on in personam jurisdiction based on Internet contacts is inconsistent and incoherent at several levels. Fundamentally, the method of analysis of the significance of contacts via., the Internet is still unclear. The court in Zippo analyzed the defendant's contacts by looking at the number of Pennsylvania residents using the defendant's Internet service. In Granite Gate the court looked at the number of Minnesota residents accessing defendant's Web site and the frequency of use by several Minnesota-based Web gamblers. Other courts have referred to the number of times the defendant's Web site was "accessed" by the forum state's residents, or the number of Internet users in the state.

It is submitted that the issue cannot be solved by any objective standard as to contact, but rather requires an analysis of both the quantity and quality of Internet contacts. This would involve the examination of several components, for example, the number of "Hits" a Web site receives, and the number of forum state citizens accessing the site. However, an evaluation cannot stop at this.

All hits are not of equal weight for jurisdictional purposes, so courts and commentators need to develop a hierarchy of different types of Internet contacts in order to evaluate the totality of a defendant's contacts with a forum.

Evolution of a new system

One of the suggestions that has been made towards the resolution of this rather troublesome problem, is the evolution of new and entirely independent rules to govern jurisdiction on the Internet. These regulator structures should treat cyberspace as a distinct place for purposes of legal analysis. This suggestion originates from the conception that cyberspace has its own sovereign jurisdiction. By developing a uniform law governing cyberspace transactions, it will be much easier to determine, which rules regulate one's online activities, rather than deciding, which territory's laws apply.

The next question that arises from this-approach is who is to develop and enforce these rules. It is suggested that the Internet community can, "develop its own, effective legal institutions." The proponents of system suggest that since the Internet was implemented through a system of self-governance those persons can establish a system to govern themselves. Yet, the determination of those who would have the "ultimate" right to control the p>!-uncertain. Another criticism of this suggestion is its sheer impracticably. I Inmatci must decide jurisdiction it only to regulate their sphere of influence and decision-m power. An independent set of rules, ignoring geographical factors, is unlikely to be workable in this context. Another suggestion has been the creation of some mechanism for alternative dispute resolution. In this regard, there has emerged the Vitual Magistrate Project.

Like other arbitration schemes, the Virtual Magistrate must obtain jurisdiction over parties by consent. This consent can be obtained in at least two ways, consent by explicit agreement and implied in fact consent. Under this first method, parties may manifest consent entirely through electronic means. The implied in fact agreements would involve consenting to jurisdiction through a term of the contract between the service providers and subscribers. As a result, once an event had been noticed for Virtual Magistrate resolution, the service provider could compel participation. If successful, the Virtual Magistrate would be a big step toward the establishment of a cyberspace jurisdiction.

Conclusion

The Indian Code of Civil Procedure, 1908, bases territorial jurisdiction 17 on two principles first, the place of residence of the defendant, and second, the place where the cause of action arises. However, there are no clear guidelines as to how these are to be determined. In the context of the Internet, residence of the defendant may well include either his place of physical residence, or the place where the web-site server is located.

Similarly, the cause of action may be said to arise at a variety of places where the site is accessed or where its server is located. But in the absence of airy statutory clarification, courts will be forced to rely upon precedents, such as those described above.

The review of the decisions seems to indicate that any active attempt to utilize the World Wide Web to reach its vast audience will likely subject the publisher to a lawsuit in a distant forum. The growing popularity of interactive sites enabling the browsers to do business with the publisher from their desktops alone will almost certainly provide a basis for jurisdiction in the plaintiffs chosen court.

Furthermore, a web site coupled with a toll-free number will almost certainly indicate an intention to reach the widest possible market, also permitting a court to exercise jurisdiction over the defendant. "The effect of this could be to force web site owners to attempt to restrict access to their sites to local persons, thus affecting the global reach of the Internet-one of its primary aims. Parties to a contract may select a prefer-red forum, or a preferred choice of law, as a part of their agreements with each other. Similarly, parties to a lawsuit, or a potential lawsuit, may select a forum or applicable law after the fact, in order to smoothen matters at trial.

In the absence of dear choice-of-law rules, courts could benefit by abiding by the wishes of the parties and enforcing valid forum-selection clauses." Thus, if one is concerned about jurisdiction in connection with commercial transactions, it may be advisable to create on-line agreements that govern those transactions and to specify the jurisdiction in, which any disputes will be litigated and the law that will be applied. It is also probably advisable to require users to manifest their assent to such agreements before they enter into any transactions (in order to help avoid "shrink\vrap"-type arguments that the agreement unenforceable).

Generally, a forum is safe in applying its own law to a controversy being tried in its courts. After all, if the suit is proceeding in a forum, it must have a sufficient relationship to the transaction to have jurisdiction over the parties." Thus, often, a forum that is torn between two conflicting laws often chooses to apply its own law. Although this reaction is certainly understandable-a forum will always be most familiar with the nuances of its own laws-such a rule, on the whole, would be unwise.

This could give rise to forum shopping by plaintiffs. If forum shopping is allowed on a global scale, it could lead to situations, which are not entirely equitable- for example, plaintiffs would sue in nations where the defendants are unable to respond, either due to absence of resources, or due to unfavourable legal conditions in that particular forum.

Until the law in this area becomes clearer, there are at least some lessons we can learn from the cases that have been decided so far. For instance, there may be some jurisdictions in, which you will not want to do business at all if the nature of your business requires that users be a certain age or if' your business is banned or regulated in certain areas (for example, gambling), then it may be necessary to identify all users before they can be permitted to engage in transactions, and to prohibit transactions with certain users and in certain jurisdictions".

Other strategies to minimize risk include:

1. Lin-tit the Degree of Interaction, because the provision of "goods" in the four transmitted data or information requested by a user, or the acceptance of purch orders through the Web site, may suffice to establish specific jurisdiction relating to that transmission or transaction.

2. Limit the Amount of Non-Interest Promotion and Solicitation, so that the courts are unable to identify the vital 'other contact" that they mostly rely upon to obtain jurisdiction.

3. Decline Business from Remote Locales, by making it clear that the site is only directed at persons from a particular region or locality. This would do away with the "purposeful availment" requirement of the minimum contacts test.

Further, site owners can limit the site's interactivity. Inviting consumers to sign on for services, post messages and order products from a Web site may increase the chances that a court will find purposeful availment.

Jurisdiction under the IT Act, 2000

The IT Act, passed in India, is illustrative of the prevailing confusion in the area of jurisdiction in the context of the Internet. The Act begins by saying, in clause (2) to section 1, that it shall extend to the whole of India and, save as otherwise provided in the A applies also to any offence or contravention thereunder committed outside India by person.

Clause (2) of Section 75 of the Act also simply states that this Act shall apply in offence or contravention committed outside India by any person if the act or conduct constituting the offence or contravention involves a computer, computer system; computer network located in India." Provisions of this nature are unlikely to be free for a number of reasons.

Firstly, it is unfair to suggest that the moment an Indian computer system is used, an a defined by Indian laxvs as an "offence" would be subject to the jurisdiction of India'.

To illustrate, let us consider a web site located in a foreign country. The site may host content that would be perfectly legal in its home country, but may be considered offensive or illegal in India. If an Indian chooses to view this site on a computer situated in India, does that mean that the site can be prosecuted in an Indian Court?

This would appear to violate principles of justice. As explained earlier, the judicial trend of examining the amount of activity that a site undertakes in a particular jurisdiction is a far more equitable method to determine jurisdiction.

Further, even if Indian Courts are to claim jurisdiction and pass judgments on the basis of the principle expostulated by the IT Act, it is unlikely that foreign Courts will enforce these judgments since they would not accept the principles utilized by the Act as adequate to grant Indian Courts jurisdiction. This would also render the Act ineffective.

In this context, it is necessary that Indian courts take a leaf out of the books of American counterparts and develop justifiable grounds on, which extraterritorial jurisdiction may be validly exercised, The times ahead promise to be very interesting.

13

Computer Crimes and the Act

Introduction

World over there is a great concern due to various types of crimes committed by using computers and on the Internet.

Almost everyday there is an international story about some or the other portal attacked or credit card fraud or some virus bringing down the system.

Broadly such crimes can be classified as:

- Unauthorized access
- Unauthorized interception
- Unauthorized use of computer, computer system
- Computer related fraud
- Computer forgery
- Damage to computer data
- Computer sabotage

The Information Technology Act covers in detail various types of computer crimes and the penalties provided for such crimes.

Some of the important provisions of the Act in respect of the crimes and offences are as under:

S/43. Penalty for damage to computer, computer system, etc. S/43 If any person without permission of the owner or any other person who is in charge of a computer, computer system or computer network-

(a) accesses or secures access Explanation

(b) downloads, copies or extracts any data,

(i) "computer database! means a representation of

computer data base or information	information, knowledge, facts, concepts or instructions in text, image, audio, video that are being prepared or have been prepared in a formalized manner or have been produced by a computer, computer system or computer network and are intended for use in a computer, computer system or computer network.
(c) introduces or causes to be introduced any computer contaminant or computer virus	(ii) "computer contaminant" means any set of computer instructions that are designed- (a) to modify, destroy, record, transmit data or programme residing within a computer, computer system or computer network, or (b) by any means to usurp the normal operation of the computer, computer system, or computer network; (iii) "computer virus" means any computer instruction, information, data or programme that destroys, affects the performance of a computer resource or attaches itself to another computer resource and operates when a programme, data or instruction is executed or some other event takes place in that computer resource:
(d) damages or causes to be	

damaged any computer, computer system or computer network, data, computer data base or any other programmes
(iv) "damage" means to destroy, alter, delete, add, modify or rearrange any computer resource by any means.

(e) disrupts or causes disruption.

(f) denies or causes the denial of access to any person authorized to access.

(g) provides any assistance to any person to facilitate access in contravention of the provisions of this Act, rules or regulations made thereunder.

(h) charges the services availed of by a person to the account of another person by tampering with or manipulating

He shall be liable to pay damages by way of compensation not exceeding one crore rupees to the person so affected.

REMEMBER KEVIN MITNICK?

Kevin Mitnick, a software programmer in the US, was involved in what was probably one of the most sensational computer crimes. He was a famous hacker who hacked into the files of Shimomura a security expert at the San Diego computer centre. The FBI later arrested him.

Mitnick was sentenced to serve one year in jail, being credited for the seven-and-a-half months he spent incarcerated before his plea. He was then to enter a rehabilitation programme in Los Angeles to be treated as a "computer addict".

Some of the important provisions of the Act in respect of the crimes and offences are as under in, which penalties as well as punishment with imprisonment for different terms are prescribed.

Sec. No.	*What Offence*	*Penalty*	*Remarks*
65	Tampering with computer source documents	shall be punishable with imprisonment up to three years, or with fine, which may extend up to two lakh rupees, or with both.	Explanation-For the purposes of this section, "computer source code" means the listing of programmes, computer Commands, design and layout and programme analysis of computer resource in any form.
66	Hacking with Computer System	Whoever commits hacking shall be punished with imprisonment up to three years, or with fine, which may extend up to two lakh rupees, or with both	Whoever with the intent to cause or knowing that he is likely to cause wrongful loss or damage to the public or any person, destroys or deletes or alters any information residing in a computer resource or diminishes its value or utility or affects it injuriously by any means, commits hacking.
67	Publishing of	shall be punished	Whoever publishes

	information which is obscene in electronic form	on first conviction with imprisonment of either description for a term, which may extend to two years and with fine, which may extend to one lakh rupees and in the event of a second or subsequent conviction with imprisonment of either description for a term, which may extend to ten years and also with fine, which may extend to two lakh rupees.	or transmits or causes to be published in the electronic form, any material, which is lascivious or appeals to the prurient interest or if its effect is such as to tend to deprave and corrupt persons who are likely, having regard to all relevant circumstances, to read, see or hear the matter contained or embodied in it.
70	Protected system (1) The Appropriate Government may, by notification in the Official Gazette, declare that any computer, computer system or computer network to be a protected system.	shall be punished with imprisonment of either description for a term, which may extend to ten years and shall also be liable to fine.	Any person who secures access or attempts to secure access to a protected system in contravention of the provisions of this section.

71	Penalty for misrepresentation	shall be punished with imprisonment for a term, which may extend to two years, or with fine, which may extend to one lakh rupees, or with both.	Whoever makes any misrepresentation to, or suppresses any material fact from, the Controller or the Certifying Authority for obtaining licence or Digital Signature Certificate, case may be.

Hackers Beware

64. Recovery of penalty

A penalty imposed under this Act, if it is not paid, shall be recovered as an arrear of land revenue and the licence or the Digital Signature Certificate, as the case may be, shall be suspended till the penalty is paid.

For instance in Maharashtra such penalty can be recovered under the Maharashtra Land Revenue code inter alia by one or more of the following process: (S./176)

- by serving a written notice of demand on the defaulter,
- by distrait and sale of the defaulter's moveable property.
- by attachment and sale of defaulter's immovable property,
- by arrest and imprisonment of the defaulter.

S/45. Residuary penalty- Whoever contravenes any rules or regulations made under this Act, for the contravention of, which no penalty has been separately provided, shall be liable to pay a compensation not exceeding twenty-five thousand rupees to the person affected by such contravention or a penalty not exceeding twenty-five thousand rupees.

80. Power of police officer and other officers to enter, search, etc: -

(1) Notwithstanding anything contained in the Code of Criminal Procedure, 1973, any police officer, not below the rank of a Deputy Superintendent of Police, or any other officer of the Central Government or a State Government authorized by the Central Government in this behalf may enter any public place and search and arrest without warrant any person found therein who is reasonably suspected or having committed or of committing or of being about to commit any offence under this Act.

Explanation- For the purposes of this sub-section, the expression "public place" includes any public conveyance, any hotel, any shop or any other place intended for use by, or accessible to the public.

(2) Where any person is arrested under sub-section (1) by an officer other than a police officer, such officer shall, without unnecessary delay, take or send the person arrested before a magistrate having jurisdiction in the case or before the officer-in-charge of a police station.

(3) The provisions of the Code of Criminal Procedure, 1973 shall, subject to the provisions of this section, apply, so far as may be, in relation to any entry, search or arrest, made under this section.

U/s 76. Any computer, computer system, floppies, compact disks, tape drives or any other accessories related thereto, in respect of, which any provision of this Act, rules, orders or regulations made thereunder has been or is being contravened, shall be liable to confiscation subject to the proviso.

Some of the things, which can be confiscated are:

Hardware, which can include any data-processing devices (such as central processing units, memory typewriters, "laptop" or "notebook" computers); internal and peripheral storage devices (such as fixed disks, external hard disks, floppy disk drives and diskettes, tape drives and tapes, optical storage devices, transistor-like binary devices, and other memory storage devices), peripheral input/output devices (such as keyboards, printers, scanners, plotters, video display monitors, and optical/readers); and related communications devices (such as modems, cables and connections,. recording equipment,. RAM or Rom units, acoustic couplers, automatic dialers, speed dialers, programmable telephone dialing or signaling devices, and electronic tone-generating devices).

Under S/75. Act to apply for offence or contraventions committed outside India by any person if the act or conduct constituting the offence or contravention involves a computer, computer system or computer network located in India.

The Act also has provision for amendment of the Indian Penal Code (I.P.C.) Various sections of I.P.C. will be amended to take care of offences related to electronic records. Some of the amendments are provided for covering:

- making false electronic record,
- forgery
  1. for purpose of cheating.
  2. of court or public register, etc.
  3. for purpose of harming reputation

- forged electronic record
- falsification accounts

This also clearly shows the urgent need in India for computer savvy police, lawyers, judiciary, computer security experts and computer forensic experts, who can help prevent, detect and fight these crimes. Most forensic computer examiners while investigating the computer crimes normally perform at least the following:

(1) make the equipment operate properly;

(2) retrieve information;

(3) unblock "deleted" or "erased" data storage devices;

(4) bypass or defeat passwords;

(5) decipher encrypted data.

There is need for such legal and computer experts who can help prosecute the case with advice about how to present computer-related evidence in court, give expert advise, help prepare the case and also may protect an innocent victim. The virus "I Love you" has shown the world the vulnerability of the computer systems, which are prone to computer crimes because of connectivity, lack of security measures, absence of legislation in various countries. The COUNCIL OF EUROPE has released a "Draft Convention on Cyber-Crime" on crime in cyberspace for public discussion. It aims to harmonize national legislation in this field, facilitate investigations and allow efficient levels of co-operation between the authorities of different countries. There is an urgent need for uniform legislation regarding computer crime and more co-operation between different countries in combating such activities.

14

Case Laws on Internet and Computer Crimes

Los Angeles Man Sentenced to Prison for Role in International Computer Hacking and Internet Fraud Scheme.

A Los Angeles man who admitted to defrauding computer distributor Ingram micro, Inc. and numerous Online retailers, including Hewlett-Packard. Corn and office Depot. Com., was sentenced on Wednesday to 33 months in federal prison.

Thomas Pae 20, was sentenced on charges of wire fraud, conspiracy and credit card fraud for his involvement in an international computer hacking and internet fraud scheme targeting ingram Micro, the largest global wholesale distributor of technology products, based in Santa Ana, California. Pae pleaded guilty to the charges and admitted that in 2001 he participated in a scheme involving Computer hackers in Romania who had gained unauthorized access to ingram micro's online ordering System and placed hundreds of dollars of fraudulent orders for computer equipment. The equipment was sent to locations controlled by Pae and his co-conspirators in - the Los Angeles area and then Repackaged and sent to Eastern Europe.

Pae also admitted that he purchased credit card numbers from hackers on the Internet and used the Cards to purchase computer chips, hard drives, personal digital assistants and other items from Handspring. Corn, amagon, Corn and egghead.com, Pae admitted that he and his co-conspirators Attempted to purchase over 500,000 in computer equipment and other items from Ingram micro and the other online retailers.

Pae was sentenced by United States district judge Lourdes G. Baird who also ordered Pae to pay $ 324, 061 in restitution to the victims of his crimes. In addition, once released from prison, judge Baird imposed significant restrictions on his use of computers while he is under supervised release for a period of three years. Six other defendants involved in the scheme have also pleaded guilty to federal charges and three are awaiting sentencing.

This case was investigated by the Los Angeles field office of the FBI, Cyber crimes squad.

Former Employee Indicted on Charges of password Trafficking and Computer Damage

United States Attorney Mary Beth Buchanan announced today, February 26, 2003, that a resident of Greensburg, Pennsylvania, has been indicted by a federal grand jury in Pittsburgh on password trafficking And computer damage.

The two-count indictment named Kenneth Patterson, age 38, of 615 Cherry Street, Greensburg, Pennsylvania, 15601.

According to the indictment presented to the court, Patterson, a former employee of American Eagle Outfitters, was charged with trafficking in passwords and similar information that would have permitted Others to gain unauthorized access to the American Eagle Outfitters computer network, when patterson Posted and maintained at a Yahoo hacker group posing board the username and password combinations of certain legitimate American Eagle personnel and corrective actions were implemented that limited their intended economic impact.

Assistant United States Attorneys Paul E. Hull and Luke E. Dembosky, who presented the case to the grand jury, indicated that the law provides for a maximum total sentences of 11 years in prison, a fine of $ 350,000 or both. Under the Federal Sentencing Guidelines, the actual sentences imposed would be based upon the seriousness of the offences and the prior criminal history, if any, of the defendant.

Agents from the High Technology Crimes Task Force conducted the investigation leading to the indictment in the case together with the invaluable cooperation and assistance of American Eagle Outfitters' staff employees.

An indictment is only a charge and is not evidence of guilt. A defendant is presumed innocent and is entitled to a fair trial at, which the government must prove guilt beyond a reasonable doubt.

U.S. Convicts Kazakhastan Hacker of Breaking into Blookberg L.P.'s Computers and Attempting Extortion.

JAMES B. COMY the United States Attorney for the Southern District of New York, and KEVIN P DONOVAN, the Assistant Director in charge of the New York Field Office of the FBI, announced that OLEG ZEZEV, a/k/a/, "Alex", a Kazakhastan citizen, was convicted in Manhattan Federal court today on charges that he schemed to hack into Bloomberg L.P.'s ("Bloomberg") computer system in order to steal confidential information, and then attempted to extort $ 200,000 from Bloomberg by threatening to disclose the confidential information to Bloomberg's customers and the media in an effort to harm Bloomberg's reputation.

After a three and a half week jury trial, before United States District Judge KIMBA M. WOOD, ZEZEV was found guilty of all four counts against him-one count of attempted extortion, one count of sending extortionate threats, one count of conspiracy to commit extortion and one count of computer instrusion.

Judge WOOD scheduled May 23, 2003 for ZEZEV's sentencing. According to the evidence at trial, Bloomberg L.P. is a multinational financial data company that provided its customers in the international financial community with timely financial information and trading data through a computer network. The company was founded in 1981 by Michael Bloomberg, currently Mayor of the City of New York, who also was the President and Chief Executive Officer of Bloomberg, Inc. the general partner of Bloomberg.

According to the evidence introduced at trial, ZEZEV was the chief information technology officer at Kazkommerts Securities ("Kazkommerts") located in Almaty, Kazakhastan. In the Spring of 1999, Bloomberg provided database services to Kazcommerts. As a result, Kazcommerts was provided with Bloomberg's software needed to gain access to Bloomberg's services over the Internet. Those services were cancelled by Bloomberg in 1999 because Kazcommerts did not pay its bill. The evidence at trial demonstrated that in March, 2000, ZEZEV manipulated Bloomberg's software to bypass Bloomberg's security system in order to gain unauthorized access to Bloomberg's computer system so that he could pose as different legitimate Bloomberg customers and employees. On 11 separate occasions during March, 2000, ZEZEV manipulated Bloomberg's software to bypass Bloomberg's security system in order to gain unauthorized access to Bloomberg's computer system so that he could pose as different legitimate Bloomberg customers and employees. On 11 separate occasions during March, 2000, ZEZEV illegally entered Bloomberg's computer system and accessed various accounts, including Mihale Bloomberg's personal account as well as accounts for other Bloomberg employees and customers. ZEZEV copied various information from these accounts including e-mail in-box screens, Michael Bloomberg's credit and numbers and screens relating to internal functions of Bloomberg. He also accessed various internal information from Bloomberg that was only accessible by Bloomberg employees.

According to the evidence at trial, on March 24, 2000, ZEZEV sent Michael Bloomberg an e-mail from Kazakhastan using the alias "Alex" attaching various screen he had copied from Bloomberg's computer system demonstrating his ability to enter the bloomberg computer system as any user. He wrote in an attachment to the e-mail that he had "all possibilities. I can log under the name of any Bloomberg user including Super Users such as yourself." He then asked for payment and threatened

"There a lot (sic) of cleave but mean heads in the world who will use their chance to destroy your system to the detriment of your worldwide reputation. ZEZEV ended the letter with "Your security and reputation are in your hands. The evidence at trial established that Michael Bloomberg then decided the contract the FBI. Under the FBI's direction, Michael Bloomberg communicated with ZEZEV via e-mail during The Spring and The Summer of 2000.

The evidence demonstrated that ZEZEV sent an e-mail on April 17, 2000, to Michael Bloomberg threatening that if Michael Bloomberg did not send him $ 200,000 he would disclose to the media and Bloomberg's customers that he was able to gain unauthorized access to Bloomberg's computer system.

According to the evidence trial, Michael Bloomberg, acting in conjunction with FBI agents, sent ZEZEV e-mail saying that if ZEZEV wanted the money he would have to meet with Michael Bloomberg and some of bloomberg's computer specialists in London and explain to them how he was able to break into Bloomberg's computer system.

The evidence demonstrated that the e-mails themselves came from two e-mail accounts at a company called Hot-mail, which ZEZEV had registered under a false name. The e-mails were traced back to Kazkommerts Securities, where ZEZEV worked. After receiving the first e-mail, Bloomberg computer specialists were able to piece together how ZEZEV had broken in, and rewrote the software on the Bloomberg system to prevent him from accessing the system again.

The evidence showed that in August 2000, ZEZEV and an associate, Igor Yarimaka (who has also been indicted on attempted extortion and conspiracy charges) travelled from London to meet with Bloomberg. On August, 10, 2000, Michael Bloomberg, Tom Secunda, the Head of Technology at Bloomberg, and a British undercover agent posing as Michael Bloomberg's bodyguard met with ZEZEV and Yarimaka in London. The meeting was recorded by an undercover videotape. At the meeting, ZEZEV introduced himself as "Alex". Michael Bloomberg told ZEZEV and Yarimaka that they were extorting his company. ZEZEV and Yarimaka were arrested after the meeting.

The evidence demonstrated that on August 12, 2000, after ZEZEV and Yarimaka were arrested, Michael Bloomberg's e-mail account received more threatening e-mails. In one of these e-mails, a co-conspirator states that he has not heard from ZEZEV and Yarimaka for 24 hours, and if bloomberg does not do something about it, "I begin severe measures against you!!!! The truth about you is learned with all world !!!"

On May 17, 2002, ZEZEV and Yarimaka were extradited from England to the United States to face the charges in the Indictment.

ZEZEV faces up to 5 years in prison on the conspiracy charge, up to 20 years in prison on the interference with commerce by using extortion charge; 2 years in prison for the extortion of a corporation using threatening communications charge; and 1 year in prison for the unauthorized computer intrusion charges.

ZEZEV faces a maximum fine of $ 250,000 to twice the gross gain or loss resulting from the crime for each count.

Yarimaka is scheduled to be tried before Judge WOOD on March 10, 2003.

Mr. COMEY praised the investigative efforts of the Federal Bureau of Investigation's Computer Hacking and Intellectual Property Squard. The Kazaldiastan Bureau of Special Services, the General Prosecutor's Office in Almaty Kazakhastan and the London Metropolitan Police of the New Scotland Yard. Mr. COMEY also expressed his appreciation to Michael Bloomberg and Bloomberg., L.P. for their cooperation.

Mr. COMEY stated "The Internet is a powerful communication tool in helping international commerce. This case demonstrates law enforcement's commitment to prosecute vigorously those individuals, wherever they are located, who seek to abuse this tool to their own ends. It further illustrates how important it is that victims of cyber-crime report these kinds of crimes to the FBI."

Ex-employee of Airport Transportation Company Arrested for Allegedly Hacking Into Computer, Destroying Data.

A man previously employed at the administrative and operations centre of the Airline Coach Service and the Sky Limousine Company in Inglewood was arrested this morning on federal charges of hacking into the companies computer system and Wiping out critical data. The hack wiped out the companies' customer database and other records, and effectively shut down the companies' computer server, Internet-based credit card processing system and web site.

Alan Giang Tran, 28, of Fountain Valley, was arrested pursuant to a criminal complaint filed on Tuesday in United States District Court in Los Angeles. The complaint accuses Tran of international causing damage to a protected computer and recklessly causing damage by internationally accessing a protected computer. These violations are alleged to have occurred between 22 December 2002 and January 6, 2003.

According to court documents, Airline Coach Service and Sky Limousine are jointly owned companies with a combined gross annual revenue of approximately $ 8.5 million. Tran was the network administrator at the companies' facility in Inglewood, where he had administrator-level passwords and privileges for all of the companies' computer operations.

Tran was terminated by the companies.

On January 5, 2003, the companies' computer system was attacked; passwords on the system were changed and specialized software applications were deleted. Because employees could not use the computer system, the companies were unable to dispatch drivers to pick up clients and the companies suffered thousands of dollars in losses.

Federal investigators last week executed a search warrant to Tran's home, where they found several computers, a file folder marked "retaliation" and information regarding the companies' computer systems.

A criminal complaint contains allegations that a defendant has committed a crime. Every defendant is presumed innocent until and unless proven guilty beyond a reasonable doubt.

Tran made his initial appearance this morning in United States District Court in Los Angeles, where a Magistrate Judge ordered him released on a $ 10,000 bond that has various conditions, including restricted access to computers. Tran was ordered to appear on March 17 for an arraignment. The two counts alleged in the criminal complaint carry a maximum possible sentence of 15 years in Federal prison.

The case against Tran was investigated by the Federal Bureau of Investigation Cyber-crimes Squad.

Ohio Man Attacked NASA Computer System Shutting Down Email Server

Emily M. Sweeney, United States Attorney for the Northern District of Ohio, today announced that a one-count information was filed in U.S. District Court in Cleveland, Ohio, Charging Dino A. Amato, age 37, of 6820 Lafayette Road, Medina, Ohio, with Knowingly violating the regulations and orders of the Administrator of NASA for the protection and security of property and equipment in the custody of NASA, and property and equipment under contract with NASA.

According to Court documents, between 5 November 2001 and 14 November 2001 Dino A. Amato, while employed as a contract employee with Affiliated Computer Services at the NASA Glenn Research Centre in Cleveland, Ohio, knowingly and wilfully violated NASA regulations by downloading a compressed or 'zipped' computer file called 'ZIP-42' from the Internet, and transmitted said zipped file to an e-mail account on the NASA e-mail server on at least seven different occasions, knowing that the zipped file in question would cause the computer system to drastically slow down or completely stop processing e-mail message at the Glenn Research Centre.

According to Court documents, Amato's actions caused a disruption in the flow of electronic communications on the Glenn Research Centre e-mail server, and NASA's computer security department incurred losses of approximately $12,000 in inspecting, diagnosing and repairing the e-mail server.

The maximum statutory penalty for a violation of Title 18, United States Code, Section 799 (Violating the Rules and Regulations of NASA) is up to 1 year imprisonment, a fine of up to $100,000, or both.

This case is being prosecuted by Assistant U.S. Attorney W. Kern, following an investigation by NASA's Office of the Inspector General.

An information is only a charge and is not evidence of guilt. A defendant is entitled to a fair trial in, which it will be the government's burden to prove guilt beyond a reasonable doubt.

Former Employee of Viewsonic Arrested on Charges of Hacking into Company's Computer, Destroying Data.

A man previously employed at the Walnut office of the Viewsonic Corporation was arrested this morning on Federal charges of hacking into the company's computer system and wiping out critical data, acts that shut down a computer server that was central to the company's foreign operations.

Andy Garcia, 39, of Montebello, was arrested pursuant to an indictment returned January

28 by a federal grand jury in Los Angeles. The indictment accuses Garcia of unauthorized access to a protected computer and of being a convicted felon in possession of a firearm.

Viewsonic Corporation is a manufacturer of computer monitors that generates more than $ 1 billion a year in revenues. Garcia was the network administrator at Viewsonic's Walnut office, where he was in charge of several computer servers and had access to system passwords for management employees.

According to court documents, on April 14, 2002, approximately two weeks after Garcia was terminated, Garcia allegedly accessed Viewsonic's computer system and deleted critical files on one of the servers that he had maintained while employed by the company. The loss of these files rendered the server inoperative, and Viewsonic's Taiwan office was unable to access important data for several days.

Gracia was also charged with possession of a semi-automatic assault weapon found at his home. His possession of such a weapon is unlawful because he was previously convicted of two felonies. An indictment contains allegations that a defendant has committed a crime. Every defendant is presumed innocent until and unless proven guilty beyond a reasonable doubt.

Garcia is expected to make an initial appearance on the charges this afternoon in United States District Court in Los Angeles. If convicted, she faces a maximum possible sentence of 15 years in federal prison.

The case against Garcia was investigated by the Federal Bureau of Investigation.

Pittsburgh, Pennsylvania Man Convicted of Hacking a Judge's Personal E-mail Account.

United States Attorney Mary Beth Buchanan announced today, January 23, 2003, that after deliberating 2 hours, a jury of five men and seven women found Brain T. Ferguson guilty of three courts of unauthorized access to a protected computer.

Ferguson, age 43, of 414 Dewalt Drive was tried before Chief United States District Judge Donetta W. Ambrose in Pittsburgh, Pennsylvania.

According to Assistant United States Attorney Paul E. Hull, who prosecuted the case, the evidence presented at trial established that Ferguson broke into the America Online account of Common Pleas Court Judge Kim D. Eaton on three occasions. He obtained personal e-mail messages belonging to Judge Eaton, files, and other information that were part of her AOL account.

Judge Ambrose scheduled sentencing for April 11, 2003 at 10:00 a.m. The law provides for a total sentence of 3 years in prison, a fine of $ 300,000, or both. Under the federal sentencing Guidelines, the actual sentence Imposed is based on the seriousness of the offence and the criminal history, if any, of the defendant. Pending sentencing, Ferguson remains free on bond.

The federal bureau of Investigation's High Technology crime Task Force and the Allegheny County District Attorney's Office conducted the investigation that led to the prosecution of Ferguson.

St. Joseph Man Charged in District's First Computer Hacking Indictment.

KANSAS CITY, Mo.-Todd P. Graves, United States Attorney for the Western District of Missouri, announced today that a St. Joseph man has been indicted for unauthorized computer intrusion. Graves noted that this is the first case of computer hacking ever prosecuted in the Western District of Missouri, which launched a new Cyber Crimes and Child Exploitation Unit.

Richard W. Gerhardt, 43, of St. Joseph, Mo. was charged in an indictment returned under seal by a federal grand jury on 19 December 2002. That indictment was unsealed and made public today upon Gerhardt's arrest and initial court appearance before U.S. Magistrate Judge Sarah W. Hays.

The indictment alleges that Gerhardt gained unauthorized access to the network computer system of Nestle USA while employed as an information systems consultant, working primarily at the Friskies Petcare plant in St. Joseph. Friskies Petcare is a corporate subsidiary of Nestle USA, which in turn is a subsidiary of Nestle S.A. of Vevey, Switzerland.

On Five separate occasions between 12 August 2001, and 10 June 2002, the indictment alleges, Gerhardt gained access to the Nestle network computer system without authorization and in excess of his authorized access. Gerhardt allegedly downloaded approximately 5000 user account passwords from Nestle's system, costing the firm more than $5000 to conduct a damage assessment of; verify the security of, and restore the integrity of its computer system.

The various offices and facilities of Nestle USA and Nestle S.A. throughout the United States and the world, including the Friskies Petcare plant in St. Joseph, are linked together by a network computer system. Any computer or server connected to that system, Graves explained, is thus a "protected computer" under federal law.

Gerhardt allegedly used a password-cracking software called "LophtCrack" to retrieve the passwords for user accounts on the system. Gerhardt then created a database containing the user account passwords, the indictment alleges, and stored the database in a file on a computer servert connected to the system and in a file located on a laptop computer issued to him by Nestle.

While on the system, Gerhardt allegedly ran at least one password recovery utility program and then stored the results in the least one zip file, creating a file, which contained passwords he had obtained.

Without authorization, the indictment alleges, Gerhardt located and installed a program called "pwdump.exe" on the Nestle network computer system and on the laptop computer issued to him by Nestle. According to the indictment, the "pwdump.exe" program is associated with an automated command that, at a preset time each day, communicated to other computers on the Nestle network computer system and downloaded active accounts and passwords. On June 3, 2002, Gerhardt allegedly caused the output from the "pwdump.exe" program to be stored on a computer server connected to the Nestle computer network system. Approximately 5000 passwords associated with users of the Nestle computer network system were allegedly accessed and stored by Gerhardt.

The indictment alleges that on June 4, 2000, Gerhardt used a dial-up connection to log onto the Nestle network computer system from a rem6te location. While on the system Gerhardt allegedly created a new and unauthorized administrator account.

Graves cautioned that the charge contained in the indictment is simply an accusation, and is not evidence of guilt. Evidence supporting the charges must be presented to a federal trial jury, whose duty is to determine guilt or innocence.

The case is being prosecuted by Assistant U.S. Attorney Gene Porter. The case was investigated by the Federal Bureau of Investigation.

U.S. Arrests Queens, New York Man on Computer Fraud Charges

JAMES B. COMEY United States Attorney for the Southern District of New York, accounted today that JUJU Jiang, 24, of Flushing, Queens, New York, was arrested on charges of computer fraud for attempting to gain access to the accounts of nemerous subscribers of GoToMyPC.com, a computer services company that provides subscribers, which remote computer access, and successfully taking control of one of those accounts.

According to the one-count complaint filed today, JIANG, operating from his home in Flushing, and using a computer program designed to record computer passwords and user names, attempted to gain access to the computer accounts of approximately 15 subscribers of Go To My PC.

As described in the complaint, Go To My PC is a company that offers individuals the ability to remotely access their personal computers from any computer connected to the Internet. According to the complaint, JIANG obtained these users' passwords and user names by installing computer software for this purpose at a kinko's located on Seventh Avenue in Manhattan. JIANG then used passwords and usernames in attempts to gain access to those subscribers' personal computers in order to obtain credit card and other information stored on those computers, it was alleged.

As described in the Complaint, JIANG's alleged fraud came to light after a subscriber of Go To My PC (the "Victim"), who was at home, heard his personal computer ("PC") turn on without any action the subscriber's parts and then observed the cursor of the PC move around the screen and files on the PC being accessed and opened as if by remote control.

Afterwards, as alleged in the Complaint, the Victim observed his computer access a web site known as www. Neteller.com ("Neteller"), an online payment transfer service, and observed an account in his name being opened at Neteller, also without his authorization.

A short time later, Victim allegedly observed his computer accessing the web site for the American Express Corporate card and, using information stored on his computer, saw his computer attempt to access his corporate American Express card account file.

According to the Complaint, upon viewing this unauthorized activity, the Victim manually regained control of his PC, terminated the computer session, and contacted officials of Neteller in order to direct them to close the unauthorized Neteller account that had been opened in his name.

According to the Complaint, computer records maintained by Go To My PC traced the unauthorized intrusion of the Victim's account to JIANG's home. The complaint alleged that, upon searching JIANG's Flushing residence, agents observed one of JIANG's computers executing a program known as a "brute force attack," a program frequently used by computer hackers to gain unauthorized access to other person's computers.

If convicted, JIANG faces a maximum sentence of 5 years in prison and a $250,000 fine.

Mr. COMEY praised the investigative efforts of the United States Secret Service Electronic Crimes Task Force. He said the investigation is continuing. Assistant United States Attorney JOSEPH V. DE MARCO is in charge of the prosecution.

The charges contained in the Complaint are merely accusation, and the defendant is presumed innocent unless and until proven guilty.

Disgruntled UBS Paine Webber Employee Charged with Allegedly.

Unleashing "Logic Bomb" on company computers.

NEWARK- A disgruntled computer systems administrator for UBS paine Webber was charged today with using a "logic bomb" to cause more than $3 million in damage to the company's computer network, and with securities fraud for his failed plan to drive down the company's stock with activation of the logic bomb, U.S. Attorney Christopher J Christie announced.

Roger Duronio, 60, of Bogota, N.J., was charged today a two-count Indictment returned by a federal grand jury, according to Assistant U.S. Attorney William Devaney.

The Indictment alleges that Duronio, who worked at Paine Webber's offices in Weehawken, N.J., planted the logic bomb in some 1,000 of Paine Webber's approximately 1,500 networked computers in branch offices around the country.

Duronio, who repeatedly expressed dissatisfaction with his salary and bonuses at paine

Webber resigned from the company on Feb. 22, 2002. The logic bomb Duronio allegedly planted was activated on March 4, 2002.

In anticipation that the stock price of UBS Paine Webber's parent company, UBS, A.G. would decline in response to damage caused by the logic bomb, Duronio also purchased more than $21,000 of "put option" contracts for UBS, A.G.'s stock, according to the charging document. A put option is a type of security that increases in value when the stock price drops. Market conditions at the time suggest there was no such impact on the UBS. A.G. price.

Paine Webber promptly reported what had happened to government investigators and the U.S. Attorney's Office, and has been helpful and cooperative in the investigation by the U.S. Secret Services Electronic Crime Task Force.

Duronio is scheduled to make an initial appearance in court at 2 :00 before U.S. Magistrate Judge Madeline Cox Arleo.

"Cybercrime against financial institutions is a significant issue", Christie said. "Although the damage was contained in this case, the potential for catastrophic damage in other cases is always there. We will prosecute cyber criminals and put them in prison."

The Indictment alleges that, from about November, 2001 to February, Duronio constructed the logic bomb computer program. On March 4, as planned, Duronio's program activated and began deleting files on over 1,000 of UBS Paine Webber's computers. It cost Paine Webber more than $3 millions to assess and repair the damage, according to the Indictment.

As one of the company's computer system administrators, Duronio had responsibility for, and access to, the entire UBS Paine Webber computer network, according to the Indictment. He also had access to the network from his home computer via secure Internet access.

Million fine. He is charged in Court Two with Fraud and Related Activity In Connection with Computers. That charge carries a maximum prison sentence of 10 years and a fine of $250,000 or, alternatively, two times the gain made by the defendant or the loss suffered by the victim.

In February and March, 2002, according to the Indictment, Duronio spent approximately $21, 762 when purchasing 318 put option contracts for the stock of UBS A.G., all due to expire on March 15. A "put option" contract is a security that gives the purchaser the right to sell 100 shares of stock in a company for a fixed per-share price at a specified date. The lower the stock price falls, the more valuable the put option contract becomes. If the contract is sold on or before the expiration date with the stock at or below a specified "strike Price", a profit is earned.

Page Four of the Indictment gives a table listing Duronio's purchases of the put options leading up to the activation of the logic bomb. Despite Indictment, every defendant is presumed innocent, unless and until found guilty beyond a reasonable doubt following a trial at, which the defendant has all of the trial rights guaranteed by he U.S. Constitution and federal law. A grand jury may vote on Indictment if 12 or more jurors find probable cause to believe that the defendant has committed the crime or crimes charged.

Christie credited Special Agents to the U.S. Secret Services Electronic Crimes Task Forces, under the direction of Jan Gilhooly, Special Agent in Charges of the Secret Service in New Jersey with bringing the case against Duronio. Christie also credited the assistance of UBS Paine Webber in the investigation.

The Government is represented by Assistant U.S. Attorney Devaney.

Defence Counsel Justin Walder, Esq. Roseland

15

Cybersquatting and Trademark Infringement

Introduction

"Cyberlaw" is fast evolving into its own discipline, and "traditional" law firms are keen to enter the lucrative new legal area. To date, the most active area for legal skirmishes has been domain name disputes that involve accusations of trademark infringement, usually by cybersquatters. Until recently there has been no legislation governing trademark introduce cyberspace-specific trademark legislation with the Anti-cybersquatting Infringement Act of 1999 (ACPA), which is not part of U.S. trademark law.

Trademark law has evolved to ensure the consumer is not mislead about the source of a product, in this sense a trademark acts as a kind of quality assurance for the consumer. The benefits of a trademark acts as, a kind of quality assurance for the consumer. The benefits of a trademark represent a significant amount of goodwill in the form of consumer recognition and trust.

Trademarks are therefore valuable business assets that their owners are keen to protect. However, as soon as the Internet become a valuable commercial tool, companies have been plagued by cybersquatters, who register trademark as domain names, thereby preventing trademark owners from establishing web sites using their own mark. Thus, the emerging area of cyberlaw has concentrated chiefly on trademark issues, with the greatest emphasis on domain name disputes with a gradual expansion towards other Internet uses of trademarks, such as meta tags.

Because domain name disputes involve trademarks, courts have applied "traditional" trademark law, as well unfair competition, defamation, misleading and deceptive practices, passing off, and similar laws (1) transposing such laws into the realm of cyberspace, however, presents an unprecedented difficulty; cyberspace is not "real" space, and the constraints of geography, political boundaries, legal jurisdiction, and even time considerations of real space do not apply. Add to this the uncontrollable global reach of cyberspace, and it is clear that traditional law applied to cyberspace is bound to run into difficulties.

Nevertheless, courts have managed to deal reasonably well with trademark infringements in domain names, simply because this problem is analogous on the horizon with disputes involving the use of trademark in practices such as meta tagging and linking, but these issues are beyond the scope of this paper.

An added complications, which is starting to emerge fully only now, is that there is no convenient break-up of jurisdiction in cyberspace. Cyberspace is global in the broadest sense, its reach is not curtailed by international treaties or geographical or political boundaries. Indeed any computer anywhere can connect to the Internet, as long as the necessary infrastructure is available, and even infrastructure limitations are rapidly decreasing with the advance of satellite communication.

Cyberspace is virtually everywhere and in reality nowhere. Its non-territorial ubiquitousness gives rise to jurisdictional issues and related problems, such as conflict of laws and enforceability issues. Although cyberspace development of cyberlaw has proceeded from a U.S. centric perspective, mostly due to the historical reason that the Internet originated in the United States. This caused few problems when Internet use, particularly in the commercial area, was concentrated in the U.S. However, it is questionable whether this trend will be allowed to continue, given the increasing presence and commercial importance of non-U.S. users.

This paper will look at the phenomenon of trademark infringement through cybersquatting and discuss how the Anticybersquatting Consumer protection act contributes to regulating cyberspace-related trademark infringement. Because the ACPA is U.S. law, the cases touched on are U.S. cases. Finally, the paper will consider the issue of jurisdiction concerning domain name disputes, both on a national and at international level. The paper concludes that "real space" based legislation such as the ACPA may be relatively effective for cyber offences that mirror the kinds of offences found in "real" space. However, given the global reach of cyberspace, traditional law that depends on legal and territorial boundaries may become less relevant.

Domain names disputes

Rearly has there been such a rapid spurt of growth in any business activity as in domain name registration. In 1993 the Internet was still in its infancy, with few businesses realizing the commercial opportunities it offered. Surprisingly, even large corporation were slow to identify the commercial opportunities offered by the new technologies of the Internet Patrick Gunning reports that 100000 domain names were registered world-wide in 1995 and 5 million at the beginning of 1999. This figure jumped to fifteen million domain names by the year 2000. The battle for domain names representing trademarks has heated up accordingly. The arbitration and Mediation Centre of WIPO reports a total of 904 cases field with it by the end of July, 2000. What is telling is not so much the number of cases as the rate at, which domain names cases are increasing. According to WIPO cases filings, 182 cases were filed in June, 2000, a 550% jump up from January's 28 cases filing. Apart from WIPO, there are also numerous court cases concerning domain name disputes, especially in the U.S.

As this proliferation of cases suggests, domain names are more than mere addresses. They can be closely identified with the company itself in the sense that customers believe that a domain name should reflect the company name, as the court suggested in Cardservice Intl'v McGee ("A customer who is unsure about a company's domain name will often guess that the domain name is also the company's name. And in MTV Networks Inc V. Curry (a domain name mirroring a corporate name may be a valuable corporate asset, as it facilitates communication with a customer base).

Domain names frequently represent a company's intellectual property in the form of trademarks, either registered or common law, or words and phrases associated with the company. Trademarks as domain names are not only contested by businesses, but also by individuals whose names have been used as trademarks (hence celebrity domain name disputes, such as juliaroberts com, sting com, and far exceeds the cost of registration was recognized early by enterprising individuals who registered domain names with the intent of selling them on (at a high price) to the companies or individuals whose trademarks the domain names represented.

Trademark Infringement

Technically, a domain name is simply the address of an individual computer connected to the Internet. From a user's point of view, a domain name is an IP address in a human-friendly form. And if the human-friendly form of the IP address coincides with the name of a business or a trademark, it becomes a valuable asset. It is unlikely that the current cybersquatting phenomenon would exist if IP address were not given human language representations. There is no magic of association-leg along trademark-with an IP address called 192, 186.0.12. But as soon as the IP address turns into something like "nike.com" (or "any well known company.com") we enter into a whole new world. That of goodwill and consumer recognition associated with a trade or service mark. As soon as it is associated with a trademark, a domain name becomes a powerful commercial tool.

Domain names can incorporate trademarks in a number of ways. The most obvious is the verbatim adoption of the mark followed by a g TLD, such as nike.com. A person who is not the trademark owner and registers the trademark as a domain name engages in relatively straightforward trademark infringement. However, trademark infringement can also take the form of trademark dilution, which is prohibited under the U.S. Federal Trademark Dilution Act (FTDA). The purpose of this act is to protect owners of famous marks against dilution and tarnishing of their mark. This spirit of this law is transposed into the Anticybersquatting Consumer Protection Act. Trademark dilution can be brought against domain name restraint, who use a variant of a famous mark for their own purposes. An example, here is the domain name gateway 20000.com that takes advantage of a typing mistake and whisks off the unsuspecting user to a pornographic site, rather than to the Gateway 2000 company site (in this instance, Gateway decided to purchase the rights to the domain name, rather than bring an action in court, which would most likely find trademark dilution.

Cybersquatting

Cybersquatting is the practice of registering a trademark as a domain name with the intent of profiting from it by selling it, usually to the trademark owner. As long as the cybersquatter owns the domain name, the trademark owner cannot register its own trademark as a domain name. In this sense, the cybersquatter breaches the fundamental rights of the trademark owner to use its trademark.

However it is important to note that there is nothing wrong with the practice of reserving a domain name. Frequently, cybersquatters register words or phrases they hope will some day be sought after by new companies or new business division. A trademark is not infringed by a domain name unless the trademark existed at the time of domain name registration. This kind of cybersquatting is speculative and legitimate. Jone D. Mercer also identifies "innocent" cybersquatting, whereby the registrant does infringe a trademark based on some unrelated interest in the word itself, without intending harm to a trademark owner, and concurrent cybersquatting, whereby the registrant uses the same trademark as another commercial entity. But not within a competing industry.

However, the harmful kind of cybersquatting involves intentional bed faith trafficking in domain names that are the same as, or a dilution of, existing trademarks. Such domain name registrants are considered "modern day extortion. Mercer offers a fitting definition 'an illegal cybersquatter should be one who acquires a domain name for the sole purpose of obtaining money or other advantage from the trademark owner, with no intent or desire to use the domain name, except as an instrument towards this purpose.

The acknowledged arch-quatter is Dennis Toeppen, who registered a host of well-known trademarks as domain names (including deltaairlines. Com, neiman-marcus. Com and numerous other famous marks), [11] and who has been unsuccessful in defending his rights to them when sued by the trademark owners. Intermatic v. Toeppen [12] and Panaui8ion v. Toeppen [13] are considered the pivotal Cybersquatting cases and have had a profound impact on the development of cybersquatting case law, as well as on the drafting of the ACPA.

Panavision illustrates some of the typical issues encountered in cybersquatting cases where trademark infringement is raised. Toeppen registered the domain name www. Panavision. Com and used the web site to display pictures of the city of Pana, Ilinois. He offered to sell the domain name to Panavision for $ 13,000. Panavision declined and brought an action under the Federal Trademark Dilution Act (FTDA). The FTDA required the plaintiff to show that the trademark in question is famous, that the defendant was using the mark in commerce, that the mark became famous before the defendant started using it, and that the "defendant's use of the mark dilutes the quality of the mark by diminishing the capacity of the mark to identify and distinguish goods and services". [14]

Toeppen argued that he was not making commercial use of the name, as he was merely displaying photographs on his web site. The court, however, decided that by having offered the domain name for sale, Toeppen had shown his intent to use the mark in commerce, which met the requirements for use in commerce test. The court further remarked on the fact that a domain name carried the reputation of a trademark.

In Intermatic, the court conceded that Toeppen was not using the trademark in commerce, as he had merely registered it, but nevertheless found infringement through dilution. Importantly, the court in Intermatic recognized that if Toeppen were allowed to operate the web site intermatic. com, Intermatic's "name and reputation would be at Toeppen's mercy."

The rulings in Panavision and Intematic affirmed that "traditional" trademark and trademark dilution law applied in cyberspace. It is not only the "unadulterated" trademark that can be protected, but also any variation of it that is likely to confuse or deceive, or in some way dilute the "distinctive Act incorporates the dilution and tarnishment provisions of the FTDA, but without the FTDAs requirement for use in commerce. This significantly broadens the concept of trademark infringement.

Anticybersquatting Consumer Protection Act

Is cyberlaw based on "traditional" law really the best way to regulate the proliferation of cyber-offences? The fact that the United States thought it wise to enact legislation that specifically targets trademark infringements in cyberspace arguably indicates a growing awareness that the Internet is indeed a different kind of legal space and may require cyberspace-specific law [16] Although the Anticybersquatting Consumer Protection Act is cyberspace specific, it is still based on "traditional" legal principles of trademark law, and importantly, refers to jurisdictional parameters of domestic law, which are defined by "real" territorial boundaries. Moreover, the ACPA fails to account for the global reach of cyberspace, and the Act reads as if the Internet were confined to the U.S. This is because the ACPA is a milestone in the regulation of cyber offences and provides a useful blueprint for similar regulations (ICAN's Uniform Dispute Resolution process, which has also been adopted by the WIPO Mediation and Arbitration Centre, is substantially similar to the ACPA).

According to the U.S. Sentence the ACPA was enacted "to protect consumers and American businesses. To promote the growth of online commerce, and to provide clarity in the law for trademark owners by prohibiting the bad-faith and abusive registration of distinctive marks as Internet domain names with the intent to profit from the goodwill associated with such marks-a practice commonly referred to as 'cybersquatting.' "[17] The Act states that cybersquatting when the person registering a domain name containing a trademark "has a bad faith intent to profit from that mark" and "registers, traffics in, or uses" a domain name that contains the trade mark, either verbatim or in a diluted form ("identical or confusingly similar to or dilutive of that mark"). [18]

The ACPA lists nine non-exclusive factors that courts may consider when determining whether the plaintiff has acted with bad faith intent: -

(I) The trademark or other intellectual property rights of the person, if any, in the domain name;

(II) The extent to, which the domain name consists of the legal name of the person or a name that is otherwise commonly used to identify that person;

(III) The person's prior use, if any, of the domain name in connection with the bona fide offering of any goods or services;

(IV) The person's bona fide non-commercial or fair use of the mark in a site accessible to a site accessible under the domain name;

(V) The person's intent to divert consumers from the mark owner's online location to a site accessible under the domain name that could harm the goodwill represented by the mark, either for commercial gain or with the intent to tarnish or disparage the mark, by creating a likelihood of confusion as to the source, sponsorship, affiliation, or endorsement of the site;

(VI) The person's provision of material and misleading false contact information when applying for the registration of the domain name the person's international failure to maintain accurate contact information, or the person's prior conduct indicating a pattern of such conduct;

(VII) The person's registration or acquisition of multiple domain names, which the person knows are identical or confusingly similar to marks of others that are distinctive at the time of registration of such domain names, or dilutive of famous marks of others that are famous at the time of registration of such domain names, without regard to the goods or services of the parties; and

(VIII) The extent to, which the mark incorporated in the person's domain name registration is or is not distinctive and famous.

20. It appears that the Act nudges the courts towards finding bad faith intent. In fact, the only reason that no bad faith intent is when the defendant "believed and had reasonable grounds to believe that the use of the domain name was a fair use of otherwise lawful". With the ACPA the cards are undeniably stacked against the cybersquatter.

21. As mentioned above, the Act incorporates elements of the Federal Trademark dilution Act, which is meant to protect "famous" marks. As mentioned before, under the ACPA trademark infringement in domain name cases is not confined to use in commerce, but can also be found when the defendant "disparages" or "tarnishes" the trademark for, whichever reason. [19] While the FTDA suggest a series of non-exclusive tests to determine that a mark is famous, the ACPA does not give any guidelines. As a result, the interpretation of what is a "famous" mark is left even more open than under the FTDA, to the extent that prohibition against trademark dilution can arguably apply

to virtually any mark, famous or obscure. Finding the element of fame in a mark, it now appears, is left to the discretion of the courts. This of course broadens the reach of the act considerably. Provided that something is considered a trademark infringement, or dilution and tarnishment, both of, which are incorporated into the ACPA.

22. A case that illustrates the power of the dilution and tarnishment provision in the ACPA is Toys "R" Us v Akkaoui. Here, the defendant registered the domain name adultsus.com and used the emponymos web site to sell sexual devices over the Internet. The court found that the domain name adultsrus.com "tarnishes the R Us' Family of marks by associating them with a line of sexual products that are inconsistent with the image Toys R Us has striven to maintain for itself; and issued an injunction against the defendant. This kind of case is somewhat worrying, in the sense that it is difficult to see how it could cause consumer confusion, as the two businesses were in different industries altogether. Here, however, it was enough that the domain name shared some elements of a trademark, even in a non-competing industry.

23. Despite its name, the ACPA is not strictly about cybersquatting, as Sporty's Farm L.L. C. v. Sportman's Market, Inch-the first case to be tried under the ACPA demonstrates. Sporty's concerns one party's blatant attempt to take commercial advantage of a well known registered trademark by trying to obtain a declaration prohibiting the trademark owner from using its own trademark in a domain name. Though this case does not fit the traditional cybersquatting pattern the domain name owner did not try to sell the name to the trademark owner, it nevertheless contains elements that fit perfectly with the ACPA.

    The domain name in dispute was sportys.com "Sporty's" was a mark used by Sportman's Market throughout its catalogues and advertisements over many years. The plaintiff owned the domain name and brought an action against Sprotman's Market seeking a declaration that the trademark owner had no rights to the domain name Sprotys.com was first registered by the plaintiff's parent company, Omega, which intended eventually to compete in the same market as Sportsman's Market (selling aviation goods via catalogues). Sporty's Farm was established solely to demonstrate its rights in the domain name and did not operate in the same market as sportsman's (Sporty's Farm grew Christmas trees).

    However, it emerged that the intention of the plaintiff's parent company was to transfer the domain name to a yet to be formed subsidiary that would compete directly with Sportsman's Market. Sportsman's brought a counter claim for trademark dilution, trademark infringement and unfair competition. The district court found for the defendant on the basis of the Federal Trademarks Dilution Act (the ACPA was not yet in force) and enjoined the domain name owner from using it.

    One appeal, the court applied the ACPA, as the legislation was law by the time the appeal, the court applied the ACPA, as the legislation was law by the time the appeal was heard, and affirmed the district courts, order on the grounds that the mark "Sporty's" was distinctive, that sportys.com was confusingly similar to the mark, and that the domain name owner acted with bad faith intent and sought to profit from the mark. This combination places the plaintiff's conduct squarely into the reach of the ACPA. (Oddly, the court did not order transfer of the domain name to Sport'sman's Market).

24. The act specifically points out that it is not necessary that the registrant use the domain name for any purpose at all apart from having a "bad faith intent" to profit from it. The mere fact that he has possession of domain name means that the trademark owner can bring an action against him, provided the trademark owner can show bad faith intent. The only defences left to the domain name owner is that he "believed and had reasonable grounds to believe that the use of the domain name was a fair use of otherwise lawful.

The ACPA and Free Speech

25. Although generally welcomed by trademark owners, ACPA has been criticized for its potential to limit free speech. This danger is inherent in the Act's recognition of tarnishment and dilution as trademark wealthy enough to bring law suits against individuals whose only "crime" has been to register a domain name that happened to be a variation of a trademark.

26. The issue of fee speech and fair use of a trademark arises in cases involving so-called sucks sites or gripe sites where domain name holders incorporate a trademark into their domain name, usually as a form of protest against the trademark owner (for example, famouscompanysucks.com) The ACPA, it is feared, can be used to sue sucks site owners criticizing or parodying a trademark.

27. Whether there is trademark infringement in the case of sucks sites depends on a variety of factors that may outweigh the free speech defence. These include confusing the consumer regarding sources of the site (even causing initial confusion). Trademark dilution and tarnishment, and defamation. While fair use provisions would allow a site to publish a critical editorial about a company, it appears that many sucks sites are de-mobilized by the courts, to the delight of the trademark owners.

28. To deter disgruntled consumers from tarnishing the goodwill of their trademark in cyberspace, many companies go out of their way to register every conceivable undesirable variation on their name. Start-up companies do the same in anticipation of critical sites that may spring up in the future. As verizon Wireless demonstrates, this exercise can be futile. A hacker magazine attempted to register verizonsucks.com, only to find that verizon itself owned the domain name. The magazine then registered verizonerallysucks.com, upon, which Verizon threatened to bring an action under

ACPA. Undeterred, the magazine declared it was not making unlawful use of the name and proceeded to register other Verizon related names, including verizondoesreallysuck.com. In the end, verizon conceded that the magazine's use of the trademark was fair.

Undoubtedly, Verizon's zeal in trying to stamp out the offending sucks site only contributed to a proliferation of further ducks sites incorporating the verizon trademark. This case indicates that the dilution and tarnishment provisions of the ACPA are unsatisfactory to both trademark owners and people who use the trademark to exercise free speech.

29. Furthermore, given that further gTLDs are in the offing, the effort required to register a plethora of related names in an effort to stem the tide of future such sites in daunting indeed. In addition, the ephemerality of the Internet makes it near impossible to keep tabs on all possible trademark infringements, as web sites may appear, disappear and reappear at a moment's notice.

A further complication occurs when sucks sites are registered by registrars into based in the United States. It is questionable whether a sucks site owner in a foreign jurisdiction could be sued effectively by the offended company on the basis of the dilution and tarnishment provision of the ACPA. This brings us to the issue of jurisdiction, which the ACPA appears to envisage as a U.S. specific problem to, which it offers a U.S. specific solution.

Jurisdiction and enforcement

30. An innovative feature of the ACPA is that it enables in rem jurisdiction in domain names disputes-this means that the trademark owner does not have to sue the domain name owner personally, but can take action against the domain name itself. This provision recognizes that cybersquatters frequently give out false contact information, presumably in anticipation of possible law suits Normally, in U.S. law, a person who cannot be located cannot be sued. And since domain name registrars are not liable for registering domain names that infringe trademarks, the fact that the registrant cannot be located would be prejudicial to the rights of the trademark owner to claim infringement.

31. To take advantage of the in rem provision the trademark owner must take steps to satisfy the courts that the registrant cannot be found. For straightforward cybersquatting offences the in rem provision in useful. However, in cases where there is a genuine question whether the domain name infringes the rights of the trademark owner, the desirability of the provision is another matter. On the other hand, if the plaintiff uses the in rem provision he cannot claim damages, as the only remedies available are cancellation or transfer of the domain name. This it is more beneficial for the plaintiff to obtain personal jurisdiction if the infringing domain name caused material damage

to the trademark. In a related matter, it needs to be pointed out the most trademark owners prefer to use ICANN's Uniform Dispute Resolution Policy (whose provisions are similar to those of ACPA) rather than face the expense of litigation. This route is popular among trademark owners who do not so much want to use the domain name themselves as to prevent others from using it. Like action under the ACPAs in rem provision, the Uniform Dispute Resolution policy permits only cancellation or transfer of the domain name, not damages. Thus for more grievous cases and to recover damages the plaintiff would still need to go to court and sue the cybersquatter personally.

32. In rem jurisdiction depends on the location of the gTLD registrar. Until recently, the only official registrar was Network solutions, Inc. Gradually, other registrars were permitted to register gTLD names (.com .net, .org), including foreign registrars. As long as the trademark owner wants to bring an in rem action against a domain name registered with a U.S. registrar, the ACPA is adequate. But what happens if the registrar is located outside the U.S. and has no intention (for whatever reason) to assist the complainant? If a registrar in Korea registered a famousinth US.com" domain name and the web site is widely accessible to United States users, what is the likelihood of the trademark owner winning his suit in court? And in, which court could he sue effectively, and whose laws would apply? How would a U.S. court claim jurisdiction, and even if it succeeded to do so, how would it be enforced? In theory, the U.S. court could order the deletion of the domain name from the central registry. But this action would be extremely undesirable for the sake of international harmony. Such strong-arm tactics would doubtlessly be resented by the Internet community. In this sense, the usefulness of the ACPA even for U.S. based companies are stops at the U.S. border.

Whose Cyber law?

33. Until recently, the commercial use of cyberspace was the purview of relatively few countries that shared similar Socioeconomic and political backgrounds (i.e., democratic first world countries) and were reasonably familiar with each other's legal systems. But what will happen when the commercial use of the Internet becomes more wide spread, when more and more countries with various legal political and economic backgrounds start on the path of e-commerce? Trademark owners will need to increase their vigilance to preserve the integrity of their marks.

34. This brief run-down of some of the problems encountered with domain names and trademarks can only hint at the myriad legal issues yet to arise in cyberspace. Perhaps the most pressing question now is whether reliance on domestic laws is adequate in addressing cyberspace squabbles. So far, most case law has come from the United States. But it is hardly to be excepted that foreign courts will adopt U.S. court decisions as precedents, especially if foreign courts would normally decide the issues differently.

While following U.S. precedents is probable among common law countries. It is less likely in countries with different legal traditions. International law governed by treaties and conventions is difficult enough to administer, and it is doubtful that international agreements on cyberlaw will prove to be an exception. Furthermore, because of the internet's literally boundless "territory" it is unlikely that anything like an international cyberlaw would be achievable as long as geographical, legal and political jurisdiction need to be considered.

35. Scholarly opinion on the future direction of cyberlaw ranges from the conservative to the extravagant. "Traditional" legal commentators believe that cyberspace is no different than any other "space" occupied by telecommunications. National telecommunication laws are well developed, so why should cyberspace laws be any different? Thus, Jack Goldsmith believes that cyberlaw should follow in the footsteps in international law, whereby each nation remains responsible for regulating harms that cause effects locally.

36. Goldsmith's idea, however, has its drawbacks in the global non-space of the Internet. If cyberspace were to be governed by something like international law, all countries active on the Internet would need to enter into an agreement with all other Internet using countries. Furthermore, achieving uniformity of law and application would entail adopting a kind of transnational law that domestic courts would need to adhere to even if such a law should contradict local law. Achieving owner cannot control the dissemination of material, it would be potentially unfair to allow the application of local law (in a conflicts of law case, for instance).

For example, consider what would happen to international relations if a country with Islamic law were to claim jurisdiction over a web site owner resident in a common law state who, either internationally or inadvertently, publishes material considered blasphemous under Islamic law, which is somehow accessible to residents of the Islamic law country. The degree of ill feeling such a case would elicit can only be imagined. Nor would the solution Goldsmith suggests be particularly useful to the earlier mentioned hypothetical U.S. trademark holder taking issue with a domain name registered in Korea, as suing in a Korean court under Korean law would be not only expensive but also uncertain. Give the inevitability of jurisdictional squabbleson an international level, combined with the notion that cyberspace is non-territorial, self-regulation of some issues, at least, may be an answer.

37. One of the more interesting (and controversiable) cyberlaw scholars is David Post. In essence, Post suggests that cyberspace should remain free of any geographical legal boundaries, because cyberspace is an a geographical space where time and distance constriction are minimal due to the almost real-time quality of Internet communication. He also contends that many events and transactions on the internet have no recognizable tie at all to physical places but take place only on that network

itself, which, by its very nature, is not a localizable, phenomenon and that the very concept of location is meaningless in cyberspace where space is only in reference to a virtual space consisting of the address of the machines between, which messages and information are routed; this machine addressing system is entirely independent of the physical address or location of those machines.

38. It appears that the non-geographical location and a temporality of cyberspace is a difficult concept to fit into the confines of traditional law that governs real space. It is understandable that the metaphors used to describe cyberspace mirror real space and time. Virtual space becomes real space (and therefore familiar when we talk about Internet addresses.

    Chat rooms that we can enter and leave sites that we can visit, and so on. This is not surprising, as all new ventures require metaphors rooted in the familiar to make the new phenomenon intelligible. Similar metaphors taken from familiar legal territory are necessary for the development of new law. As post comments, cyberspace is not a system designed for the convenience of lawyers.

39. Trademark infringement through cybersquatting has a far been regulated by adopting the law of real space to that of cyberspace. The anticybersquatting Consumer Protection Act is an example of this kind of real space based legislation that transposes the familiar to the unfamiliar. This practice is useful to litigants as long as courts are able to claim jurisdiction and ensure reinforcement of their orders.

    However, as a trademark infringement in cyberspace is bound to proliferate globally, national legislation is unlikely to be effective. On the other hand, relying on the kind of international Sale of Goods-may not work well in cyberspace, as this would entail shutting out non-signatory countries from the Internet. The global reach of the Internet cannot is curtailed without profoundly effecting the very technology that makes the Internet possible.

Meta Tags, Sale of Keywords, Framing and Linking

The practices like sale of keywords, meta-tagging, linking, or framing are necessary for facilitating easy access to information on the Internet. But these practices because of the purpose that they serve and the way they work, give rise to certain trademark disputes.

A growing body of jurisprudence is developing in some countries, as courts determine the limits of legal activity in this field (This is evidenced by the replies to the WIPO Questionnaire "Hypothetical Cases Concerning the Use of Trademarks on the Internet", summarized in WIPO document SCT/312 (1999), paras 16-21.). While there are divergences of approach between countries based on their distinct national laws relating to trademarks, trade practices and unfair competition, it is difficult for enterprises to formulate a coherent marketing strategy for their activities in e-commerce.

A. Meta tags

A 'meta tag' or 'meta data' is a keyword or phrase embedded in a web site's HTML (hypertext markup language) code as a means for Internet search engines to identify and categorize the contents of the web site. Being HTML code they are not visible to the naked eye.

When search engines prepare their indexes, they index various sites on the basis of the content of the site, its domain name and its meta-tags. In the race for getting more users to access their site, what entities do is that they use their competitor's trademark, or phrases or words similar thereto in the meta-tags of their web site. By doing so they ensure that whenever a user searches for the competitors trademark through a search engine, their web site gets ranked higher in the search engine results than the competitor's web site, thus increasing the chances of users landing up at their web site. This is where the conflict arises. The trademark owners allege that use of their trademark in the meta4ags amounts to infringement.

The question that arises is can use of trademarks in meta-tags constitute infringement. Two most important ingredients of infringement are 'use in the course of trade', and 'use in relation to goods or services.' (Sub-section 1, 2 and 4 of Section 29 of the Trademarks Act 1999). As meta-tags are invisible to the user, it can hardly be said that use of trademarks in meta-tags satisfies the first element of trademark infringement. Therefore in my view such use cannot be termed as trademark infringement.

If we consider the tort of passing off, we realize that for passing off there has to be a misrepresentation in relation to goods of services in such a manner as to lead to confusion. In my view, use of a trademark in meta-tags does constitute misrepresentation, as it represents one party's web site to be that of the other. In addition it causes something, which is called as 'initial interest confusion'. Thus use of a trademark in meta tags should be actionable as passing off (As for example in Road Tech Computer Systems Ltd. v. Mandata (management and Data Services) Ltd., (2000) Masons CLR 35; and Reed Executive plc. v. Reed Business Information Ltd., (2002) Masons CLR 40).

What 'initial interest confusion' means is when the user is searching for the plaintiff's web site using his trademark as a search term; he might land up at the defendant's web site dealing in similar products. He might like those products and might decide not to look for the plaintiff's site.

In Promatek Industries Ltd. V. Equitrack Corp., 2002 US Appeal Lexis 22217 (7th Circuit October 18 2002)) the court reaffirmed the propriety of applying the initial interest confusion doctrine in the meta-tag context. The court held 'it is not the case that trademarks can never appear in meta-tags, but they may only do so, where a legitimate use of the trademark is being made.

In some jurisdiction, the courts have found that companies' use of competitors' names as meta-tags constitutes unfair competition. The Indian case of Tata Sons Limited v. Bodacious Tatas (Tata Sons Limited v. Bodacious Tatas & ors, unreported ex-parte interim injunction order of the Delhi High Court dated January 25, 1999 referred to by Pravin Anand, First WIPO E-Commerce Conference (September 1999).), and the Italian case of Genertel SpA v. Crowe Italia Sri (Genertel SpA v. Crowe Italia Sri, (January 18, 2001), in International IT and New Media Update, Freshfields Bruckhaus Deringer, (Summer 2001).). In the United States of America, in the case of Brookfield Communications Inc. v. West Coast Entertainment Corp (Supra note 71. See Brookfield Communications Inc. v. West Coast Entertainment Corp, 50 U.S.P.Q. 2d 1545 (9th Cir. 1999). A similar approach is taken in the decision by the Tribunal de grande instance de Paris (March 24, 1999) in Societe Kaysersberg Packaging v. Societe Kargil; and in the judgment of the Landgericht Mannheim, 7 0 291/97 (August 1, 1997), involving the trademark "ARWIS."), the Court regarded the practice of meta tagging as potential trademark infringement, stating that such use might suggest sponsorship or authorization by the trademark owner, or that consumers looking for the products of the trademark owner might be misdirected and diverted to a competitor's web site and be at least initially confused in their search for the trademarked goods (Supra note 71. 'Initial interest confusion' was described by the District Court in the American case of Playboy Enterprises, Inc. v. Netscape Communications Corp. (55 F. Supp. 2d 1070 (C.D. Ca., 1999) at 1073) as follows "Generally speaking, initial interest confusion may result when a user conducts a search using a trademark term and the results of the search include web sites not sponsored by the holder of the trademark term, but rather of competitors. (citing Brookfield Comm., Inc. v. West Coast Ent. Corp., 174 F 3d 1036, 1062-64 (9th Cir. 1999)).

The Ninth Circuit reasoned that the user may be diverted to an unsponsored site, and only realized that she has been diverted upon arriving at the competitor's site. Once there, however, even though the user knows she is not in the site initially sought, she may stay. In that way, the competitor has captured the trademark holder's potential visitors or customers." See generally Yelena Dunaevsky, "Don't Confuse Metatags with Initial Interest Confusion," 29 Fordham Urban. Law School Journal, p.1349 (February 2002).).

One of the defenses that are often raised in meta-tag cases is that of nominative fair use. Several cases address whether meta-tag use of another's mark constitutes nominative fair use, but their somewhat inconsistent results suggest that the ultimate determination depends upon a fact specific analysis of what constitutes a reasonable use.

However, while as a general rule the unauthorized use of a trademark as a meta-tag is considered unlawful, this approach is not universal. A number of cases brought by Playboy Magazine illustrate the complexity of the law in this area, and the diversity of outcomes even within one legal jurisdiction. In the American cases of Playboy Enterprises Inc. v. Calvin Designer Label (985 F. Supp. 1220 (N.D. Cal. 1997)), and Playboy Enterprises, Inc. V. Asia Focus International, Inc. (1998 U.S. Dist. LEXIS 10459 (E.D. Va. 1998)), the Courts prevented the defendants from using the marks 'Playboy' and 'Playmate' as meta tags on their web sites, as well as in related domain names. In the case of Playboy Enterprises Inc. v. Welles, it was held that use as a meta tag of the Playmate trademark by a former Playmate of the year, to enable consumers to locate her web site, was a fair use (See Playboy Enterprises Inc. v. Welles, 7 F Supp. 2d 1098, 47 U.S.P.Q. 2d 1186. See also Bemina of America V. Fashion Fabrics International, 2001 U.S. Dist. LEXIS 2122, at pp.7-8.55 F. Supp. 2d 1070 (C.D. Cal.) affirmed -without opinion 202 F. 3d 278 (9th Cir. 1999)). Similarly, in Playboy Enterprises V. Netscape Communications, the Court found that the use of trademarks as meta-tags by the defendant's search engines, which linked adult entertainment advertisements to the trademarked terms, was in fair use.

In is becoming clear that the courts may allow the use of trademarks as meta tags where such use is not misleading or unfair; Bihari V. Gross, 119F. Supp. 2d 309 (S.D.N.Y 2000).

Finally adequate remedies for meta-tag infringement remain elusive, since mere removal of the plaintiffs mark from the meta tags is insufficient, to prevent the site from appearing in search results of search engines whose records are not regularly updated. The consent order entered in Bayer Corporation v. Custom School frames LLC (F. Supp. 2d 503 (E. D. La 2003)) may present the best remedy trademark owners are generally likely to obtain an order that the defendant request removal from all search engines of its site as a result of searches for the plaintiffs mark (Supra note 78.).

B. Keywords

Keywords are words used by a search engine to formulate their index of web sites. This index is in turn used by the search engine to answer a user's query. Thus when a user enters a word into the search engine, the search engine software checks up that word in its keyword index and brings up a list of web sites featuring that word. On the Internet, more the number of clicks that a web sites gets higher are- the amount of advertisements that it gets. In a thirst for getting more clicks and in turn more advertisements, what web site owners do is that they buy certain keywords from a search engine. Thus the search engine agrees with the buyer that whenever a particular keyword is entered into it, the buyer's web site will be displayed. But this at times gives rise to trademark disputes. Invariably what happens is that one person buys a keyword, which is the trademark of his competitor. Thus he is able to divert his competitors customers to his web site, and thus profits out of the competitor's reputation.

This gives rise to trademark infringement as well as dilution claims. Such keywords could either be the actual trademark, or phrases containing a part of the trademark. The other kind of cases are wherein the search engine sells the keyword to an advertiser, so that whenever the keyword is searched for, along with the search results, the advertisers advertisement is also displayed. This is called 'word specific banner advertising.' The question that now arises is whether buying keywords constitutes trademark infringement. Considering the unique way in, which the search engines work on the Internet, it is not possible to give a definite answer to this question. However, it is my view that a person who buys a keyword being the trademark of his competitor could be said to commit the tort of passing off. In each case, the possibility of confusion shall vary according to the facts.

The legal treatment of such cases is still developing. In the case of Playboy Enterprises Inc. v. Netscape Communications Corporation & Excite Inc, the Court denied preliminary relief stating that the 'Playboy' and 'Playmate' keywords sold by the defendant were used by searchers as common or generic words, not the marks (Playboy Enterprises Inc. v. Netscape Communications Corp., 2000 U.S. Dist. Lexis 13418 (C.D. Cal. 12 Sept. 2000)).

In its final decision the court held that such use of the word 'Playboy' by Excite does not constitute trademark use, because the search engine is not using the trademark to identify its or its customers goods or services, but only to refer to Playboy in a comparative manner. Moreover the court held that any such use was not likely to confuse consumers. This ruling, if it stands effectively validates a long-standing business practice of many search engines. The case has been appealed to the Ninth Circuit (Supra note 78.).

There have been certain cases wherein the Courts have ruled in favour of the trademark owner (German case of Estee Lauder, Excite and Ibeauty; Washington post Newsweek Interactive Co., LLC v. The Gator Corporation, 2002 U.S. Dist. Lexis 20879 (E.D. Va. July 16 2002).). However, a large number of cases are currently pending before various Courts, especially in the US. Their outcome could help develop the law in this area (Mark Nutritionals, Inc v. Alta Vista, Inc. and Overture, Inc., et al., No. 02 CV 00087 (W.D.Tx., complaint filed 1,28/02); Plasma Net, Inc. v. Overture; Novak v. Overture.).

The question that remains to be answered is whether it is the duty of a search engine to carry out a trademark search before it sells keyword to buyers. The popular search engine Google has filed a case in U.S. District Court in San Jose, Calif., on Nov.26, 2003. In this case it seeks declaratory judgment that its current policy regarding the sale of keyword-triggered advertising does not constitute trademark infringement.

C. Framing:

Framing involves incorporation of material from one web site into another by using a link and a window or a frame to display the content from the linked site. Framing gives rise to trademark claims because of the ability of the person creating the frame, to avoid the linked web sites trademark from appearing in the frame, which could lead the user to conclude that there is some association between the material displayed in the frame and the site that he is currently viewing.

In usual cases involving trademarks the plaintiff is aggrieved because the defendant is trying to use the plaintiff's trademark in relation to the defendant's goods or services. But the cases of framing are unique in the sense that here the plaintiff is aggrieved because the defendants framing tactics could lead to passing off the plaintiffs web site as that of the defendant. Thus claims arising out of framing are an antithesis of usual trademark claims

There have been cases involving allegations that the defendants framing tactics lead to trademark infringement and dilution claims. In the American case of The Washington Post v. Total News, Inc., six major news organizations whose content had been framed by the defendant alleged misappropriation, trademark dilution and infringement, false and deceptive advertising, unfair trade practices, copyright infringement, and tortious interference with their advertising contracts. The defendant in this case had framed news content from the plaintiff's sites with advertisements that it had itself sold, thereby diverting advertising revenue and, by maintaining its own site address for the material, made it appear that the news originated from its site. A settlement was reached that permitted the defendant to maintain its links to the news sites, upon agreement to cease framing the plaintiff's material in association with any third party advertising or its URL (Washington Post Co. v. Total News, Inc., No.97 Civ. 1190 (PKL) (S.D.N.Y). A line of cases in trademark law on the repackaging of trademarked goods also offers support for the contention that framing may violate trademark law.

But as most of the cases were settled, the Courts have not had a chance of laying down any principles on this issue.

D. Linking:

By clicking on an underlined term or a coloured word on a web page, the user gets transported to another page within that site, or to the home page of another site or to a page within another site. This is called as linking and in the case of a page within another site, as deep linking. The technical term for this is hyper-linking.

Law on the conflict between linking and trademarks has been particularly silent in the past few years because most of the controversies have got settled outside court.

Linking can give rise to trademark issues either because the link itself contains the trademark, or the link takes the user to the plaintiff's site, which could constitute passing off.

Coming to the first case, the question that arises is whether one should be able to use another's trademark in text or logo form on one's web site to link to another's web site. One might argue that she merely makes a 'fair use' of another's logo when using it merely as a link. On the other hand the trademark owner might argue that use of the text link is permissible, but use of a logo in a link is not permissible because the logo is truly a source identifying mark to, which the 'fair use' or 'nominative use' defense does not apply.

According to a line of recent US case authority, the trademark owner should prevail in this argument. Indeed in a recent case involving the alleged fair use of a famous trademark via the Internet, the US Circuit Court of Appeal for the Ninth Circuit has defined a three-factor test to apply to the 'nominative use defense'.

First the product or service in question must be one not readily identifiable without use of the trademark; second only so much of the mark or marks may be used as is reasonably necessary to identify the product or service; and third the user must do nothing that would, in conjunction with the mark suggest sponsorship or endorsement by the trademark holder (Playboy Enterprises v. Welles 279 F. 3d 796, 801 (Ninth Circuit 2002)).

Therefore it appears that the nominative use defense will not apply in cases where the defendant has utilized the plaintiff's logo as a link, though it will apply if defendant merely uses a text link and satisfies the remaining elements of such defense (Supra note 78).

In several German cases trademark law has been relied upon to deal with situations where the link incorporated trademarked material. In Symicron V. Fachhochschule Oldenburg (Ibid; L.G. Braunschweig, September 6 2000, Germany.) the defendant a college was found liable for incorporating a trademarked name in a link used by its students to point to software products. Contrary to this decision was a later case Swabedoo (Supra note 78; OLG Schleswig, 19 December 2000 Germany.). The court found that the link provider was not liable for trademark infringement because there was non-commercial use of trademarked terms in a link- the link provider did not seek any payment for the links that he provided.

Coming to the second category, it is my view that linking can lead to trademark disputes, where there is likelihood that a user who by using link is transported to a deep link within another web site, will associate that page with the original web site. This could lead to passing off.

In my view, sites that incorporate links to other web sites or to pages within other web sites can include a short note against each link, intimating the user that the site hosting the link does not have any association with the linked site.

There have been cases where the Courts have held linking to constitute trademark infringement (Supra note 78; Jeri-Jo Knitwear v. Club Italiana, 94 F. Supp. 2d 457 (S.D.N.Y 2000).), but the law in this area yet needs to be defined.

In a recent decision of the Swedish Appeals Court 21st March 2003, Sony Sweden had posted links to its subsidiaries web site on its web site. On reaching the subsidiaries web site the trademark of the plaintiff "i-Link" was displayed. Sony was held liable as if it had displayed the trademark on its web site, because it was transferring users to the site where the trademark was displayed.

In the case of Ford Motor Company v.2600 Enterprises (Ford Motor Company v.2600 Enterprises, et al., 177 F. Supp. 2d 661, 2001 U.S. Dist. Lexis 21302 (E.D. Michigan, December 20, 2001).), however, the Court denied the claims for alleged unfair competition and trademark dilution as a result of linking, because the defendants had not used the plaintiff's mark in commerce, nor in connection with the sale, or advertising for sale, of any goods or services.

E. Solutions

The extent to, which the use of meta-tags, keywords, framing and linking causes confusion will depend upon how sophisticated the user is. Keeping in mind the phenomenal role that these techniques play in simplifying access to information, web site owners cannot be expected to cease using them.

However, in order to avoid any disputes, what web site owners can do is to display sufficient number of notices at conspicuous places on their web sites as would indicate their identity. Such notices should ideally be displayed against links and frames, so as to help the user distinguish between the content of different web sites.

F. POP UP ADVERTISEMENTS

A pop-up ad is a window, not initiated by the user that appears on top of the content page when a site is loaded. A user who clicks on the pop-tip graphic will be redirected to the advertiser's web site, otherwise, and unless closed by the user, the pop-up window will close automatically after a short period of time. Pop-up ads are used as marketing tools designed to capture consumers' attention.

In the American case of Washington post Newsweek Interactive Co. v. Gator Corp., the Court issued a preliminary injunction, that prohibited the defendant from enabling third-party advertising to appear on a user's computer screen while the user was viewing web sites owned or affiliated with the plaintiffs, who were 16 online news companies (Washington post Newsweek Interactive Co. v. Gator Corp., E.D. Va., Civil Action No. 02-909-A, July 16, 2002. The Court found that the software violated the plaintiffs' trademarks by causing pop-up advertising to appear in proximity to them.

A notable decision is the one in U-Haul International Inc. v. When U. corn Inc. (68 U.S.P.Q. 2d 1038, 2003 U.S. Dist. LEXIS 15710 (E.D. Va. Sept 5 2003).) wherein the court held that while pop up adds are a burden, they are legal. Currently U-Haul is considering its options under appeal (Supra note 78.).

In my view, in most of the cases when an advertisement pops-up while a user is viewing a site, there is least likelihood of him associating it with the site that he is viewing. 'Thus there can be no confusion and the pop-up advertisement will not be violating the web site owner's trademark in any way.

G. POTENTIAL AREAS OF CONFLICT

Web rings

A web ring is a group of web sites, which cater to a common theme or interest. They are usually linked to each other. Due to the large number of users that they attract and specific interests that they cater to, they attract a large number of advertisements. These advertisements and the linking that exists between the sites serve a potentially fertile ground for trademark infringement and other claims.

Blogs

A blog is an abbreviated term for a Web log. It is a chronological publication that contains commentary by the author and frequently features links to relevant sites. Although there are no reported trademark cases on bl$_9$gs, this is an area worth watching (Ibid).

Conclusion

The growth of the Internet, while providing a fertile ground for those aspiring to tap the world market, poses various challenges to trademark owners. As the Internet evolves, and as advanced techniques of accessing information unfold, the existing trademark law might not be able to cope with them. Therefore, the International community as well as the Indian legislature has to be proactive and enterprising in developing suitable legislation. In absence of such efforts, the community of trademark owners might continue to sail in the sea of uncertainty.

16

Digital Signature

Introduction

A digital signature is an electronic replacement of a physical "wet" signature, created by software. It uses the technology of public key cryptography to provide for data integrity. This feature prevents the contents of an electronic file from undergoing modification. Digital signatures are also used for authentication as they prove the identity of the person who has applied the signature. A user needs a digital certificate to create a digital signature. Digital certificates are issued to end-users by certifying authorities. For a digital certificate to be considered valid, it must be issued by a certifying authority.

To digitally sign a document, a user is expected to log on to the software with either a password, a smart card or using bio-metric technology (such as fingerprints on a palm reader) that authenticates his/her identity.

Digital Signature and electronic records under the Information Technology Act, 2000

The Act provides for legal recognition of electronic records and of digital signature.

Written Signature v/s Digital signature

In India the law places a lot of emphasis on written signature. The written signature binds the person to the writing signed. The first thing when a person signs is a presumption that the person has read and applied his mind to the content that he is about to sign. By signing the person authenticates the writing and binds himself. The person is stopped from repudiating the writing. By the signature the outside world is able to attribute and associate the writing to the person who has signed it and can rely on it. In the digital world where there is no scope of handwritten signatures. There is a need of technology by, which the world can bind a person, and attribute the electronic record to the person and be sure that the electronic record is not tempered with during the transmission. There are various technology such as symmetric crypto system, asymmetric crypto system, biometrics system, scanning the handwritten system, etc.

Legal recognition of digital signature under Act, S. 5.

Where any law provides that information or any other matter shall be authenticated by affixing the signature or any document should be signed or bear the signature of any person then, notwithstanding anything contained in such law, such requirement shall be deemed to have been satisfied, if such information or matter is authenticated by means of digital signature affixed in such manner as may be prescribed by the Central Government. The Information Technology Act gives legal recognition to electronic records and to digital signature u/ss. 4 and 5.

Something more on digital signature

Digital Sign is not like your handwritten signature. It is jumble of letters and digits. It looks something like this.

...... BEGIN SIGNATURE ......

Uz5xHz7DxFwvBAh24zPAQCmOyhT47gvuvzO0YbDA5txg5
bN1Ni3hgPgnRz8FwxGU0Dnj7aw17BwSBeW4MSG7/3NS70ZyD/
AWO1Uy2dYD4Uqt/w3d6D21l1v3L8EOiHiH+5K8Gpe5zK5CLV+
zBKwGY47n6Bpi9jCYXz5YwXj4JxTT+y8 = gy5N

...... END SIGNATURE ......

- Your e-mails can be digitally signed.
- It is difficult to forge Digital sign.
- Digital Affidavits, Digital Notary, Digital company seal possible in future.
- Digital Sign can be used in WAP enabled mobile phones.

17

Domain

Getting a good domain name...(Almost everything is taken!)

So you've decided to setup a web site? Why not? Everybody is doing it. Hire some web space, get a good domain name and you are on... Wait a minute, did I say good domain name? I must be out of my mind. Last time I checked it felt like almost every English dictionary word was taken. I decided to look for a good Hindi domain name.

No luck again, whatever came to mind had already been registered. Our clients then came up something, which was sort of a compromise. It was definitely not in the league of a business.com or an internet.com, but what the heck; the site had to go up....

So what does one do'? How does one get a good domain in a world where thousands of domain names are being registered everyday? Well, there is no simple answer to that, but there are some rules you can follow to construct a good domain name. These rules will help you systematically search for a good domain name. But let's first look at what is a good domain name.

A good name must have the following qualities It must be easy to remember. (Most Important) It must as closely describe the web site content as possible (This can really help you get good rankings on a search engine). Though there are exceptions to this rule (Yahoo.com being the most notable exception). It must be as short as possible. It must be easy to spell. (you don't want your visitors to misspell their way to other sites). It must be sufficiently different from the names of other popular sites (at least different from the names of popular sites in the same category as you). It must NOT be the name used by a famous brand or company. If your site is international in nature, make sure the domain name is not considered offensive in some country.

Now let's say how one can construct a good, possibly available, domain name Let's say your site is a general information site about books, so your main keyword would be books.....

First you will try books.com, and unless you are really, really lucky you will not get it. Next maybe you'd give a shot to books.net (no luck again! huh!). If your site is India specific maybe you can try pustak.com or kitaab. com, but if your site is international in nature, you would have a problem at your hands. The only choice now would be to use prefixes or suffixes with your keyword and see if the resulting domain name was available for registration.

While adding prefixes or suffixes to your keyword avoid the use of hyphens. This causes a problem when you rely on word of mouth publicity for your web site. When people recommend your site to others, they might not mention the hyphen and the person would not be able to reach your web site at all. Getting a good domain name..(Almost everything is taken!) (cont.)

Here's how your domain name would look when attached with some common prefixes for information web sites....

aboutbooks .com

allaboutbooks.com

knowbooks.com

books.com

ebooks.com

Here's how your domain name would look when attached with some common suffixes for information web sites .....

booksonline.com

booksonthenet.com

bookssite.com

If you are India specific, then you could try for indiabooks.com or booksindia.com. If you feature books of a specific type you could try prefixing an adjective to your keyword. For e.g. oldbooks.com, classicbooks.com, rarebooks.com, etc. All these domain meet the criteria mentioned on top. In addition these type of domain names are in vouge.

Net savvy surfers directly try these domain names when they are looking for information on the net. This might become a common practice, as the use of the webs grows and more and more peoples gain expertise. These domain names will surely become extremely valuable in a couple of years. Remember domain names like business.com have fetched millions of dollars when their original owners sold them.

Of course you could have many more prefixes and suffixes and therefore a lot more combinations would be possible. This as you will realize could be a lot of hard work. Specially, if you are using a conventional web based who is query tool to check for domain name availability. Almost every site, which lets you register a domain name provides a web based who is query tool. Some sites like qwho.com or betterwhois.com are dedicated exclusively to this purpose.

Such sites are fast and return detailed information about the registered domain name.

Detailed information, which includes registrant name and address, helps you contact the owner of the domain name in case you want to purchase the domain name from him/her.

But what you really need is a tool to, which helps you make who is query for multiple domain names at the same time. The best tool available at the moment is at register.com. Who is query tool at register.com lets you specify one or two keywords. It also lets you specify the type of content your web site would host. Then using this information it automatically constructs domain names and gives you a report within seconds.

The problem with web based tools are that they are slow and cannot be customized. They are now software applications available, which make searching for a good domain name a breeze. ITAZ DomaiNIC is one of the new fast and easy to use tools available. It is first of its kind because it is actually a set of tools, which help you quickly choose a good available domain name. It features a quick multi domain who is query tool, a fast, intelligent and fully customizable domain name generator and domain name research tool.

The DomaiNIC research tools lets you quickly survey the kind of domain names already registered for your keyword.

Dispute of Ownership of DOMAIN NAME

Q.1. What is a domain name?

Ans. Each host computer providing Internet services ("Web Site") has a unique Internet address. Users seeking to exchange digital information (electronic mail ("email"), computer programs, images, text, etc.) with a particular Internet host require the host's address in order to establish a connection. Hosts actually possess two fungible addresses a numeric "IP" address such as 123.456.123.12, and an alphanumeric "domain name" such as http ://www.lawfirmofkhonas .com/ with greater mnemonic potential.

Here "LawFirmOfKhonas" is a domain name. Domain names are the familiar, easy to remember names for computers on the Internet (such as LawFirmOfKhonas.com). Domain names are used generally as a convenient way of locating information and reaching others on the Internet.

Q.2. What does it mean to "register" a domain name?

Ans. The Internet domain name system (DNS) consists of a directory, organized hierarchically, of all the domain names and their corresponding computers registered to particular companies and persons using the Internet. When you register a domain name, it will be associated with the computer on the Internet you designate during the period the registration is in effect.

Q.3. How can I get a domain name in. com, .net or .org?

Ans. Domain names ending with .com, .net or .org can be registered through many different companies (known as "registrars"). ICANN is the new non-profit corporation that is assuming responsibility from the U.S. Government for co-ordinating certain Internet technical functions, including the management of Internet domain name system. Domain names are registered on a first come first serve basis.

Q.4. What is involved in registering a domain name in .com, net or org.?

Ans. To register a domain name, you will be asked to provide the registrar you select with the various contact and technical information that makes up the registration. The registrar will then keep records of the contact information and submit the technical information to a central directory known as the "registry".

This registry provides other computers on the Internet the information necessary to send you e-mail or to find your web site. You will also be required to enter a "Registration Agreement" with the registrar, which sets forth the terms under, which your registration is accepted and will be maintained. It is upmost important that you are named and addressed as the "Registrant" when you give all the information to register your Domain Name. Nobody "owns" a domain name.

There is no way that Registrar can determine whether you are entitled to register a domain name or not. But the person who registers it for all practical purposes controls the usage of the name, e.g. to register 'LawFirmOfKhonas" the Author being one of the partners should register herself as the "Registrant".

Q.5. Will your name and contact information be publicly available?

Ans. Yes, Information about who is responsible for domain names is publicly available to allow rapid resolution of technical problems and to permit enforcement of consumer protection, trademark, and other laws. The registrar will make this information available to the public on a "Who is" site.

Q.6. Someone else has registered your company's name as a .com domain name. What is the remedy available to you?

Ans. Domain name mirroring a corporate name may be a valuable corporate asset, as it facilitates communication with a customer base.

All ICANN-accredited registrars follow a "Uniform domain name dispute resolution policy". The policy, which is in effect at present inter alia provides that the Registrar will cancel, transfer or otherwise make changes to domain name registrations under the following circumstances:

a. On their receipt of written or appropriate electronic instructions from you or your authorized agent to take such action;

b. their receipt of an order from a court or arbitral tribunal, in each case of competent jurisdiction, requiring such action; and/or

c. their receipt of a decision of an Administrative Panel requiring such action in any administrative proceeding to, which you were a party and, which was conducted under this Policy or a later version of this Policy adopted by ICANN.

In disputes arising from registrations allegedly made abusively (such as "cybersquatting" and "cyberpiracy"), [see clause c above] the uniform policy provides an expedited administrative procedure to allow the dispute to be resolved without the cost and delays often encountered in court litigation. In these cases, you can invoke the administrative procedure by filing a complaint with one of the dispute-resolution service providers. Currently Three organizations have been appointed (a) World Intellectual Property Organization (WIPO) at Geneva (b) National Arbitration Forum in Minneapolis and (c) Resolution in Montreal as dispute-resolution service providers.

Q.7. What is "Cybersquatting"?

Ans. It is the action of registering domain names sometimes in bulk without actually using them except to ultimately to sell it to a real user by making profit over and above reasonable out-of-pocket expenses.

Q.8. What do you have to prove before the "dispute-resolution service providers" for dispute over a domain name registered by some third party if you are the complainant?

Ans. In the administrative proceeding, the complainant(you) must prove that each of the following three elements are present:

(i) disputed domain name is identical or confusingly similar to a trademark or service mark in, which the complainant(you) has rights; and

(ii) the present domain name registrant has no rights or legitimate interests in respect of the domain name; and

(iii) your domain name has been registered and is being used in bad faith.

Q.9. What is Evidence of "Registration and Use in Bad Faith"?

Ans. The following circumstances, in particular but without limitation, if found by the "dispute-resolution service provider's Panel to be present, shall be evidence of the registration and use of a domain name in bad faith:

(i) circumstances indicating that the third party have registered or you have acquired the domain name primarily for the purpose of selling, renting, or otherwise transferring the domain name registration to the complainant(you) who is the owner of the trademark or service mark or to a competitor of that complainant for valuable consideration in excess of your documented out-of-pocket costs directly related to the domain name; or

(ii) third party have registered the domain name in order to prevent the owner of the trademark or service mark from reflecting the mark in a corresponding domain name, provided that third party have engaged in a pattern of such conduct; or

(iii) third party have registered the domain name primarily for the purpose of disrupting the business of a competitor; or

(iv) by using the domain name, third party have intentionally attempted to attract, for commercial gain. Internet users to your web site or other on-line location, by creating a likelihood of confusion with the complainant's mark as to the source, sponsorship, affiliation, or endorsement of his web site or location or of a product or service on his web site or location.

Q.10. How to Demonstrate Your Rights to and Legitimate Interests in the Domain Name in Responding to a Complaint?

Ans. When you receive a complaint, any of the following circumstances, in particular but without limitation, if found by the Panel to be proved based on its evaluation of all evidence presented, shall demonstrate your rights or legitimate interests to the domain name:

(i) before any notice to you of the dispute, your use of, or demonstrable preparations to use, the domain name or a name corresponding to the domain name in connection with a bona fide offering of goods or services; or

(ii) you (as an individual, business, or other organization) have been commonly known by the domain name, even if you have acquired no trademark or service mark rights; or

(iii) you are making a legitimate non-commercial or fair use of the domain, without intent for commercial gain to misleadingly divert consumers or to tarnish the trademark or service mark at issue.

Q.11. Can I go to Court for protecting my rights and interests?

Ans. Yes, Indeed you can go to court of Competent Jurisdiction for protecting my rights and interests. You can do so even if proceedings have commenced before the Panel and are pending subject to para 4(k) of the policy.

All other disputes between you and any party other than the Registrar regarding your domain name registration that are not brought pursuant to the mandatory administrative proceeding provisions of the policy shall be resolved between you and such other party through any court, arbitration or other proceeding that may be available.

Q.12. Is there any decision taken, which can highlight some of the legal implications?

Ans. Following are the details of the case decided by WIPO in the month of January, 2000.

Administrative Panel Decision

World Wrestling Federation Entertainment, Inc. (Complainant) V. Michael Bosman(Respondent)

The domain name at issue is worldwrestlingfederation.com,

Factual Background

The complainant has provided evidence of the registration of the following marks:

1. Service Mark-WORLD WRESTLING FEDERATION, registered for a term of 20 years from January 29, 1985, with the United States Patent and Trademark Office;
2. Trademark-WORLD WRESTLING FEDERATION, registered for a term of 20 years from November 7, 1989, with the United States Patent and Trademark Office.

On October 10, 1999, three days after registering the domain name at issue, respondent contacted complainant by e-mail and notified complainant of the registration and stated that his primary purpose in registering the domain name was to sell, rent or otherwise transfer it to complainant for a valuable consideration in excess of respondent's out-of-pocket expenses.

Parties' Contentions (in brief) were

A. Complainant

Complainant contended that respondent had registered as a domain name a mark, which is identical to the service mark and trademark registered and used by complainant, that respondent has no rights or legitimate interests in respect to the domain name at issue, and that respondent has registered and is using the domain name at issue in bad faith.

Because respondent offered to sell the domain name to complainant "for valuable consideration in excess of" any out-of-pocket costs directly related to the domain name, respondent has "used" the domain name in bad faith as defined in the Policy.

B. Respondent

Respondent had not contested the allegations of the Complaint.

Decision

The Panel decided that "the domain name registered by respondent is identical or confusingly similar to the trademark and service mark in, which the complainant has rights, and that the respondent has no rights or legitimate interests in respect of the domain name, and that the respondent's domain name has been registered and is being used in bad faith".

Accordingly, pursuant to Paragraph 4,i of the Policy, the Panel requires that the registration of the domain name worldwrestlingfederation.com be transferred to the complainant.

18

Uniform Domain Name Disputer Resolution Policy

1. Purpose: This Uniform Domain Name Dispute Resolution Policy (the policy has been adopted by the internet corporation for assigned names and numbers (ICANN) is incorporated by reference into your Registration Agreement, and sets forth the terms and conditions in connection with a dispute between you and any party other than us (the registrar) over the registration and use of an internet domain name registered by you. Proceedings under paragraph 4 of this policy will be conducted according to the Rules for Uniform Domain Names Dispute Resolution Policy (the "Rules of Procedure"), and the selected administrative-dispute-resolution service provider's supplemental rules.

2. Your Representations: By applying to register a domain name, or by asking us to maintain or renew a domain name registration, you hereby represent and warrant to us that the statements that you made in your registration agreement are complete and accurate; to your knowledge, the registration the domain name will not infringe upon or otherwise violate the rights of any third party; you are not registering the domain name for an unlawful purpose; and you will not knowingly use the domain name in violation of any applicable laws or regulation. It is your responsibility to determine whether your domain name registration infringes or violates someone else's right.

3. Cancellations, Transfers, and Changes: We will cancel, transfer or otherwise make changes to domain name registrations under the following circumstances

   a. subject to the provisions of paragraph 8, our receipt of written or appropriate electronic instructions from you or your authorized agent to take such action;

   b. our receipt of an order from a court or arbitral tribunal, in each case of competent jurisdiction, requiring such action, and/or.

   c. our receipt of a decision of an Administrative Panel requiring such action in any administrative proceeding to, which you were a party and, which was conducted under this policy or a later version of this policy adopted by ICANN. (See Paragraph 4(I) and (K) below.)

We may also cancel, transfer or otherwise make changes to a domain name registration in accordance with the terms of your Registration Agreement or other legal requirements.

4. Mandatory Administrative Proceeding.

   This Paragraph sets forth the type of, which you are required to submit to a mandatory admimstrative-disput-resolution service providers listed at www.Icann.Org/udrp/approved-providers.htm(each, a "provider").

   a. Applicable Disputes: You are required to submit to a mandatory administrative proceeding in the event that a third party (a complaint) asserts to the applicable provider, in compliance with the Rules of procedure, that

      (i) Your domain name is identical or confusingly similar to a trademark or service mark in, which the complainant has rights, and

      (ii) You have no rights or legitimate interest in respect of the domain name; and

      (iii) Your domain name has been registered and is being used in bad faith.

      In the administrative proceeding, the complaint must prove that each of these three elements are present.

   b. Evidence of Registration and Use in Bad faith: For the purposes of Paragraph 4(a) (iii), the following circumstances, in particular but without limitation, if found by the panel to be present, shall be evidence of the registration and use of a domain name in bad faith:

      (i) circumstances indicating that you have registered or you have acquired the domain name primarily for the purpose of selling, renting, or otherwise transferring the domain name registration to the complaint who is the owner of the trademark or for valuable consideration in excess of your documented out-of-pocket costs directly related to the domain names; or

      (ii) You have registered the domain name in order to prevent the owner of the trademark of service mark from reflecting the mark in a corresponding domain name, provided that you have engaged in a pattern of such conduct; or

      (iii) You have registered the domain name primarily for the purpose of disrupting the business of a competitor; or

      (iv) By using the domain name, you have internationally attempted to attract, for commercial gain, internet users to your web site or other on-line location, by creating a likelihood of confusion with the complainant's mark as to the source, sponsorship, affiliation, or endorsement of your web site or location or of a product of service on your web site or location.

c. How to Demonstrate: Your rights to and Legitimate Interests in the Domain Name in Responding to a complaint, When you receive a complaint you should refer to Paragraph 5 of the Rules of Procedure in determining how your response should be prepared. Any of the following circumstances, in particular but without limitation, if found by the Panel to be proved based on its evaluation of all evidence presented, shall demonstrate your rights or legitimate interests to the domain name for the purposes of Paragraph 4 (a) (ii):

   (i) before any notice to you of the dispute, your use of or demonstrable preparation to use, the domain name in connection with a bona fide offering of goods or services; or

   (ii) you (as an individual, business, or other organization) have been commonly known by the domain name, even if you have acquired no trademark or service mark rights; or

   (iii) you are making a legitimate non-commercial or fair use of the domain name, without intent for commercial gain to misleadingly divert consumers or to tarnish the trademark or service mark at issue.

d. Selection of Provider: The complainant shall select the provider from among those approved by ICANN by submitting the complaint td that Provider. The select Provider will administer the proceeding, except in cases of consolidation as described in Paragraph 4 (f).

e. Initiation of Proceeding and Process and Appointment of Administrative Panel: The Rules of Procedure state the process for initiating and conducting and for appointing the panel that will decide the dispute (the "Administrative Panel").

f. Consolidation: In the event of multiple disputes between you and a complaint, either you or the complaint may petition to consolidate the disputes before a single Administrative Panel appointed to hear a pending dispute between the parties. This Administrative Panel may consolidate before it any or all such disputes in its sole discretion, provided that the disputes being consolidated, are governed by this Policy or a later version of this Policy adopted by ICANN.

g. Fees: All fees charged by a Provider in connection with any dispute before an Administrative Panel pursuant to his Policy shall be paid by the complainant except in cases where you elect to expand the Administrative Panel from one to three panelists as provided in Paragraph 5 (b) (iv) of the Rules of Procedure, in, which cases all fees will be split evenly by you and the complainant.

h. Our Involvement in Administrative Proceedings: We do not, and will not, participate in the administration or conduct of any proceeding before an Administrative Panel. In additi6n, We will not be liable as a result of any decisions rendered by the Administrative Panel.

i Remedies: The remedies available to a complainant pursuant to any proceeding before an Administrative Panel shall be limited to requiring the cancellation of your domain name or the transfer of your domain name registration to the complainant.

Notification and Publication: The Provider shall notify us of any decision made by an Administrative Panel with respect to a domain name you have registered with us. All decisions under this policy will be published in full over the Internet, except when an Administrative Panel determines in an exceptional case to redact portions of its decision.

k. Availability of Court Proceedings: The mandatory administrative proceeding requirements set forth in Paragraph 4 shall not prevent either you or the complainant from submitting the dispute to a court of competent jurisdiction for independent resolution before such mandatory administrative proceeding is commenced or after such mandatory administrative proceeding is commenced or after such proceeding is concluded. If an Administrative Panel decides that domain name registration should be cancelled or transferred we will wait ten (10) business Days (as observed in the location of our Principal office) after we are informed by the applicable Provider of the Administrative Panel's decision before implementing that decision. We will then implement the decision unless we have received from you during that ten (10) business days period official documentation (such as a copy of a complaint, file-stamped by the clerk of the court) that you have commenced a lawsuit against the complainant in a jurisdiction to, which the complainant has submitted under Paragraph 3(b) (xiii) of the Rules of procedure. (In general, that jurisdiction is either the location of our principal office or of your address as shown in our who is database. See Paragraph 1 and we will take no further action until we receive (i) evidence satisfactory to us of a resolution between the parties; (ii) evidence satisfactory to us that your lawsuit has been dismissed or withdrawn; or (iii) a copy of an order from such court dismissing our lawsuit or ordering that you do not have the right to continue to use your domain name.

5. All Other Dispute and Litigation. All other disputes between you and any party other than us regarding your domain name registration that are not brought pursuant to the mandatory administrative proceeding provisions of Paragraph 4 shall be resolved between you and such other party through any court, arbitration or other proceeding that may be available.

6. Our Involvement in Disputes. We will not participate in any way in any dispute between you and party other than us regarding the registration and use your domain name. You shall not name us as a party or otherwise include us in any such proceeding. In the event that we are named as a party in any such appropriate and to take any other action necessary to defend ourselves.

7. Maintaining the Status Quo: We will not cancel, transfer, activate, deactivate, or otherwise change the status of any domain name registration under this Policy except as provided in Paragraph 3 above.

8. Transfers During a Dispute.

   a. Transfers of a Domain Name to a New Holder. You may not transfer your domain name registration to another holder: (i) during a pending administrative proceeding brought pursuant to Paragraph 4 or for a period of fifteen (15) business days (as observed in the location of our principal place of business) after such proceeding is concluded; or (ii) during a pending court proceeding or arbitration commenced regarding your domain name unless the party to whom the domain name registration is being transferred agrees, in writing to be bound by the decision of the court or arbitrator. We reserve the right to cancel any transfer of a domain name registration to another holder that is violation of this subparagraph.

   b. Changing Registrars: You may not transfer your domain names registration to another registrar during a pending administrative proceeding brought pursuant to paragraph to Paragraph 4 or for a period of fifteen (15) business days (as observed in the location of our principal place of business) days (as observed in the location of your principal place of business) after such proceeding is concluded. You may transfer administration of your domain name registration to another registrar during a pending court action or arbitration provided that the domain name you have registered with us shall continue to be subject to the proceeding commenced against you in accordance with the terms of this Policy. In the event that you transfer a domain name registration us during the subject to the domain name dispute policy of the registrar from, which the domain name registration was transferred.

9. Policy Modifications: We reserve the right to modify this Policy at any time with the permission of ICANN. We will post our revised Policy at <URL> at least thirty (30) calendar days before it becomes effective. Unless this Policy has already been invoked by the submission of a complaint to a provider, in, which event the version of the Policy in effect at the time it was invoked will apply to you until the dispute is over, all such changes will be binding upon you with respect to any domain name registration dispute, whether the dispute arose before, on or after the effective date of our change. In the event that you object to a change in this Policy your sole remedy is to cancel your domain name registration with us, provided that you will not be entitled to a refund of any fees you paid to use, this revised Policy will apply to you until you cancel your domain name registration.

Internet Domain Name Disputes: Questions and Answers

Service for country has top-level domains-for example, VE for Venezuela and TV for Thvalu-further increasing reliability among Domain names on the Internet.

WIPO is now addressing of protection for identifiers other than trademarks, such as geographical indications-for wine-producing regions, for example-persons-names (considering protection other than as a recognized trademark, for, which they may already qualify under the UDRP), trade names, and names or acronyms of international intergovernmental organizations.

Developments in the fields of domain names and related dispute resolution are extremely dynamic.

What is a domain name?

A domain name is the address of a web site that is intended to be easily identifiable and easy to remember, such as yahoo.com or wipo.int. These user-friendly address for web sites help connect computers-and people-on the Internet. Because they are easy to remember and use, domain names have become business identifiers and, increasingly, even trademark themselves, such as amazon.com. By using existing trademarks for domain names-sony.com for example-business attract potential customers to their web sites.

What is the nature of the disputes?

Domain name disputes arise largely from the practice of cybersquatting, which involves the pre-emptive registration of trademarks by third parties as domain names. Cyberequatters exploit the first come, first served nature of the domain name registration system to register names of trademarks. Famous people of business with, which they have no connection since registration of domain names is relatively simple and inexpenseive-less the US $ 100 in most cases cybersquatters often register hundreds of such names as domain names.

As the holders of these registrations cybersquatters often then put the domain names up for auction, or offer them for sale directly to the company or person involved, at prices far beyond the cost of registration. Alternatively, they often keep the registration and use the good name of the person or business associated with that domain name to attract business for their own sites.

Why so many disputes?

There is no agreement within the Internet community that would allow organizations that register domain names to pre-screen the filing of potentially problematic names. The reasons vary, ranging from allowing easy registrations to stimulate business to the practical difficulties involved in determining who holds the rights to a name, to the principle of freedom of expression.

Furthermore, the increasing business value of domain names of the internet has led to more cybersquatting, which results in more disputes and litigation between the cybersquatters and the business or individuals whose names have been registered in bad faith.

How did WIPO get involved in the resolution of disputes?

The Internet grew rapidly over the last decade as a place to do business, although no international legal standards existed to resolve domain name disputes. The Internet Corporation for Assigned Names and Numbers (ICANN), the organization responsible for, among other things, management of the generic top level domains such as com, net and org, was in urgent need of a solution to the dispute resolution problem.

The process of negotiating a new international treaty was considered too slow and new national laws would most likely be too diverse. What were needed were internationally uniform and mandatory procedures to deal with what are frequently cross-border disputes.

With the support of its Member States WIPO-which is mandated to promote the protection of intellectual property world-wide-conducted extensive consultations with members of the Internet community around the world, after, which it prepared and published a report containing recommendations dealing with domain name issues. Based on the reports recommendations, ICANN adopted the Uniform Domain Name Dispute Resolution Policy (UDRP). The UDRP went into effect on December 1, 1999, for all ICANN accredited registrars of Internet domain names.

Under the UDRP, WIPO is the leading ICANN accredited domain name dispute resolution service providers. As of the end of 2000, some 65 per cent (about 1850) of all the cases filed under the UDRP were filed with WIPO. Additionally a growing number of registrars of country code top-level domains have designed WIPO as a dispute resolution service provider.

How does the UDRP work?

The UDRP permits complaints to file a case with a resolution service provider, specifying:

a. The domain name is question.

b. The respondent or holder of the domain name.

c. The registrar with whom the domain name was registered.

d. The grounds for the complaint.

Such grounds include, as their central criteria, the way in, which the domain name is identical or similar to a trademark to, which the complaints has rights; why the respondent should be considered has rights; why the respondent should be considered as having no rights of legitimate interests in respect of the domain name that is the subject of the complaint, and why the domain name should be considered as having been registered and used in bad faith.

Who makes the decisions and how does WIPO ensure that there is no conflict of interest?

Taking into account the specific circumstances of each dispute, such as the specific circumstances of each, WIPO appoints an expert "neutral" or panelist, (from a roster of some 200 independent individuals qualified for deciding such cases) to review dispute and issue a decision. Either party to the dispute may opt to have one of three panelists assigned to the case.

Panelists must confirm to WIPO the absence of any potential conflict of interest before taking a case, as well as disclose in written statement any and all facts that should be considered prior to appointment. In the event that one of the parties involved in a case raises a specific objection to a panelist, WIPO will consider offering a replacement.

What factors guide the panelists' decisions?

a. Whether the domain name is identical or confusingly similar to a trademark or service mark in, which the complainant has rights.

b. Whether the respondent has any rights of legitimate interests in the domain name (for example, the legitimate offering of goods and services under the same name).

c. Whether the domain name was registered and is being used in bad faith.

What accounts for WIPO's popularity as a resolution service provider?

WIPO's resolution service offers highly qualified neutral panelists, through expeditious administrative procedures, and overall impartiality and credibility.

Dispute resolution at WIPO is much faster than normal litigation in the courts. A domain name case filed with WIPO is normally concluded within two months, using online procedures, whereas litigation can take much longer.

Fees are also much lower than normal litigation. There are no in person hearings, except in extraordinary cases. Minimal filing requirements also help reduce costs. For resolution of a case involving one of five domain names, with a single panelist, the cost is US$ 3000. For six to ten domain names, the cost is US$ 2000 for a single panelist and US$ 4000 for three panelists.

What are the resolutions offered by WIPO, and are they binding?

A domain name is either cancelled, transferred, or sustained (i.e., the complaint is denied and the respondent keeps the domain name). Some examples of cases that received significant media attention include juliaroberts.com and jimihendrix.com, which were transferred to the individuals or their families. A complaint involving sting.com, filed by the singer known as Sting, was denied for a variety of reasons principally that the domain name registrant was also known by the same nickname, as-well-as the fact that the name is a common word in the English language and is not necessarily an exclusive trademark.

Domain name disputes, and no injunctive relief is available. The accredited domain name registrars-which have agreed to abide by the UDRP-implement a decision after a period of ten days, unless the decision is appealed in that time.

The resolution offered by WIPO are mandatory in the sense that accredited registrars are bound to take the necessary steps to enforce a decision, such as transferring the name concerned. However, under the UDRP, either party retains the option to take the dispute to a court of competent jurisdiction for independent resolution.

Will UDRP dispute resolution stifle the Internet?

On the contrary, domain name registration procedures remain flexible and open to everyone. In fact, the number of disputes-just under 2,000 cases were filed with WIPO by year-end 2000-represent a mere fraction of the more than 33 million domain names in use on the Internet today. With the success and reputation of WIPO's dispute resolution services, awareness is increasing among Internet users that abusive practices regarding domain names will no longer go uncontested, and that a quick and simple recourse exists. This helps assure a general reliability of domain names on the Internet.

What is WIPO doing to further improve the reliability of domain names?

The UDRP was originally designed for settling disputes in generic top-level domains such as.com, and org. however, some country code domain name registrars also have started to adopt the UDRP or similar policies, and WIPO has begun providing dispute resolution.

Many owners of creative works do not have the means to pursue the legal and administrative enforcement of copyright, especially, given the increasingly world-wide use of literary, musical and performance right. As a result, the establishment of collective management organizations or societies is a growing trend in many countries. These societies can provide members the benefits of the organization's administrative and legal expertise, in for example, collecting, managing, and disbursing royalties gained from international use of a member's work.

Cable, or satellite;

Its translation into other languages, or its adaptation such as a novel into a screenplay.

Many creative works protected by copyright require mass distribution, communication, and financial investment for their dissemination (for example, publications, sound recordings, and films); hence, creators often sell the rights to their works to individuals or companies best able to market the works in return for payment. These payments are often made dependent on the actual use of the work, and are then referred to as royalties.

These economic rights have a time limit, according to the relevant WIPO treaties, of 50 years after the creator's death. National law may establish longer time limits. This limit enables both creators and their heirs to benefit financially for a reasonable period of time. Copyright protection also includes moral rights, which involve the right to claim authorship of a work, and the right to oppose changes to it that could harm the creator's eputation.

The creator-or the owner of the copyright in a work-can enforce rights administratively and in the courts, by inspection of premises for evidence of production or possession of illegally made-"pirated"-goods related to protected works the owner may obtain court orders to stop such activities, as well as seek damages for loss of financial rewards and recognition.

The WCT and the WPPT must be ratified by 30 les before they enter into force. As of the end of the WCT had been ratified by 12 countries and PPT by 11.

V of the important new norms provided by the WCT and the WPPT, it is essential for the development of the Internet and electronic commerce that they enter into force without delay. Moreover, in order for the treaties to be fully effective in the borderless world of cyberspace they must become widely adopted in countries around the world. WIPO is therefore devoting and types success to promoting the treaties and to governments on their implementation entering force by thereof the dealt.

A meantime the treaties are meaningful as a statement of widely accepted norms. They represent broad international agreement as to the appropriate approach to copyright and related rights in the digital environment As such they save today as a guide and as a model for national legislation.

Genera- In December, 1996, two new treaties were concluded. At the World Intellectual Property organization (WI PO performances and phonograms Treaty (WIPPT).

Together, these treaties represent a milestone and related rights. Ushering that system into the digital age.

Back ground.-Copyright law provides protection for literary artistic works giving their creators the ability to control certain uses of their works. The law of related rights (That is, rights related to copyright) provides similar protection for the creative contributions of parties involved in presenting works to the public such as performers, phonogram producers, and broadcasters. National laws in individual countries provide copyrights and related rights. International treaties link the various national laws by ensuring that at least a minimum level of rights will be granted to creators under each national law. The treaties do not themselves grant rights, but rather require the countries that join the treaties to grant certain rights specified on a non-discriminatory basis.

The purpose of the two WIPO treaties is to update and improve the protection of the already existing treaties date back more than a quarter of a century to the days before more than a quarter of a century to the days before the development of personal computers and the Internet. The WCT and WPPT contain computers and the Internet. New standards and serve to clarify the older treaties. Most important, the WCT and WPPT provide responses to the challenges of the new digital technologies. For this reason this have come to be known as the "Internet treaties."

Main Elements of the Treaties- The WCT protects literary and artistic works such as books, computers programs, music, photography, paintings, sculpture and films.

The WPPT protects the rights of the producers of phonograms or sound recordings (e.g. records, cassettes, CDs) as well as the rights of perform whose performers whose performance is fixed in sound recordings.

Both treaties require countries to provide to a framework of basic rights allowing creators to control and/or be compensated for the various ways in, which their creations are used and enjoyed by others. Most important at the owners of those rights will continue to be adequately and effectively protected when their works are disseminated through new technologies and communications systems such as the Internet.

The treaties thus clarify first that the traditional right of reproduction continues to apply in the digital environment including to the storage of material in digital forma in an electronic medium. Second they clarify that the owners of right can control whether and how their creations are made available online to individual consumers at a time and a place chosen by the consumer, e.g. at home via the Internet.

To maintain a fair balance of interests between the owners of rights and the consuming public the treaties further clarify and that countries have reasonable flexibility in establishing exceptions or limitations to rights in the digital environment grant exceptions for uses deemed to be in the public interest, such as for nonprofit educational and research purposes.

The two treaties also break new ground by requiring countries to provide not only the rights themselves, but also two types of technological adjuncts to the rights. These are intended to ensure that right holders can effectively use technology to protect their rights and to licenses their works online.

The first known as the "anti-circumvention" provision tackles the problem of "hacking" it requires countries to provide adequate legal protection and effective remedies against the circumvention of technological measures (such as encryption) used by right holders to protect their rights when their creations are disseminated on the Internet the second type of technological adjunct safeguards the reliability and integrity of the online marketplace by requiring countries to prohibit the deliberate alteration or deletion of electronic "rights management information", that is, information, which accompanies any protected material available online and which identifies the work its creator performer or owner and the terms and conditions for its use.

Both treaties deal with other matters as well, not specific to the digital environment. These include rights of distribution and rental the right to receive payment for certain form of broadcasting or communication to the public and an obligation for countries to provide adequate and effective measures allowing rights holders to enforce their rights against infringement.

19

Computer Software and Copyright

Introduction

Computer software is valuable, but easy to copy, pirate and crack.

Hence we need to look at what kind of protection the law provides against the unauthorized copying and against piracy.

We will discuss the provisions of the Copyright Act, 1957 as it applies to computer programs.

What is Copyright?

Copyright is a bundle of rights given by the law to creators of literary, dramatic, musical and artistic works and producers of cinematography films and sound recordings.

Copyright in respect of computer program is:

U/S 14 "copyrigh" means the exclusive right subject to the provisions of this Act, to do or authorize the doing of any of the following acts in respect of a work or any substantial part thereof, namely -in the case of a computer programme-

1. to reproduce the work in any material form including the storing of it in any medium by electronic means,
2. to issue copies of the work to the public not being copies already in circulation,
3. to perform the work in public, or communicate it to the public,
4. to make any cinematography film or sound recording in respect of the work,
5. to make any translation of the work,
6. to make any adaptation of the work,
7. to do, in relation to a translation or an adaptation of the work, any of the acts specified in relation to the work in sub-clauses (i) to (vi).
8. to sell or give on hire, or offer for sale or hire, any copy of the computer programme, regardless of whether such copy has been sold or given on hire on earlier occasions.

U/S 2(ffc) "computer programme" means set of instructions expressed in words, codes, schemes or in any other form, including a machine readable medium, capable of causing a computer to perform a particular task or achieve a particular result.

Owner of the Copyright

- An individual author who writes a programme is the owner of copyright. A programme developed by several individuals, in, which the contribution of one author is not distinct from the contribution of the others, all the individuals are joint authors and own the copyright jointly.
- Under the Act "author" means- In relation to any literary, dramatic, musical or artistic work, which is computer-generated, the person who causes the work to be created.
- Contract of service

  In case of programme made under a contract of service as an employee then the employer will be the first owner of the copyright unless there is any agreement to the contraiy
- Contract for service

  Programmes written by people who have been appointed as independent contractor on contract for service will have the first right as owners unless such copyright is expressly assigned to the party taking their services.

How to protect your copyright?

Copyright subsists in all original published or unpublished computer programmes,

The copyright in computer programmes made within the lifetime of the author until sixty years from the year in, which the author dies.

It is not compulsory to register the copyright in India but it can be a good idea to register. But one needs to take proper professional advise before registering.

Registration with the registrar of Copyright is helpful in an infringement suit.

Copyright notice

As per the Berne Convention (to, which India is a signatory) for protection of literary and artistic works, use of copyright notice is optional. It is a good idea to incorporate a copyright notice.

A Copyright notice consists of the following:

1. The symbol © (letter "c" in a circle) or the word "Copyright",
2. The copyright owners name, and
3. The year of first publication.

For example below this article the author can write : ©Zarana Khona 2000.

The copyright notice should be placed on computer programme copies in such a way as to give reasonable notice of the owner of the copyright.

You can also put the copyright notice on your web site in the similar fashion.

How to register a programme with the Registrar of Copyright

Copyright Office regards computer programmes as literary works for, which one has to file the following duly completed along with requisite fees:

1. Form W-Application for Registration of Copyrights,
2. Statement of Particulars,
3. Statement of Further Particulars,
4. Three complete copies of the works (one has to be very cautious here to submit appropriate works after taking professional help as giving away whole of the source code can be harmful as after registration your application is open to public for inspection).

Assignment of the Copyright

U/S 18. The owner of the copyright in an existing work or prospective owner of the copyright in a future work may assign to any person the copyright, either wholly or partially in the following manner: -

1. for the entire world or for a specific country or territory; or
2. for the full term of copyright, or part thereof; or
3. relating to all the rights comprising the copyright or only a part of such rights.

U/S 19. Mode of assignment-

(1) No assignment of the copyright in any work shall be valid unless it is in writing signed by the assignor or his duly authorized agent.

(2) The assignment of copyright in work shall identify such work, and shall specify the rights assigned and the duration and territorial extent of such assignment.

(3) The assignment of copyright in any work shall also specify the amount of royalty payable, if any,

(4) Where the assignee does not exercise the rights assigned to him under any of the other sub-sections of this section within a period of one year from the date of assignment, the assignment in respect of such rights shall be deemed to have lapsed after the expiry of the said period unless otherwise specified in the assignment.

(5) If the period of assignment is not stated, it shall be deemed to be five years from the date of assignment.

(6) if the territorial extent of assignment of the rights is not specified, it shall be presumed to extend within India.

Infringement of Copyright

Copyright in work is considered to be infringed-

A. When any person without a license granted by the owner of the Copyright or the Registrar of copyrights or in contravention of the conditions of a license so granted or of any conditions imposed by a competent authority under Copyright Act-

1. does anything, the exclusive right to do, which is by Copyright Act conferred upon the owner of copyright, or
2. permits for profit any place to be used for the communication of the work to public where such communication constitutes an infringement of the copyright in the work.

B. When any person-

1. makes for sale or hire, or sells or lets for hire, or by way of trade displays or offers for sales or hire, or
2. distributes either for the purpose of trade or to such an extent as to affect prejudicially the owner of the copyright, or
3. by way of trade exhibits in public, any infringing copies of the work, or
4. Imports into India any infringing copies of the work for the private and domestic use of the importer.

Remedies for copyright infringement

Courts are empowered to grant the following reliefs: -

1. Temporary and permanent injunctions
2. Impounding and destruction of all infringing copies, including masters
3. Imprisonment of the accused or imposition of fine or both.
4. Actual monetary damages plus the infringor's profits

U/S 64 of the Copyright Act, any police officer, not below the rank of a sub-inspector, may, if he is satisfied that an offence in respect of copyright in any work has been, is being, or is likely to be committed, seize without warrant, all copies of the work, and all plates used for the purpose of making infringing copies of the work, wherever found and produce them before a Magistrate as soon as practicable. U/S 66 of the Copyright Act, the Court trying any offence, may, whether the alleged offender is convicted or not, order that all copies of the work in the possession of the alleged offender, which appear to be infringing copies be delivered up to the owner of copyright.

20

Laws relating to Online Transactions

The Aims & Salient Provisions of the Law

So much is available on the computers that the eagerness to sabotage is high. To avoid these so called hackers, who spoil the show, we have the Cyber laws. It is a very wide term that includes:

- computers
- computer networks
- the Internet
- data
- software etc.

Cyber law includes laws relating to:

1. Electronic and Digital Signatures
2. Computer Crime
3. Intellectual Property
4. Data Protection and Privacy
5. Telecommunications Laws

Let us discuss each of them in brief:

Electronic and Digital Signature Laws

Electronic Signatures especially Digitally Signatures are fast becoming the de-facto standard for authentication of electronic records, Electronic Data Interchange, Emails etc. Comprehensive laws are required so that uniform standards and procedures can be established.

These laws relating to Electronic Signatures e.g. the Electronic Signatures in Global and National Commerce Act of the USA are part of cyber law.

Computer Crime Law

Our governing dependence on computers and the Internet has made us all potential victims of Internet threats.

Some countries have enacted legislations that especially deal with computer crime and yet others have adapted their existing laws to make computer crime an offence under existing statutes.

Intellectual Property Law

Cyber law covers the intellectual property laws that relate to cyber space and its constituents.

This includes:

- Copyright law in relation to computer software, computer source code etc.
- Trademark law in relation to domain names
- Semiconductor law which relates to the protection of Semiconductor Design and Layouts
- Patent Law in relation to computer hardware and software.

Data Protection and Privacy laws

Many nations have enacted legislation relating to data protection and privacy within their jurisdictions. It is pertinent to note that due to the nature of the Internet and the amount of information that may be accessed through it, such legislation is critical to protect the fundamental rights to privacy of an individual.

These laws would probably play a vital role, as the dependence of insecure networks such as the Internet grows further.

Telecommunication Laws

As has been seen above cyberspace does not only include the Internet and computes, but is present where two or more cables or wires etc. meet. Telecommunications systems also call within the ambit of cyber space and therefore would form an integral part of cyber laws. The word cyber and its relative dot.com pare probably the most commonly used terminologies of the modern era.

In the information age the rapid development of computers, telecommunications and other technologies has led to the evolution of new forms of trans-national crimes known as "cyber crimes". They may be defined as "any crime with the help of computer and telecommunication technology", with the purpose of influencing the functioning of computer or the computer systems.

The extent of loss involved worldwide of cyber crimes is tremendous as it is estimated that about 500 million people who use the Internet can be affected by the emergence of cyber crimes. Cyber crimes are a very serious threat for the times to come and pose one of the most difficult challenges before the law enforcement machinery.

Most cyber crimes do not involve violence but rather greed, pride or play on some character weakness of the victims. It is difficult to identify the culprit, as the Net can be a vicious web of deceit and can be accessed from any part of the globe. For these reasons, cyber crimes are considered as "white-collar crimes". To understand cyber crime as a significantly new phenomenon, with potentially profoundly new consequences, it is necessary to recognize it as a constituent aspect of the wider political, social and economic reconstructing currently effecting counties worldwide.

This new technology not only provides opportunities for the profitable development of an international information market but has also raised the specter of new criminal activities to exploit them. The very technology that enables multinationals to do business more effectively and challenge the individual controls and regulations of nation states, also offers the prospect of globally organized criminal networks.

Moreover the free flow of uncensored information on electronic networks and web-sites is an attractive Just as crimes have changed with the growth of information technology so have the categories of criminals who engage in such crimes. There are three basic categories of criminals who engage in such crimes, ranging from hackers, information merchants and mercenaries, to terrorists, extremists and deviants.

The types of Cyber Crimes: The following are the possible cyber crimes.

Hacking

It is the most common type of Cyber crime being committed across the world. Hacking has been defined in section 66 of the Information Technologies Act, 2000 as follows "whoever with the intent to cause or knowing that he is likely to cause wrongful loss or damage to the public or any person destroys or deletes or alters any information residing in a computer resource or diminishes its value or utility or affects it injuriously by any means commits hacking".

Punishment for hacking under the above mentioned section is imprisonment for three years or fine which may extent to two lakh rupees or both. A Hacker is a person who breaks in or trespasses a computer system. Hackers are of different types ranging from code hackers to crackers to cyber punks to freaks. Some hackers just enjoy cracking systems and gaining access to them as an ordinary pastime; they do not desire to commit any further crime. Whether this itself would constitute a crime is a matter of fact. At most such a crime could be equated with criminal trespass.

Security Related Crimes

With the growth of the internet, network security has become a major concern. Private confidential information has become available to the public. Confidential information can reside in two states on the network. It can reside on the physical stored media, such as hard drive or memory or it can reside in the transit across the physical network wire in the form of packets. These two information states provide opportunities for attacks from users on the internal network, as well as users on the Internet.

Network Packet Sniffers

Network computers communicate serially where large information pieces are broken into smaller ones. The information stream would be broken into smaller pieces even if networks communicated in parallel. These smaller pieces are called network packets. Since these network packets are not encrypted they can be processed and understood by any application that can pick them off the network and process them. A network protocols specifies how packets are identified and labeled which enables a computer to determine whether a packet is intended for it.

The specifications for network protocols such as TCP/IP are widely published. A third party can easily interpret the network packets and develop a packet sniffer. A packet sniffer is a software application that uses a network adapter card in a promiscuous mode (a mode in which the network adapter card sends all packets received by the physical network wire to an application for processing) to capture all network packets that are sent !across a local network.

A packet sniffer can provide its users with meaningful and often sensitive information such as user account names and passwords.

IP Spoofing

An IP attack occurs when an attacker outside the network pretends to be a trusted computer either by using an IP address that is within its range or by using an external IP address that you trust and to which you wish to provide access to specified resources on your network. Normally, an IP spoofing attack is limited to the injection of data or commands into an existing stream of data passed between client and server application.

Password attacks

Password attacks can be implemented using several different methods like the brute force attacks, Trojan horse programmes. IP spoofing can yield user accounts and passwords. Password attacks usually refer to repeated attempts to identify a user password or account. These repeated attempts are called brute force attacks.

Distribution of sensitive internal information to external sources: At the core of these security breaches is the distribution of sensitive information to competitors or others who use it to the owners' disadvantage. While an outside intruder can use password and IP spoofing attacks to copy information, an internal user could place sensitive information on an external computer or share a drive on the network with other users.

Man-in-the-middle-attacks

This attack requires that the attacker have access to network packets that come across the networks. The possible use of such attack are theft of information, hijacking an ongoing session to gain access to your internal network resources, traffic analysis to drive information about one's own network and its users, denial of service, corruption of transmitted data and introduction of new information into network sessions.

Fraud On the Internet

This is a form of white collar crime. Internet fraud is a common type of crime whose growth has been proportionate to the growth of internet itself. The internet provides companies and individuals with the opportunity of marketing their products on the net. It is easy for people with fraudulent intention to make their messages look real and credible. There are innumerable scams and frauds most of them relating to investment schemes and have been described in detail below as follows:

Online investment newsletters

Many newsletters on the internet provide the investors with free advice recommending stocks where they should invest. Sometimes these recommendations are totally bogus and cause loss to the investors.

Bulletin boards

This is a forum for sharing investor information and often fraud is perpetrated in this zone causing loss of millions who bank on them.

E-mail scams

Since junk mail (E-mail which contains useless material) is easy to create, fraudsters often find it easy to spread bogus investment schemes or spread false information about a company.

Credit card fraud

With the electronic commerce rapidly becoming a major force in national economies it offers rich pickings for criminals prepared to undertake fraudulent activities. In U.S.A. the ten most frequent fraud reports involve undelivered and online services; damaged, defective, misrepresented or undelivered merchandise; auction sales; pyramid schemes and multilevel marketing and of the most predominant among them is credit card fraud.

Something like half a billion dollars is lost to consumers in card fraud alone. Publishing of false digital signature. According to section 73 of the I.T. Act 2000, if a person knows that a digital signature certificate is erroneous in certain particulars and sill goes ahead and publishes it, is guilty of having contravened the Act. He is punishable with imprisonment for a term that may extended to two years or with fine of a lakh rupees.

Making available digital signature for fraudulent purpose

This is an offence punishable under section 74 of the above mentioned act, with imprisonment for a term that may extend to two years or with fine of two lakh rupees or with both.

Alteration & Destruction of digital information

The corruption and destruction of digital information is the single largest menance facing the world of computers. This is introduced by a human agent with the help of various programmes which have been described in detail below as follows: virus Just as a virus can infect the human immunity system three exist programs, which can destroy or hamper computer systems.

A computer virus is a programme designed to replicate and spread, generally with the victim beging oblivious to its existence. Computer viruses spread by attaching themselves to programs like word processor or spreadsheets or they attack themselves to the boot sector of a disk. When an infected file is activated or when the computer is started form an infected disk, the virus itself is also executed.

Pornography on the net

The growth of technology has flip side to it causing multiple problems in everyday life. Internet has provided a medium for the facilitation of crimes like pornography. Cyber porn as it is popularly called is widespread. Almost 50% of the web sites exhibit pornographic material on the Internet today.

Pornographic materials can be reproduced more quickly and cheaply on new media like hard disks, floppy discs and CD-ROM's. The new technology is not merely an extension of the existing forms like text photographs and images. Apart from still pictures and images, full motion video clips and complete movies are also available. Another great disadvantage with a media like this is its easy availability and accessibility to children who can now log on to pornographic web-sties from their own houses in relative anonymity and the social and legal deterrents associated with physically purchasing an adult magazine from the stand are no longer present.

Furthermore, there are more serious offences which have universal disapproval like child pornography and far easier for offenders to hide and propagate throught the medium of the internet.

Laws in India

India has enacted the first I.T. Act, 2000 based on the Unciral model recommended by the general assembly of the united nations by a resolution dated 30th Jan 1997. The preamble to this Act gives a very clean picture in this regard. The various offences which are provided under this chapter are:

- Tampering with Computer source documents
- Hacking with Computer systems
- Access to protected system
- Access to protected system
- Misrepresentation
- Breach of Confidentiality and Privacy
- Fraud

The elementary problems, which are associated with cyber-crimes are:

1. Jurisdiction is the highly debatable issue as to the maintainability of any suits which has been filled. Today with the growing arms of cyberspace the growing arms of cyberspace the territorial boundaries seems to vanish thus the concept of territorial jurisdiction as envisaged under S.1 of C.P.C and S.2. of the I.P.C. will have to give way to alternative method of dispute resolution.
2. Loss of evidence is a very common & expected problem as all the data are routenly destroyed. Further collection of data outside the territorial extent also paralyzes this system of crime investigation.
3. Cyber Army-There are also an imperative need to built a high technology crime & investigation infrastructure, with highly technical staff a the other end.
4. A law regulating the cyber-space which India has done.
5. Though S.75 provides for extra-territorial operations of this law, but they could be meaningful only when backed with provision recognizing orders and warrants for Information issued by competent authorities outside their jurisdiction and measure for cooperation for exchange of material and evidence of computer crimes between law enforcement agencies.
6. Use of incepted messages, virtually private networks etc. also create a big problem to trace the activities of cyber criminals.
7. Cyber savvy judges are the need of the day. Judiciary plays a vital role in shaping the

enactment according to the order of the day. One such stage, which needs appreciation, is the P.I.L., which the Kerela High Court has accepted through an email.

8. The procedural obligation which have to be fulfilled as lettertrography U/s 166A & 166B of the Cr. P.C. and bar in case of crimes committed outside India. (i.e. prior approval of the central government.)

'Perfect' is a relative term. Nothing in this world is perfect. The persons who legislate the laws & by-laws also are neither perfect. The laws therefore enacted by them cannot be perfect. This law has emerged from the womb of globalization. It is at the threshold of development. In due course of exposure through varied & complicated issues it will grow to be a piece of its time legislation. The Information and Technology Act 2000 seeks to introduce some sort of control over the use of encryption for communication in India.

The use of the cryptography and encryption in India is a relatively new phenomenon. The use of this technology for the purposes of communication has begun only over the last 15-20 years in India. According to a recent report in India there are very few companies involved in the development of cryptography. Further, cryptography remains within the domain of the defense sector. It is only as late as 1995 that India introduced a list of items that required licensing before export. The list only included encryption software for telemetry systems in specific and did not relate to encryption software in general.

The information and Technology Act 2000 makes the publishing of information which is obscene in electronic form punishable as under:

"Whoever publishes or transmits or causes to be published in the electronic form, any material which is lascivious or appeals to the prurient interest or if its effect is such as to tend to corrupt persons who are likely, having regard to all relevant circumstances, to read, see or hear the matter contained or embodied in it, shall be punished on first conviction with imprisonment of either description for a term which may extend to five years and with fine which may extend to one lakh rupees and in the event of a second or subsequent Conviction, with imprisonment of either description for a term which may extend to ten years and also with fine which may extend to two lakh rupees."

This new law will operate upon anyone who is within its jurisdiction net. Any one within the country or the area of operation of the law who is carrying on a business of cyber porn will liable under section 67 of the above mentioned Act. Apart from this, a multi-layered governance program should be ushered in.

This will mainly include a mixture of national and international legislations and self imposed regulations by internet service providers and users like parents for their children, hotlines and special organizations to report pornographic content. In this way the balance between the freedom of the individual and the greatest good of the society can be maintained.

Taxation Issues in Electronic Commerce

As the commercialization of the Internet expands, so too inevitably will the taxation of electronic commerce. For a long time Internet users believe the Internet should remain free of governmental regulation or taxation.

According to one oft-repeated Internet message: "Governments of the Industrial World, you weary giants of flesh and steel, I come from Cyberspace the new home of Mind. On behalf of the future, I ask you of the past to leave us alone. You are not welcome among us. You have no sovereignty where we gather."

However, taxation of electronic commerce is not a future issue, but a present reality. It is not surprising that state income tax laws apply to income earned from electronic commerce transactions. It is less widely known that many states also impose sales and taxes on electronic commerce transactions.

Overview of State Sales Tax Rules

Four-fifths of the states impose a sales tax on the "transmission" component of electronic commerce – the interstate telecommunications and/or intrastate telecommunications. About one-half of the states impose a sales tax on specific categories of on-line "content" such as the electronic transmission of canned software or cable television. About one-quarter of the states impose a broader-based sales tax on numerous categories of on-line "content" such as electronic information or computer services. For example, Texas (USA) imposes its sales tax on numerous forms of electronic commerce including electronically downloaded software, Internet access, creation of Web home pages, posting of Web home pages, cable television services, credit reporting services, information services and data processing services.

Similarly, New York imposes its sales tax on numerous forms of entertainment or information services provided by telecommunications, such as stock quotes, credit reports, computer bulletin board systems, tax or stock market advisory and analysis reports, legal information and sports highlight lines. To be sure, these jurisdictions with expansive sales tax based did not set out consciously to tax the Internet – for the obvious reason that the Internet was virtually unknown to the general population until the early 1990s.

To date, no single state has comprehensively addressed the many sales tax and nexus issues related to electronic commerce. Rather, these states impose sales taxes on certain categories of electronic commerce as the result of a hodgepodge of existing laws frequently intended to tax other types of activities such as sales of telecommunications, canned software, cable television, information services, computer services and data processing. In many cases, states are attempting to use a mid-twentieth century tax system – designed largely for manufacturers and vendors of tangible personal property – to tax a technologically advanced 21st century service industry.

The Internet is exploding with new concepts and terminology such as TCP/IP digital assistants, packet switching, web crawlers, routers, hyperlinks and encryption. Not surprisingly, these old tax rules are often ill suited to taxing electronic commerce.

Complex State Tax Issues Related to the Internet

Due to complex intangible and interstate nature of electronic commerce, the rapid growth of the Internet and the information highway raises more issues for state income and transactional taxation than for federal taxation. Present and future state taxation of electronic commerce touches upon some of the most controversial and cutting edge issues in state taxation including:

Should services be subject to sales and use taxes as extensively as tangible personal property? If so, what rules should be applied to the complex fact patterns of many services – particularly electronic services?

Should sourcing rules for corporate income tax purposes be revised withr egard to the sourcing of the sales of services or intangibles?

Even if an activity is subject to a sales or income tax, there is no filing requirement unless nexus is established. Accordingly, should nexus rules be extended so as to apply to remote sellers with minimal physical presence, economic presence, intangible property presence, or attributional presence (i.e., activities or presence of third parties attributed to the taxpayer)?

The future state taxation of electronic commerce

1. General Issues: The state taxation of electronic commerce is in its infancy and there are many unresolved issues and statutory and regulatory ambiguities. There are already stark differences in approaches taken by various states that are creating considerable confusion and a lack of uniformity in state tax rules. In many cases, states are attempting to adapt a mid-twentieth century tax regime – developed for manufacturers and vendors of tangible personal property – to a technologically advanced 21st century service industry. In response to both the phenomenal growth of the Internet and the general inadequacies of state tax rules regulating this type of economic activity, many states are in the process of evaluating their approach to the taxation of electronic commerce.

   The effectiveness of state tax rules in adapting to electronic commerce will likely have a major impact on public opinion toward state tax policy in the early twenty-first century. Ironically, in drafting tax policies, the states are caught between two conflicting forces – one prodding them toward avoiding or delaying the taxation of electronic commerce; the other compelling them to continue or expand the taxation of cyberspace.

2. Cautionary Pressures: First, there is pressure on states to proceed cautiously so

that they do not adversely impact the entrepreneurial businesses that are commercializing the Internet and other forms of electronic commerce.

Given the low entry barriers to interstate commerce by means of the Internet, these new businesses may be disproportionately small or medium-size companies that are ill-equipped to handle the compliance burdens of multi jurisdictional corporate and sales and use tax filing responsibilities. The inclination to proceed deliberately with new tax rules on the Internet is also reflective of the sheer novelty and dynamism of electronic commerce. There are few computer experts, let alone revenue department officials who can accurately predict how quickly or in what form electronic commerce giving serious consideration to the range of different access and content providers and the likely impact of technological developments. The go-slow approach toward extending sales tax laws to newly emerging electronic services is reinforced by the anti-tax undercurrent in the American electorate.

Those state that do not currently impose sales taxes on electronic commerce confront the reality that it is always more difficult to enact a new tax than it is to maintain the status quo that includes a broader sales tax base. This is particularly true of states that traditionally have not had broad – based sales and use taxes on services.

Retrenchment: There are a number of state that have recently reversed or delayed implementation of taxes on electronic commerce. For example, in 1993, Tennessee enacted legislation that exempted telephone-based information services from Tennessee's telecommunication sales tax. The law removed the term "value added network" from the section of the Tennessee Telecommunications Tax Act that defines the kinds of services to which the tax applies.

In the absence of such legislative action, the Tennessee tax rules could have been interpreted to tax electronic information services. Similarly, Florida has postponed implementation of new rules that would have extended the sales tax to certain types of electronic commerce. The Florida Department of Revenue had decided in 1995 that electronic commerce would be taxed as telecommunications services.

The Department took this position on the basis of a pre-existing statutory definition of "Telecommunication services" that included "teletypewriter or computer exchange service." However, Governor Lawton Chiles issued an executive order postponing the implementation of the new tax rules while a Telecommunications Taxation Task Force studies the ramifications of taxing the Internet. (Note 191) Similar Internet tax study commissions have been established in a number of sates including Massachusetts, New York and Utah. Some of these Internet taxation skirmishes are also occurring on the local level. Recently, in city of Tacoma, Washington announced that it would begin to tax Internet access providers under its telecommunications gross receipts tax.

However, after negative public reaction, the Tacoma City Council voted 8 to 1 to repeal the application of this tax to internet access providers. There has also been considerable controversy surrounding the issuance of MTC Bulletin 95 – 1 on attributional nexus. The Committed on State Taxation (COST) issued a sharp critique of the MTC bulletin - - arguing that the position asserted by the MTC and numerous states was not supported by constitutional case law. In 1996, both the California Board of Equalization (sales tax) and the California Franchise Tax Board (income tax) voted unanimously to rescind their adoption of MTC Bulletin 95 – 1. They did so in reaction to political criticism of the attributional nexus position taken by the MTC.

In many ways, these state tax actions parallel the controversy in the late 1980s and early 1990s over the extension of the sales tax to various non-electronic service categories. In that instance – both Florida and Massachusetts eventually repealed newly enacted legislation that extended the sales tax to a broad range of services. At the same time, numerous other states with longstanding sales taxation of numerous service categories left such statues intact with relatively little political unrest.

3. Expansive Influence: Conversely, despite concerns over the impact and complexity of the taxation of emerging Internet technologies, there are countervailing pressures on states to clarify or extend sales tax rules to encompass electronic commerce.

Attractive Revenue Stream: First, the anticipated revenue growth from the explosion of electronic commerce will appear very attractive to revenue – starved state governments.

For instance, a 6 percent sales tax on $100 billion of electronic commerce sales would result in $6 billion of state tax revenues – or about 5 percent of the total combined sales tax base of all states that currently impose sales and use taxes. This amount could increase significantly if electronic commerce lives up to its much-heralded potential.

This revenue stream may become increasingly desirable to state governments if the federal government succeeds in pushing down responsibilities traditionally undertaken by the federal government to the state level. For instance, the recent federal welfare reform legislation transferred federal welfare responsibilities to the states with a significant cut in federal monies available for such purposes. Other federal welfare responsibilities such as Medicaid and other health care programs may eventually be turned over to the states – without providing commensurate revenue sources.

Erosion of the Sales Tax Base: Second, if states do not broaden their sales tax statutes to encompass electronic services, states risk an erosion of their sales tax bases as taxable tangible property transactions are supplanted by largely non-taxable intangible property and service transactions. This possibility is particularly troubling to states because state sales taxes yield more revenue for state governments than any other tax - $125 billion in 1994. in 23 of 45 states imposing a sales tax, the sales tax produces more revenue than the state individual income tax. For example, as discussed above, most states tax the rental of videocassettes or the sale of magazines, but exempt the electronic transmission of motion pictures or periodicals.

Similarly, all 45 states imposing a sales/use tax, tax the sale of canned software or tangible medium but only about one-half of these states will tax the electronic transmission of such software. This is also true in the case of the sale of medical and legal research that is taxed as the sale of tangible personal property when distributed in printed form, but is frequently exempt if transmitted electronically. If electronic commerce succeeds in significantly increasing the share of products delivered directly to consumers intangible or electronic form, then states may take defensive measures just to maintain a stable sales tax revenue base.

This approach is reinforced by a philosophy among many state tax revenue base. This approach is reinforced by a philosophy among many state tax officials that goods and services should be subject to tax – regardless of the method of delivery. According to L.H. Fuchs executive director of the Florida Department of Revenue, the approach to taxation should be "based on the service and not on the method. If you're talking to somebody state to state, it shouldn't make any difference if you're talking on a cable TV system with a modem, a two-write telephone, or Dick Tracy's wrist radio. A conversion is still taking place.

Remote sellers: Third, there is pressure on the states to aggressively tax remote sellers (with instate customers) so also create a more level playing field with in-state vendors. Many state tax departments are still cafing at the restriction placed on their jurisdiction to tax mail order vendors by the U.S. Supreme Court decision in Quill Corp. As discussed above, states are trying to circumvent the limitations placed on them by the Quill Corp. decision by more aggressively pursuing minimal physical presence, attributional presence, intangible property presence and other nexus theories. Moreover, electronic commerce holds the potential to drastically increase the penetration of markets by out-of-state vendors with little or no physical presence in market states.

Locally based merchants may be at a significant competitive disadvantage if their sales are subject to both income and sales tax while their out-of-state competitors are not. While states may be sympathetic to business concerns about the complexity of tax rules as applied to electronic commerce, they may view these issues as no different – except perhaps in degree – than similar concerns that arise in conjunction with state taxation of interstate business.

In other tax areas, state governments have dealt with complexity by issuing detailed regulations and addressing unique situations on a case by case method.

4. The Prospects for Uniformity: Since electronic commerce holds the potential for significant uncertainty, inconsistency and complexity in compliance with tax rules in various states, it is likely that efforts will be made to create more uniformity among state tax rules.

While states are free to adopt their own tax rules (within federal and state constitutional parameters), there are numerous examples in both corporate and sales tax law of states modeling their status after other jurisdictions or in conformity with model uniform regulations promulgated by the Multistate Tax Commission (MTC).

Recognition of Ambiguous and Incosistent State Tax Rules: In some ways, electronic commerce would appear to be a prime candidate for state tax uniformity efforts. There is wide recognition among both states and business that the state tax rules on electronic commerce are outdated, inconsistent and potentially detrimenta, to the industry. According to a recent nationwide survey of financial and tax executives, 70 percent believe that state and local tax rules governing electronic commerce are ambiguous. In addition 50 percent of the respondents believe that this lack of clarity is inhibiting their utilization of the Internet. Moreover, the Internet is a revolutionary new technology where government/business dialogue might be most conducive to developing state tax rules that reflect the complexities of technological developments and industry practices.

As was evident with the financial services industry, a broader understanding of the different business segments (transmission and content providers) and the underlying technological architecture of the Web (servers, protocol conversion) can be of great assistance to state tax administrators in developing more workable and less burdensome state tax rules.

Obstacles to Uniformity: Nonetheless, there are significant obstacles to business and government participation in state tax uniformity efforts involving electronic commerce. First, with regard to nexus rules, there is wide disagreement among the states and businesses over what are the constitutional boundaries of a state's taxing jurisdiction. This issue is likely to be settled in many states, not at the bargaining table, but in case by case adjudication by the state and federal courts.

Second, with regard to the creation of more uniform and workable state sales and use tax rules on electronic commerce, businesses have much to gain by participating in ongoing state tax commissions studying the taxation of the Internet. Internet-related businesses frequently have technical expertise and practical experience that is invaluable to legislators or tax administrators who are considering how to revamp their existing sales tax rules as they apply to these emerging technologies.

However, cooperative efforts on sales and use tax clarification are likely to be hampered by the very different approaches taken by states on the taxation of electronic commerce. Some states impose broad-based sales taxes on Internet-related transmission and content, while other states do not tax any Internet-related activities. Still other states fall somewhere in the middle of the spectrum. As long as many states exempt most or all Internet content-related activity from the sales tax, it may be difficult for business to engage in uniformity efforts for fear that some of these states will adopt the more uniform rules and extend their sales tax bases.

In the short term, businesses are likely to oppose taxation of many Internet-related services where that is politically feasible and to engage in uniformity or clarification efforts only where the imposition of the tax is inevitable or irreversible. With regard to efforts to revise corporate income sourcing rules for Internet-related service activities, there is likely to be much more willingness on the part of business to participate in joint government/business dialogue.

As is evident from other MTC special industry apportionment regulation projects, these efforts typically lead to a change from the traditional "costs of performance" sourcing rule for service income to the "designation" or "market state consumer" rule utilized with the sales of tangible property. As discussed above, this change would generally be beneficial to electronic service businesses and is likely to be embraced by entities involved in electronic commerce.

Beneficial Approaches: While no single set of policy prescriptions is likely to gain universal support, there are a few general approaches to state tax uniformity that might prove beneficial for both at administrators and taxpayers.

First, with regard to nexus, regardless of how aggressive an individual state choose to be, it would be useful for the taxing jurisdiction to clarify its positions on "slight" physical presence, attributional nexus and intangible property and economic nexus (particularly in connection with electronic commerce fact patterns) so that taxpayers know what rules they are expected to follow (or challenge).

With regard to sales and use tax rules on electronic commerce, regardless of how broad an individual state chooses to make its sales tax base, it would be helpful for the state to clearly spell out the different types or services that it considers taxable under its statutes.

In so doing, explicit distinctions between transmission-based services and content – based services might avoid endless wrangling over definitional issues. A state should also delineate the circumstances under which it would apply the use tax to interstate electronic services. If a jurisdiction chooses to have broad-based sales taxes on electronic services – it would be useful to adopt rules on exemptions and other substantive and procedural issues that are consistent with rules utilized in conjunction with sales of tangible personal property.

For instance, where non-taxable and taxable services are bundled together, it would be constructive if a state adopted in "in conjunction with sales of tangible personal property. For instance, where non-taxable and taxable services are bundled together, it would be constructive if a state adopted an "inconsequential" rule. Under such a rule, if the taxable component of a transaction makes up less that 100 percent of the total sales value and that component is not separately stated in the sale, then the vendor would be treated as the "consumer" of the taxable portion (subject to a sale or use tax) not the vendor of a bundled taxable and non-taxable service. In connection with both sales and income tax rules, it would be advisable to develop sourcing rule that focus on where a consumer is utilizing the electronic services – not where a vendor or its computer servers are located.

A "market" state" approach would avoid creating locational disincentives for domestic-based corporations and also be more consistent with the treatment of sales of tangible personal property. The extent that a state develops a new position on the application of its sales and use tax laws to certain Internet activities, it would be desirable for the state to impose its position on a prospective basis, not a retroactive basis.

This approach would allow effecting businesses an opportunity to comply with new rules, without subjecting them to substantial back liabilities based on ambiguous statutory or regulatory interpretations. In conclusion, while many businesses would prefer that taxes not be imposed on certain electronic services.

The next best alternative is for the imposition of taxing authority to be clear and consistent. If the categories of taxable services and the principles of "nexus" are coherently set forth, then taxpayers can comply with the rules and take them into account for purposes of business decisions. This is particularly important with "trustee" taxes such as sales and use taxes where the real imposition of the tax is typically on the consumers – and the vendor is simply acting as a collection agent for the government.

In connection with sales and use taxes, if it is determined on audit examination that a tax is due, then the vendor may not be able to recover the taxes owed from the consumers and will have to assume the tax burden itself. Given the novelty and complexity of electronic commerce, state tax rules on electronic services will never be "simple" or entirely free from ambiguity.

However, if states and businesses work together, the end product is likely to be much more comprehensible and equitable.

21

Mechanism for Making Payment though Internet

Special Features Required in Payment Systems for E-Commerce?

To understand the payment system, we first must understand the Electronic Payment System (EPS). The EPS (Electronic Payment System) is an online Business process used for fund transfer using electronic means i.e. using Personal Computers, Servers, Mobile Phones and hand held devices (PDA). They are widely used in Bank whenever transactions are made in ten1IS of payment and other means.

EPS is defined as: "Any transfer of funds initiated through an electronic terminal, telephonic instrument or computer or magnetic tape so as to order, instruct or authorize a financial institution to debit or credit an account".

Thus, EPS stands in marked contract to conventional money and payment modes that rely on physical delivery of cash and cheqeus by truck, train or airplane. Some of the special features required for the importance of the electronic payments are discussed as follows.

Consumer point of view:

An EPS is a convenient way of making a purchase or paying for a service without holding cash or having to got through in process of completing a cheque producing some form of acceptable identification.

Supplier point of view :

To a supplier of goods or services an Electronic payment is the receipt or outward movement of funds, perhaps linked into an inventory management, ordering or accounting system, eliminating much of the need for large cash holdings, time consuming clerical activities and potentially offering easier management of cash flows. E-Payment represents an efficient means changing funds and cash flows, offering improved security and assurance of value.

An account/payment manager or Bank point of view:

An E-Payment is a series of processes by which value exchange is captured, verified and accepted, a series of checks, balances and reconciliation to ensure integrity. E-Payment generally requires less manual intervention, offers reduced costs and easier record storage and handlings.

Elements of online commerce and their relationships to the banking networks

1. The consumer and the associated browser to interact with the consumer.
2. The merchant system residing on an online web server with a connection to Web Browser with a connection to Web browsers on the internet.
3. An online shopping mall that may help direct consumers to the, merchant servers.
4. The background banking network to support online payments from consumers the merchant.

Working of EPS

EPS are proliferating in banking, retail, health care, online markets and even government in facts, anywhere money needs to change hands. Organizations are motivated by the need to deliver products and services more costs effectively and to provide a higher quality of service to customers.

Work on EPS can be segmented into three broad categories

1. Banking and Financial Payments
   a. Large scale or wholesale payment (e.g. Bank-to-bank transfer)
   b. Small scale or retail payments (eg. ATMs and Cash dispenses)
   c. Home Banking (Bill Payment)
2. Retailing Payments :
   a. Credit Cards (e.g. Visa or Master Card)
   b. Private Label Credit! debit cards (e.g. JC Penney Cards)
   c. Charge Cards (e.g. American Cards)
3. On-Line Electronic commerce Payments
   a. Token-based payment systems
      1. Electronic Cash (e.g. Digicash)

2. Electronic Checks (e.g. Net cheques)
3. Smart Cards or Debit Cards (e.g. Mondex Electronic Currency Cards)

b. Credit-Card based payment systems:

1. Encrypted Credit Cards (e.g. WWW form based encryptions)
2. Third part authorization numbers (e.g. First virtual)

Various types of E-Payment Systems

Following are the various types of e-payment systems:

Digital Token Based EPS

Newly developed financial Instrument "Electronic Tokens" in the form of electronic cash/ money or checks. Electronic tokens are designed as electronic analogs of various forms of payments backed by a bank or financial institutions. E- Tokens are equivalent to cash that is backed by a bank. E-Token are of three types:

1. Cash to real time: Real time payments are exchanged between buyer and seller. Here user prepays for the token that server as currency. Transactions are settled with server as e-currency.
2. Debit or prepaid: User pay in advance for the privilege of getting information e.g. smart card, electronic purses.
3. Post paid or credit: The server authenticates the customer and verified with both that funds. are adequate before the purchase of goods e.g. credit /debit card and checks.

E-Cash or Electronic Cash:

Electronic cash or E-cash digital money or digital cash provider the means to transfer money between parties ones a network such as' the internet e-cash must satisfy some general properties of digital money.

1. Independence: E-cash must not depend on c its existence in any given computer System or location.
2. Non-reusability: E-cash should not be reusable after its first use. For example, f I get e-cash for $50 and spend it to buy a shirt, then I cannot spend this money again
3. Anonymity: E-cash cannot provide information that can be used to trace the previous owner of the cash. If I buy a shirt, then there should be nothing associated with the E-cash that trace it to me.

4. Transferability: E-cash should be easily transferable from one person or party to another. This should occur without leaving any trace of who has been in possession of this money.

5. Divisibility: E-cash must be available in several denominations. It should also be divisible in a way similar to real cash. For example, 25 digital pennies should yield a digital quarter and four quarter should equal a dollar.

6. Secure Storage: E-cash should be available in such a way so it can be securely stored at the consumer's hard drive or on a smart card. It is possible to transfer this electronic cash b/w various types of parties on the Internet

Working of E-cash

The E-cash transactions take place in three district and independent phases as discussed below:

Phase I : Obtaining Electronic Cash

This phase can be described in the following steps:

1. The consumer requests his/her bank to transfer money to the e-mint to obtain e-cash.

2. The consumer bank transfer money from the consumer's a/c to the e-mint.

3. the e-mint sends e-cash to the consumer. The consumer serves his e-cash.

Phase II: Purchasing with Electronic Cash

This phase is executed whenever the consumer desires to make a purchase with ecash. It can take place after consumer transferring his money to e-cash from the emint.

4. The consumer selects the goods and transfers the e-cash to the merchant.

5. The merchant provides the goods to the consumer

Phase III: Redeeming Cash by the Merchant

This phase occurs whenever the merchant is ready to redeem the e-cash. The merchant should be capable of converting this e-cash to money for the merchant's bank a/c.

6. The merchant may send the e-cash to its bank and the bank in turn redeems the Money from the e-mint.

7. The e-mint transfers money to the merchant's bank for crediting the merchant's a/c.

Benefits

1. The potential for fraud is reduced because in proper verification is done in case e-business.
2. It can protect the customer's anonymity so that although the merchant is assured of the payment, the merchant does not need to know the details of the customer.
3. Merchant would prefer an e-cash scheme, since it prevents denial by the customer or lack of funds in a customer's account.

Currency Server:

The currency server is a special term used in EPS whereby the customer and Merchant can exchange the different currencies depending upon the machine used.

Types of Currency Server are as written below:

1. A TM Machine
2. POS Terminal
3. Card Reader, etc.

The various applications where Currency Servers are used as written below:

1. Bank Debit Card
2. Credit Card
3. Telephone Card
4. Employee Identification Card

E-Cheques

E-Chequing pertains to the use of networking services to issue and process payments that emulate real world chequeing. The payer issues a digital cheque to the payer and the payer deposits it in the bank to redeem the money. Each transaction is carried over the Internet.

1. Paying fees through the ATM network.
2. Paying bills through monthly bank account deduction.
3. Transfer of large sums of money among banks across the world.

Difference between E-Cheque and EFT:

For e-checks, electronic version of cheques are issued, received and processed. So the payer issues an electronic cheque for each payment. For EFT, automatic withdrawals are made for monthly bills or other fixed payments and no cheques are issued.

In case of e-cash, we have five primary parties: the consumer, the consumer bank, the merchant, the merchants' bank and the e-mint. For E-cheques, we have added the clearing house to process cheques among different banks.

Working of E-Cheques:

Working of e-cheques can be described in the following steps.

Steps regarding e-cheques:

The e-cheques are executed in three phases. In the 1st phase, the Consumer makes a purchase and in the 2nd phase the merchant sends the electronic cheques to its bank for redemption and in the 3rd phase, the merchants bank approaches the clearing house or the consumers bank to encash the e-cheques.

Phase- I: Purchasing Goods:

1. The consumer accesses the merchant server and the merchant server presents its Goods to the consumer.
2. The consumer selects the goods and purchases them by sending an electronic Cheque to the merchant.
3. The merchant may validate the electronic cheque with its bank for payment authorization.
4. Assuming the cheque is validated the merchant closes the transaction with the consumer.

Phase-II: Depositing Cheques at the merchant's bank:

1. The merchant electronically forwards the cheque to the bank.
2. The merchant bank forwards the e-cheque for clearing house for cashing.
3. The clearing house with the consumer's bank, clears the cheque and transfers money to the merchants bank, which updates the merchant account.
4. At last the consumers bank update the consumers with the withdraw information.

Benefits of E-cheques

1. E-Cheques works in the same way as the traditional cheques the simplifying customer education.

2. E-Cheques serve such corporate markets. Firms can use e-cheques to complete payment over the market in more cost effective than present alternatives.

3. E-Cheques are well suited for clearing micro payments. The conventional cryptography of e-cheques makes them easy to process then the system based on public-key cryptography like digital cash. The payer pays bank-authorized checks through the use public key certificate.

CREDIT CARDS (Electronic Cards):

For the online transactions, the credit cards are the easiest method of others because people are already accustomed by using them remotely. The Credit card transaction simply requires that the consumer have a valid Credit card number and expiration date when placing an order. This information has been provided through standard Internet options like e-mail/sms.

In E-Credit, conversational Credit cards may be used along with a pin. The pin is a secret code that the consumer must enter while using the credit card online. As such, it prevents misuse of the credit card in case it is stolen.

Working of E-Credit or Credit Cards:

Phase-I: Purchase of Goods: transaction starting from 1-4.

Phase-II: Settlement of transaction from 5-6.

Phase-III: Consumer update of Credit card bill in the transaction number.

SMART CARDS:

Smart cards looks very much like a traditional credit card with one major exception. There is tiny microprocessor unit [MPU like CPU] or chip on the face of the card. Smart card combines with the characteristics of the credit or debit cards. They are being offered to consumer for small purchases less than $10 or more/less for. Following are the some examples for using the Credit Cards as:

1. Prepaid telephone cards [SIM].

2. Have a cup of coffee.

3. Buy a movie ticket.

4. Buy a train ticket etc.

Smart cards are also called stored value cards uses magnetic strip technology or Integrated circuits [ICs] chip to store the consumer specific information including e-money. These cards can be used to purchase goods or services and store information, control access to a/c and performs many other functions. Smart cards offer clear! Benefits to both merchant and customer. They reduce cash hand expenses and losses caused by frauds.

Electronic Purse Digital Wallet and Debit Cards:

E-Purse or D-Purse is wallet size smart card embraced with programmable micro chip that store monitory value in form of money to be used with Point of Sale (POS) terminal.

Working:

1. After we get E-Purse from the bank we can use it for different purpose depending upon the type of POS.
2. The corresponding P~S scans the E-Purse to authenticate the E-Purse and Perform the operation corresponding.
3. The machine can send the value printing on E-Purse and perform Automatic deduction from balance of the card.
4. When the balance on the E- Purse is shown the same machine can be used to recharge the same card.

Electronic Bill:

E-Bill is similar with general bill used to pay offline exchange with merchant. It consists of digital document (Document File), which is signed by the consumer by using private key. The merchant use the payer public key to decode the digital document if the result return the receiver identification that match with the sender's identity, it means the digital documents are valid. There by the electronic version of paper cheque are issues, received and processed online.

Business issues and Economic Implications.

Ans. Business Issue: E-business world acquires various issues that must be considered by the trading partner whenever e-transaction takes place using electronic payment systems. The Business issues are basically all the legal issue exchange between two parties whenever risk management system exhibits various constrains on different electronic payment transactions. These risks associate with customer, merchant and third party etc.

Business Issue in concern with customer:

Since customer only avails the resources, the merchant is offering therefore the business are largely playa very small role during small transaction having $ 5, $ 10, $ 20, etc.

Business Issue in Concern With Merchant:

The Business issue deals with foreign policy, standardization of services, international certificate and other legal issues that the merchant has to acquire by dealing with the party. By considering the technological for various types of E-payment system, the merchant also considered all the risk mgt phases while exchanging e-currency on the net. By combining risk management option and business issue with respect to merchant the following observation should be given due care before and after making e-transaction.

Risks of the Electronic Payment System highlights are as below:

1. Risk Management Option
2. Information Privacy

Risk Management

Risk management is a methodology processing potential of future event that cause adverse effect and implement cost effective strategies deals with these Risk. .

Risk in concern with consumer :

The internet has not been viewed by most users as a safe place to use credit cards to conduct business transactions. This feeling of insecurity is primarily due to the large among of press report citing story after story about thefts of credit card information by Internet hackers.

1. Information Privacy: During the customer interaction with the merchants, the IT Act, 2000 has proposed the privacy act that maintains all the internal information of consumer in a separate block to ensure that the customer must protect from internet threats. This process is also known as Record Keeping System.

2. Timing Gap: One of potential problem of EPS System is the shifting of Credit/Debit enquiry through timing gap in the exchange of Assets. Such gaps can create float and leads to risk.

3. Operation Risk: The operation risk are due to human being interaction or the machine on fault that could be considered as fraud.

4. Security Risk: The security risk is in concern with customer are indirectly deals with the lacks of SET protocol or non implementation of their security method.

Risk in concern with Merchant:

1. Protocol Risk: Other risk management like lack of regulation policies or not implemented the protocol hierarchy sometimes leads the major problem with concern bank e.g. State Bank of Patiala.

The common problem that generally results is non-acceptance of other banks cards is also considered as the banks failure in implementing protocol.

2. Relationship Risk: In the competition world, to maintain a sound relationship with your customer, the banks have to provide a balance approach to attract more number of customers. The relationships risk can delegate the image of the Bank, if the concern bank does not offer Customer Relationship Mgt. (CRM), Partner Relationship Management (PRM) and Strategies of E-business.

3. Policies Risk: A Digital Central Bank Guarantee on settlement which involve time to time changes policies between different services e.g. Bank Loan, Mutual funds, Insurance Policy.

4. Infrastructure Risk: The E-bank also deals with infrastructure issue including hardware, software and standards.

   Hardware – Currency server

   Software – (1) Bank Away (2) Pay Away

Information Privacy

Privacy is an important issue on the Internet. Organization wants to achieve all possible data about these customers to protect the sent information about the customer. Different organizations worldwide have making efforts to lay down legislative framework for privacy on the Internet.

"ECLIP" (Electronic Commerce Legal Issue Platform) set up by European Union that defined standards for various Privacy Issue as:

Buffer—' temporary data

Cookies —. Place on client server

Principle :

1. ECLIP Guidelines says that the server data of the customer must be processed fairly lawfully.
2. Guidelines says that the use of cookies of fair processing is also be must.
3. A per son can be identified by using its If address. Therefore, it becomes Personal Information & Committee 'says that one should use dynamic IP address to protect the personal data.
4. A number of issues like taxation should be addressed.
5. Tariffs, data protection and copyrights need to be reviewed from E-prospective.

Legal Issue of E-payment system: Legal issue defines framework protocol that defines the mechanism whereby the E-transaction takes place on the Internet. The legal issue also highlights the Guidelines set up by organization concern [Visa, Dig cash, TRAI, DOT etc] while issuing the legal documents to the service provide or individual.

Legal Issue for Credit Card:

1. X-509 Certificate: These forms may be sent with each message to authenticate the sender and its messages. The certificate provides the procedure to validate the identity of the consumer, merchant, Merchant Bank.
2. The Law also makes provision to protect the Pvt. Key of Certificate Authority.
3. The Law also ensures to protect the card number, its expiry date, its PIN number, amount and other sensitive information during transaction.
4. In case of any dispute between the two parties there must be means to solve the conflicts.

Operational Risk and Credit Risk

Deals with e-cash and e-credit is concern with all operational aspect of plastic payment when use to pay online for product and services.

1. The Operational Risk in concern with e-cash includes expiry date, amount to be transferred, the number of exchange and number of transactions.
2. Operational Risk in concern with other method such as e-purse etc Sometimes during exchange of e-money certain constraints introduce by banking system and other constraints imposed by the machine mismatched as a result the strategy of reporting transaction would be inefficient for the subscribed and complete transaction process stops which result loss of customer, efforts and total number of transaction.
3. All the operational risk are indirectly linked with legal issue and other business issue when the several transaction are made concurrent.

Effective Electronic Payment System?

The components can be described as below:

Consumer and the Browser

A consumer interacts with the online commerce system through a Web-Browser. Typically a consumer first access a shopping mall and then uses the hyperlinks from the mall to access the merchants home page.

Shopping Mall

A shopping mall is where most consumers first visit for a shopping free. There will be several shopping malls, and it may pay to enlist with one or more well known malls.

Merchant System:

Consists of the Home Page and related software to manage the business.

Banking Network

Consists of several components. There is a bank that processes the online financial transaction:) for the given merchant. The bank maintains the account for the merchant, authorizes and processes the payment. The merchant bank also maintain a link with the consumers bank for verifying the transactions.

22

Security in E-Commerce

Security risks of E-commerce?

When you allow any computer to any computer over the Internet, the chances of risk becomes high. This is what is happening. There are lots of security risks over the net. Security officers have been battling worms, viruses, denial of service attacks and hackers for years now. When you add the threat of cyber-terrorism, employees using Instant Messengers and downloading full-length feature movies onto their work PCs, the list of risks is multiplying far faster than security budgets or staffs can keep pace.

The Security Risks

- Unauthorized access: Someone accesses or misuses a computer system to intercept transmissions and steal sensitive information
- Data alteration: The content of an e-commerce transaction - user names, credit card numbers and dollar amounts - is altered en route.
- Monitoring: A hacker eavesdrops on confidential information.
- Spoofing: A virtual vandal creates a fake site masquerading as yours to steal data from unsuspecting customers or just disrupt your business.
- Service denial: An attacker shuts down your site or denies access to visitors
- Repudiation: A party to an online e purchase denies that the transaction occurred or was authorized.

These dangers pose the threat of fraud, service disruption, lost sales, theft of confidential information and most damaging of all, loss of customer trust.

Types of Threats and Sources of Threats?

The different types of factors behind the threats are as follows:

- Email Attachments – Users opening an attachment could unleash a worm or virus onto the corporate network and a new evolution of viruses means that they can propagate themselves even without a user double-clicking on them

- VPN Tunnel Vulnerabilities – A hacker who worms his way into the VPN has free and easy access to the network;
- Blended Attacks – Worms and viruses are becoming more complicated and now a single one may be able to execute itself or even attack more than one platform;
- Diversionary Tactics – Hackers may strike a set of servers in a target company and then when security administrators are busy securing that, they slip in and attack another part of the network;
- Downloads from Web Sites – Workers frequently misuse their Internet access in the workplace, downloading games, movies and music and even porn. It opens the network up to attack and sucks up valuable bandwidth.
- Supply Chain and Partners Added to the Network – An administrator may grant access to the network for a partner company and then forget to close that access point when: the job is over. The same applies to employees who are leaving the company;
- Renaming Documents – An employee could save business – critical information in a different file, give it a random, unrelated name and email the information to her home computer, a friend or even a corporate competitor. Monitoring software that checks emails leaving the company might fail to pick up on the outgoing message if the subject name has been changed;
- Peer-to-Peer Applications – In a peer-to-peer environment there is an implied trust between servers. That means if a user has access to one server, he automatically has access to another if the servers share trust. Here hackers or employees can gain access to one server and move freely throughout the network;
- Music and Video Browsers – These are browsers that automatically will connect the user with related web related web sites – all without the user's permission. A music browser, for instance, may note that the user likes jazz so will connect the user to other jazz sites and exactable applications, putting the network at risk and potentially using up huge amounts of bandwidth.

Risk Management Approach

Companies are increasingly required to provide assurance that their systems are secure and conform to commercial security standards. Senior business managers arc ultimately responsible for the security of their corporate systems and for the implications in the event of a security failure.

The security risks to IT systems can be accurately assessed and controls consistently applied, only as a result of carrying out a risk analysis and management exercise.

Meeting The Regulatory Need

The process of Risk Analysis is now regarded as mandatory in many quarters. For example, by the government for all its new IT projects. Also, private industry. particularly public listed companies and those seeking a public listing, need to comply with the Turnbull Report on Corporate Governance requirements which prescribes undertaking an analysis of business risks. "A company's objectives, its internal organization and the environment in which it operates are continually evolving and as a result, the risks it faces are continually changing.

A sound system of internal control therefore depends on a thorough and regular evaluation of the nature and extent for the risks to which it is exposed. In parallel, the British Standard for Information Security Management BS7799 and the equivalent International Standard (ISO/IEC 17799) specifies that a Risk Assessment must be carried out to determine the detailed control requirements.

Similarly, the seventh principle of the Data Protection Act (1998), which came into force during 2000, requires that appropriate security controls must be implemented. Failure to comply with the Data Protection Act can result in significant fines. All commercial organizations delivering IT services to the public or to trading partners, particularly over the Internet where the risks are highest, will require that the risks 'to those systems be addressed in a systematic manner which will mean undertaking a risk analysis of the new development.

Undertaking Risk Analysis

Risk Analysis has historically been pursued in some of the larger commercial organizations and government departments by Information Security professionals who use their expertise to systematically identify the risks applying to a specified IT environment and who thereby ensure that appropriate technical and non-technical controls, including business continuity options, commensurate with the risks are implemented and managed. Like many other business activities that do not generate direct revenue streams, risk analysis has been seen as being complex, requiring specialist expertise and therefore something to be outsourced or basically delayed. This is likely to be the case for most small to medium sized businesses.

The risk analysis process encompasses significant expertise requirements:

- Measure what impact on an organization a breach of security would have
- Evaluate different categories of information such as commercial and financial. Personal and personal safety, Legal and Regulatory.
- Identify the what variety of threats that may affect the IT environment
- Determine how unburnable are the systems to the identified threats
- Select from the large number of controls that are available ones that counter the risks

- Ensure that the costs incurred need to be commensurate with the risk.

The use of an automated software tool that encapsulates the above expertise can provide an effective and economic approach to performing risk analysis.

Practical Needs for Risk Analysis: The primary benefit of undertaking a risk assessment is to provide the ability to answer fundamental questions about the nature of controls and to assist in justifying why they need to be implemented. For example:

- A new business commerce application will require user authentication logon controls
- The IT systems are required to be moved to a new data center, or even be outsourced.
- A security breach has occurred within the company and management now require that remedial action to be undertaken.

Unless controls are prioritized according to actual risk, implementing controls in a knee-jerk or haphazard fashion, and without regard for what security is needed in the rest of the environment will do little to reduce the overall risk and will be wasteful use of resources focused on one area of risk and control.

Based upon these practical needs, some of the attributes of a risk analysis process should include the ability to:

- Assess the security risks to a company in business terms.
- Justify recommended controls in relation to the value of the information that requires protection and the risks to that information
- Prioritize the implementation of controls by the level of risk.
- Be able to be applied progressively, i.e. from rapid assessment of the main concerns though to a more detailed comprehensive risk assessment but allowing any previous work to be re-used.
- Allow the implications of major IT or environment changes to be quickly assessed.
- Provide senior management with an accurate view, albeit in high-level terms of the risk to the information processed.
- To assist with the project planning process of undertaking risk analysis and implementing the recommended controls.

Companies seeking compliance with the British Standard for Information Security BS7799 will need to show they have undertaken a risk assessment. The output of the risk assessment will also need to serve as to support the BS7799 requirements. While Business Continuity is often considered a separate area of concern to IT Security, the process of analyzing business continuity requirements encompass some of the disciplines involved when performing a risk analysis.

For example the risks of business disruption and the specific need for business continuity will depend upon the business impact of for escalating unavailability time scales and the threats and vulnerabilities that could result in the unavailability or destruction occurring in the first place. Since valuation of information, threats and vulnerabilities will be evaluated as part of' the risk analysis process it is efficient to collect the business continuity requirements at the same time. The risk analysis process will also be an invaluable aid in identifying all the information and physical assets that may need to be recovered as part of the continuity plan.

Manual Risk vs Software Tool Approach

Using a manual risk analysis approach would require significant resources to meet he above needs and so may not be practical. However, a manual based approach to conducting a risk assessment may be more appropriate for the smallest of companies with a basic IT setup. Perhaps located in a single location, and where there would not likely to involve a high degree of data integrity, availability or confidentiality.

In a larger corporate environment subject to the external regulatory requirements described earlier and where new IT services are frequently being developed, perhaps over multiple sites and to many users, an interactive software tool should be capable of meeting all of the practical risk analysis needs described above. In particular, a tool will facilitate better management of the risk process and allow e-assessment of the risks in different IT environment scenarios with minimal re-working. One risk analysis and management software tool meeting the above needs, CRAMM, has extensive BS7799 support linked in, and is the preferred tool for many government bodies and commercial organizations.

The product includes a toolkit that facilitates controlled deployment within an enterprise to allow risk analysis to be carried out locally whilst maintaining consistency with a centrally defined approach. Fortunately, the most important thing you can do to secure your e-commerce sites also the simplest: Just install an electronic file called a digital certificate on your web server. Digital certificates are a kind of online passport issued by a trusted third party a certificate authority, who verifies the identity of the certificate's holder. Digital certificates authenticate that their holders - people, web sites and even network resources - are truly who and what they claim to be and protect data exchanged online from intrusion. They are tamper-proof and cannot be forged.

E-commerce security and Rational Security Policy

The basic requirements for E-Commerce security include information confidentiality, authentication, authorization, data integrity, non-repudiation and availability. Given the dynamic environment of E-Commerce, effectively meeting these requirements is not straightforward.

The challenge is to come up with the most technically and economically feasible plan for protecting E-Commerce activities, knowing that today's most secure technology will be vulnerable tomorrow. As is the case for most systems problems, the best approach is a structured one, including analyzing risk and delegating resources to protect the most valued assets of the organization.

Typically, policies are put into place to manage risk. Another framework for developing e-commerce policies uses a matrix of organizational relationships and technology. The problem with current approaches is that none address the problem of keeping up with the increasing rate of change in E-Commerce technology and applications nor do they consider how to keep such policies consistent and aligned with organizational objectives. To develop a tool that would aid in the formulation and management of E-Commerce information security policies, other tools in similarly rapidly changing business arenas were examined.

Defining Security Policy

Security policies are generally high-level, technology neutral and concern risks. Security policies set directions and procedures and define penalties and countermeasures if the policy is transgressed. Security policies must not be confused with implementation-specific information, which would be part of the security standards, procedures and guidelines.

Security policies are created by empowered representatives from group responsible for :

- Human resources
- Legal and regulatory matters
- Information systems
- Public relations
- Security
- Lines of business

Some of the most important security policies include :

- User identification and password policy
- Remote access policy
- Extranet policy
- Internet security policy
- Access to data policy
- Administration policy

- Incident response policy
- Awareness procedure policy
- User behavior policy
- Security monitoring and audit policy
- Privacy policy

Security policies must be balanced and provide tradeoffs between: Level of security User convenience and cost.

Without an equitable balance between these elements, it is not realistic to expect that the security policies will be followed. This may mean they should be modified. Today, high cost and user inconvenience far outweigh the benefits so smart cards are used instead; however, as costs decrease and usability improves biometric authentication may become a policy reality.

International Issue

One significant area of concern for E-Commerce is the international nature of the Internet. Jurisdictional issues, intellectual property rights, laws regarding particular technologies for example, encryption, local custom and local decency standards and various political and terrorist agendas, to name a few, all are cause for concern.

Industry Issue

There are a number of industry-specific challenges when it comes to security. For example, an entirely online company like Nile.com may face different threats and risks than those faced by financial services or manufacturing companies. Instead of focusing these differences, we examine application-specific issues. For example, on-line transaction security for credit card processing is critical for several different industry areas.

Policy Framework for Interpreting Risk in E-Commerce Security

Initial Policy Assessment

An organization that does not have an existing security policy always begins at this point. This may be a new organization like a start-up, a company with no security policy in place or one that is replacing existing policy.

Existing organizational strategy and policy should be referenced to gain context and to ensure that policy is created in compliance with existing business strategies and policies.

Risk Assessment Step

Risk Assessment identifies the business assets, an organization wants to protect and identifies potential threats to those assets by asking these questions:

- What am I trying to protect?
- What do I need to project against?
- How much am I willing to spend to have adequate protection?
- What is the cost versus the benefit for the business?

Risk Assessment Methodology

Risk Assessment consist of four sub-step: Conduct Security Assessment, Assess Business Risk, Develop Security Recommendations and Summarize Risk Assessment Results. Executed in sequence, these sub-steps result in a decision of whether to accept the proposed changes to security policy based on risk.

Through the risk assessment process it can be helpful to document results in a spreadsheet-based matrix.

	Asset			***Risk***	
Asset Name	Asset Type	Area to be Assessed (Technology, Platform, People)	Undersirable Event	Event History	Potential Damage
Design documents	Customer Information	NT Server network, Internet, firewall	A customer's competitor obtains access to proprietary design documents	Uncertain, no official record of it happening before, but rumors	Disclosure modifications or destruction of data, loss of customer confidence, lawsuit, fraud
Passwords	Technology	NT Server User PC, Routers, Procedures, Awareness	Stolen password misuse of authorized password	Employees have been fired for misusing access to	Unauthorized access, masquerade, all data accessible by

				commit fraud	that account is exposed and subject to disclosure, modification and destruction
OS Software and configuration data	Technology	NT Server, Procedures. Training			
Help Desk	Application	UNIX Server, Training			
Engineering and scientific information	Administrative Information	NT Server, Users PC			
Product or service marketing plans	Administrative Information	Personnel	Marketing plan revealed to competitor	Several marketing staff, suspected but not proved to be involved in industrial espionage, jumped ship to competition competion six months ago.	Disclosure could lead to not being first to market with a new offering

Conduct Security Assessment

This sub-step identifies elements in the current or proposed environment that may be subject to threats that could compromise information assets. Specific tasks include :

Asset Identification quantifies information system assets critical to the business including all forms of data and the people and technology that support information processes. Assets are then grouped to identify correspondence between the information assets and the technologies that support these assets.

Threat Assessment identifies threats to the confidentiality, integrity and availability of the identified assets. In general terms, a threat is a bad thing that can happen. Threats can also be caused by direct or indirect actions which can . originate from accidental or deliberate sources or events.

Vulnerability Assessment evaluates the target environment to identify I weaknesses within the organization's assets that could he exploited and result in a compromise of assets. In general terms, a vulnerability is the weakness that allows a threat to happen.

A variety of methods can be used to analyze the environment including review of documentation, interviews with stakeholders, site surveys or walkthroughs, automated system and/or network assessments, and surveys of targeted groups. We suggest using a combination of these approaches to achieve maximum results.

Assess Business Risk

This sub-step is an assessment of risk as it applies to business assets. Although we recommend a quantitative assessment, many organizations utilize qualitative I measurements. In either case, each asset must be given a measure, which can be either intrinsic or related to the cost of restoration if the asset were to be lost or compromised.

The value of intangible assets such as reputation and trust that do not have any intrinsic or business value must be evaluated. One way to perform this evaluation is to list all assets evaluated so far, ranked in terms of value. Based on this list, the assets with intangible and subjective value will be inserted, according to best judgment, between two assets already evaluated.

The business impact loss or damage to business assets should be evaluated and could include:

- Loss of reputation and client confidence
- Legal penalties against the company
- Cost of security failure recovery
- Cost of the unavailability of the system

This sub-step involves two tasks:

Impact Analysis and

Risk Valuation.

Analyze Impact identifies the effect on the business if the asset is harmed using two factors:

potential damage and likelihood of occurrence. Damage is rated High, Medium, or Low Potential. For example, if loss of life is a possibility - as it would be in an earthquake – the potential damage should be classified as High. Likelihood of occurrence is also rated High, Medium or Low.

Risk Valuation determines a risk factor for each asset being analyzed. Risk, the potential damage or loss of an asset, is a combination of the value the owner places on the asset, the business impact the loss of the asset would have and the likelihood that the weakness will be exploited to damage the asset.

This risk factor can be assigned by a skilled security professional or calculated using the following formula.

Risk = Potential Damage x Likelihood of Occurrence

Develop Security Recommendations:

The tasks involved with completing this sub-step are:

- Identify Security Options
- Determine Payroll and Non-payroll Cost
- Determine Priority of Options
- Verify Results

Develop Cost/Benefit Matrix

Identify Security Options determines recommendations to mitigate each identified risk. This task produces the best conclusions when skilled security professionals work together to challenge each others recommendations.

Summarize Assessment Final Results

Here results of both the Policy and Risk Assessments are documented so management can decide whether to accept the proposed change. If accepted, the life cycle for this particular proposed change continues in the Plan phase.

If rejected, but other policy changes are determined to be needed, the Plan phase follows as well. Otherwise, the life cycle resumes in the Operate phase.

The Implications

Human Performance Implications: Policy updates or alterations will inevitably change something about the way someone is working, and such changes, no matter how small, require attention. The impact of the. change must be assessed to make sure it can be successfully implemented. An understanding of the current environment is therefore vital.

While some of the security team assesses the risk involved with the proposed change, others should examine the existing organization structure, performance, and culture to determine the unique requirements of the proposed change. These questions should be asked to assess an organization's ability to successfully support a new ,security policy:

- Who is impacted?
- Does the organization structure reflect the importance of security?
- Is the culture conscious of the importance of security?
- Who are the key sponsors and advocates?
- How does the culture suggest components of a new policy and or highlight key implementation issues?
- What aspects of the culture suggest potential security risks that the new policy and implementation plan should address?
- What do you expect to happen when policy is implemented - what is the end result?

If these are not addressed, the inability or unwillingness of the organization to change represents another potential threat to security

E-commerce Implications

The process of moving business-to-consumer functions to an e-Commerce model typically involves replacing the human intermediary with software. Historically, the human intermediary served several roles including information asset protection. Today the question the organization must ask is whether software can be skeptical enough to protect valuable information assets.

But the transition to online auctions means not only business-to-consumer risks but consumer-to-consumer risks as well. Therefore the company must ask whether software can be skeptical enough to protect the information asset of personal identification.

Policy Development Methodology

Policy Development contains two sub-steps: Create/update Security Strategy and Create/ Update Security Policy.

Policy Development Create/Update Security Strategy

Security strategy is an overview of future business direction along with the security controls needed, to support these business functions. A security strategy should be held consisting of the following tasks:

- Identify future business initiatives
- Identify risks to each initiative
- Identify security options
- Prioritize security initiatives
- Document security strategy

Executive input is also vital to guarantee that security strategy is aligned with rest of the organization's business strategies. It will also ensure that security is considered when new business capabilities and acquisitions are planned, new alliances made and new markets entered. All strategies must work together.

Create/Update Security Policy:

Specific tasks of this sub-step include:

- Identify Areas for Security
- Policy Draft Security Policy
- Review Security Policy
- Publish Security Policy

Draft Security Policy creates the initial version of the security policy or security policy update. The security team should provide guidance to this person on the context and the content of the policy.

The policy draft should include, at a minimum, the following sections or attributes:

- Title — Provided by the security organization following a standard format.
- Version – number of the document so it can be version controlled.
- Purpose
- Scope and Audience – The intended audience and the environments to which it applies.
- Overview - A briefly explanation of relevant security issues including specific threats and vulnerabilities to consider.
- Roles and Responsibilities – Define who is responsible for what actions.
- Content – Identify and explain all relevant information.
- Reporting – Information for reporting all security violations and security incidents.

- Related Document
- Author and History - A record of the original author, authors of revisions and a synopsis of each revision change.

Review Security Policy ensures quality, usability and acceptance of the policy. A small review team with user, management and executive representation should review it. Their comments should be directed back to the author who will then make any updates deemed necessary. Then the final draft is forwarded to the security organization.

Finally, the Publish Security Policy task authorizes and communicates the policy. First, the security organization forwards the final draft to the executive responsible for approving the policy. Once approved, the policy is then communicated to the entire organization.

Corporate Digital Library

Today the term digital library is widely used as the generic term for diverse information strutures that provide organisations and workers access to the vast amount of internal information encoded in multimedia formats. It creates a unified repository of consistent business data for information processing. Companies can perform more substantive, accurate, and consistent analysis using the digital library as a foundation for decision support system. Digital library is focused on the utilization for the storage and retrieval of reusable data within corporate environments.

This gives significant returns in the form of cost saving, productivity gains and quality improvements. Digital library technologies are used in manufacturing industries includes aerospace, defense, biotech, automotive, consumers electronics and healthcare. A digital library is also visualized as a coordinated cluster of object oriented user level or application-level services, some of which may be owned or controlled by one or more agencies. Corporate digital libraries differ from public digital libraries in the nature of their collections.

During the lifecycle of a given product or program. corporations maintain their key technology assets in electronic form. These assets can be reports, structured memos, drawings, manuals, specifications etc. stored in formats such as page description languages, markup languages, word processor files, spreadsheets and CAD/CAM files. Corporate also includes highly unusual objects such as telemetry recordings, 3-D models, simulations, x-ray inspection images.

These electronic forms are stored in digital libraries using data conversion utilities. Corporate digital library is also refers to variety of on-line services and tools available from internal support groups such as thermal analysis, simulation and modeling etc. They are capable of giving interfaces for on-line databases.

23

Concepts and Evolution of Internet

Introduction

With the advancement of technology, man has gained lots of things, some for his personal benefits and some for his professional. Overall there has few instances where the advancement of technology has not helped the human kind.

Internet is one of them. It has benefitted the mankind tremendously. It has revolutionized the way people communicate. It is actually a network of networks. The need to communicate is innate in man and begin centuries ago. Today these primitive methods like drum codes and smoke signals have way to electric pulses. Computers are being used to send bits of information across the globe. Using telephone links data is transmitted across the countries via satellites almost instantaneously. Concept of computer networks was born around 1965. Modern technologies make use of satellites and topic fiber cables. Data can fly to distinct computers at 1.5 million bits per second.

Internet concepts

Before you understand what Internet is, you must understand what networking is. It is a method of connecting two or more computers, either by means of connecting them or through wireless. Now come to Internet. It is the network consisting of millions of machines. Millions of machines are networked together to share the data and information. Data you require may be scattered across the globe updated and kept consistent by the owner of the data and you can retrieve it when needed via Internet.

Now with the onward march of technology it is possible to keep the program that work with the data along with the data that it works on and call upon both when needed a sort of 'just in time' software that you call upon when you needed and discard when no longer required.

You no longer need to locally store and maintain the data and programmes. Internet is not just one network. It is co-ordinated union of networks. Computer users on the Internet anywhere in the world, very much like a telephone user can communicate with user anywhere in the world. So internet is also called Internet works. Internet is also the common language of different or computers dissimilar in hardware and software to communicate with each other, via a standard protocols (protocols is a set of rules and regulations for computers to communicate via networks).

Sitting on a PC at home one can trip round the globe in minutes, one can get any kind of information one needs. Internet is a large source of enjoyable, important and up to data information, which can be accessed and shared by millions of users across the world. Every information on the internet is there because some person or group of people, somewhere in the world, had an idea, developed it and then most important, made it available to the entire world using Internet. It has become a major part of business.

One can use Internet for many different purposes like as discussed below:

1. Sending and receiving E-mails (it is an instantaneous way of sending and receiving messages, called electronic mail) round the world at minimal price.
2. Finding information on any topic or can be used as educational tool. One can find information on infinite number of topics ranging from how to make a cake to how to write a program for a computer. To visit a bookstore on the Internet this all can be done on the Internet sitting at home PC.
3. One can participate in discussions on wide range of topics from recreational activities to scientific researches via a utility called Usenet news group.
4. It is also used to send data inform of files from one computer to other with the facility called FTP (File Transfer Protocol). There are sites offering information on paid basis but on the other hand there are many sites, which provide information free of cost. There are called anonymous FTP sites. The biggest advantage of FTP is one don't have to wait for days to receive some information after ordering with FTP files will be one in minutes after ordering.
5. One can use it for research purpose. With every major university connected to Internet one can be sure to find information that help in research projects.
6. It is also a form of education. Using Internet is great learning experience. One will learn things from the content one is reading and will also be more proficient at navigating computer tools, forming searches for information. Writing and typing skills also improves.
7. One can enjoy reading jokes, stories, articles, play games with other users s on Internet join with chess matches and one can enjoy Internet relay chat to talk to different people round the world.
8. On can login on to other network via as if one is a member of that network this is done through utility called Telnet. This is only possible if one get permission to log on to that network.
9. To search some topics on the Internet one can use gopher.
10. Archive is a search utility that search on the Internet based on file names or partial file names.

11. One can make profits on the Internet. Internet can be an effective medium for business communications. Services such as gopher and World Wide Web (WWW) are the best ways to distribute information about your product or service. E-mail is a great medium to communicate with contacts and customers in business.

12. To find a particular world on the Internet in text documents one can use the utility WIAS (Wide Area Information System).

13. One can have a live talk with persons all round the world and can held meetings as if sitting just by there side by video conferencing of multimedia conferencing.

Who Runs Internet?

As said earlier, Internet is Network of Networks. If fact, nobody runs or owns it. Is it not surprising? Every network that is connected to the Internet is responsible for its own part. However, there 3 main organizations which are supposed to guide and coordinate the working of Internet are:

Internet Engineering Task Force (IETF)

It develops and maintains the Internet's communication protocols, which are the methods by which computers on the Internet are connected.

Internet Research Task Force (IRTF)

It looks into long term research problems, many of which are at times critical to the Internet.

Internet Architecture Board (IAB)

This oversees the IETF and IRTF and ratifies any major change to the Internet that comes from the IETF.

Internet Funding:

The question arises that who pays Internet to make it reach us. Everyone pays for its part to use the Internet; no one pays for Internet as a whole. For example VSNL pays for the gateway assess to India and NASA pays for its NASA science Internet. Networks interconnections.

Institutions, corporate agencies and colleges pay for their connections to some regional network, which in turn pays a national provider for its access.

History of Internet

The Internet was by product of cold war. When network of computers was set up by military to ensure communication did not break in event of war. The USSR launches Sputnik in 1957, the first artificial earth satellite. In response, the United States forms the Advanced Research Projects Agency (ARPA) in 1968 within the Department of Defense (DoD) to establish US lead in science and technology applicable to the military. ARPA awarded the ARPANET contract to BBN, BBN had selected a Honeywelminicomputer as the base on which they would build the switch.

The network was physically constructed in 1969 by linking four nodes: University of California at Los Angeles, SRI (in Stanford), University of California at Santa Barbara, and University of Utah. The network was wired together via 50 Kbps circuits. The first public demonstration of ARPANET was given in October 1972. The net quickly grew to spread to entire country. From this point onwards the journey can be traced by years:

1972 The first E-mail program was created and The Advanced Research Projects Agency (ARPA) was renamed The Defense Advanced Research Projects Agency TCP/IP, it was developed by a group headed by Bob Kahn from DARPA and Vinton Cerf from Stanford. This new protocol was to allow diverse computer networks to interconnect and communicate with each other.

1974 The term Internet was used for the first time.

1976 Dr. Robert M. Metcalfe develops Ethernet, which allowed coaxial cable to move data extremely fast. This was a crucial component to the development of LANs.

1979 In 1979 USENET (the decentralized news group network) was created by Steve Bellovin (a graduate student at University of North Carolina) and programmer Tom Truscott and Jim Ellis. It was based on UUCP. The Creation of BITNET, by IBM, "Because its Time network", introduced the "store and forward" network. It was used for email.

1980 Additional networks especially LANs were connected to the ARPANET. As the scale increased finding hosts addresses became increasingly expensive so DNS (Domain Naming System) was created by University of Wisconsim to organize machines into domains and map names onto IP (Internet Protocol) addresses. This allowed packets to be directed to a domain name, which would be translated by the server database into the corresponding IP number. This made it much easier for people to access other servers, because they no longer had to remember numbers.

1981 National Science Foundation created backbone called CSNET 56 Kpbs network for institutions without access to ARPANET. Vinton Cerf proposed a plan for an inter-network connection between CSNET and the ARPANET.

1983 Internet Activities Board (IAB) was created. On January 1st, every machine connected to ARPANET had to use TCP/IP. TCP/IP became the core Internet protocol and replaced NCP entirely.

1984 In 1984 The ARPANET was divided into two networks: MILNET and ARPANET.

MILNET was to serve the needs of the military and ARPANET to support the advanced research component, Department of Defense continued to support both networks. New circuits would be T1 lines, 1.5 Mbps which is twenty-five times faster than the old 56 Kpbs lines. IBM wold provide advanced routers and Merit would manage the network. New network was to be called NSFNET (National Science Foundation Network), and old lines were to remain called CSNET. So network broke into two parts, Millnet for military sciences and smaller Arpanet for managing non military sites.

1986 The Internet Engineering Task Force to IETF was created to serve as a forum for technical coordination by contractors for DARPA working on ARPANET, US Defense Data Network (DDN), and the Internet core gateway system.

1987 BITNET and CSNET merged to form the Corporation for Research and Educational Networking (CREN), another work of the National Science Foundation.

1988 Soon after the completion of the T1 NSFNET backbone, traffic increased so quickly that plans immediately began on upgrading the network again. Merit and its partners formed a not for profit corporation called ANS, Advanced Network Systems, which was to conduct research into high-speed networking. It soon came up with the concept of the T3, a 45 Mbps line. NSF quickly adopted the new network and by the end of 1991 all of its sites were connected by this new backbone.

1990 In 1990 while the T3 lines were being constructed, the Department of Defense disbanded the ARPANET and it was replaced by the NSFNET backbone. The original 50kbps line of ARPANET were taken out of service. Tim Berners-Lee and CERN in Geneva implement a hypertext system to provide efficient information access to the members of the international high-energy physics community.

1991 CSNET (which consisted of 56kbps lines) was discontinued having fulfilled its important early role in the provision of academic networking service. A key feature of CREN is that its operational costs are fully met through dues paid by its member organizations. The NSF established a new network, named NREN, the National Research and Education Network. The purpose of this network is to conduct high speed networking research. It was not to be used as a commercial network, nor was it to be used to send a lot of the data that the Internet now transfers.

1992 Internet Society is chartered. The site http://www.worldbank.org/ comes on-line World-Wide Web released by CERN.

1993 InterNIC created by NSF to provide specific Internet services: directory and database services (by AT&T), registration services (by Network Solutions Inc.), and information services (by General Atomics/CERFnet). Merc Andreessen and NCSA and the University of Illinois develops a graphical user interface to the WWW, called "Mosaic for X".

1994 No major changes were made to the physical network. The most significant thing that happened was the growth. Many new networks were added to the NSF backbone. Hundreds of thousands of new hosts were added to the INTERNET during this time period. ATM (Asynchronous transmission Mode, 145 Mbps) backbone is installed on NSFNET.

1995 The National Science Foundation announced that as of April 30, 1995 Foundation contracted with four companies that would be providers of access to the NSF backbone (Merit). These companies would then sell connections to groups, organization, and companies. $50 annual fee is imposed on domains, excluding .edu and .gov domains which are still funded by the National Science Foundation.

1996 Internet phones catch the attention of US telecommunication companies who ask the US Congress to ban the technology (which has been around for years). Malaysian Prime Minister Mahathir Mohamad, PLO Leader Yasser Arafat, and Phillipine President Fidel Ramos meet for ten minutes in an online interactive chat session on 7 January. The controversial US Communication Decency Act (CDA) becomes law in the US in order to prohibit distribution of indecent materials over the Net. A few months later a three-judge panel imposes an injunction against its enforcement. Supreme Court unanimously rules most of it unconstitutional in 1997.

Lately Most Internet traffic is carried by backbones of independent ISPs, including MCI, AT&T, Sprint, UUnet, BBN planet, ANS and more. Currently the Internet Society, the group that controls the INTERNET, is trying to figure out new TCP/IP to be able to have billions of addresses, rather than the limited system of today. The problem that has arisen is that it is not known how both the old and the new addressing systems will be able to work at the same time during a transition period.

The WWW browser war, fought primarily between Netscape and Microsoft, has rushed in a new age in software development, whereby new release are made quarterly with the help of Internet users eager to test upcoming (beta) versions.

Internet in India

Internet was introduced in 1970s by Educational Research Network (ERNET) in India. This was set up jointly by the United Nations Development Program (UNDP) and the Department of Electronics (DoE) of Government of India. It is still operative today but still the access is restricted to educational institutes and research organizations.

Later on 15th August, 1995, Videsh Sanachar Nigam Limited (VSNL) launched the first private accessible internet services called Gateway Internet Access Service (GIAS). This was initially available only in Delhi, Mumbai, Calcutta, Madras, Bangalore and Pune but it is now available at most of the major cities of the country.

Recently even the private service providers were allowed to provide the Internet access to the public. These are called ISPs (Internet Service Provides). Some of them are: Satyam Online, Bharti Telecom, etc. There are more in the pipeline since most of these people have been given the licence to provide services on State to State basis.

There have been some moves to provide these services through the Cable Network Service providers. With more and more service providers joining the fray, the rate of connecting to the Internet is fast becoming less and less.

Web Technology and Global Publishing Concepts.

Ans. The web technology enables the web programmer to use the different programming concept like application programming, database and web programming. Organization needs to adopt various web technologies according to its requirements. Different technologies in use are: HTML, DHTML, ASP, Active Applec, IIS, COM/DCOM, COBRA, etc.

Web transactional systems use a number of associated technologies that support the integration of the heterogeneous components. Following are some Internet based advanced technologies that are used repeatedly:

HTML

HTML stands for Hypertext Mark up Language and is a computer language used to create web pages. A web page is a HTML document made of text and various HTML tags. HTML is very easy to use, specially if you are using Windows 98 onwards.

The main requirements for running HTML are as follows:

Browser to interpret the HTML documents.

1. To create HTML documents we need text editor.
2. When we save the HTML document extension should always be (.HTML) or (>HTML)
3. HTML document is composed of tags. Every tags starts with opening delineates (angle Brackets) and closed by delimiters (Closing angle bracket>)
4. We can also embedded the graphic files in the HTML documents.
5. For servelets HTML provides the basic instruction format for including servelets inside the body tags.

DHTML

DHTML means Dynamic hypertext Markup language. Dynamic means data is automatically updated. When are design web pages with the help of CSS (Cascade style scat) and script programming, the web page is called dynamic in nature. When an execute this page on the browser every timeit will give the new and updated output as prescribed in the source code. HTTP is the underlying set of rules used by WWW.

It defines how message are formatted and transmitted and what actions the web servers and browsers should take in response to various commands.

HTTP

Hypertext Transfer Protocol is a simple request/response protocol that is currently run over TCP and is the basis of the www. In short, HTTP is a protocol transferring information efficiently between the requesting client and server. When the browser or user browses the web, objects are retrieved in rapid succession from often widely dispersed servers. HTTP is used for retrieving documents in an unbounded and extensible set of formats.

To achieve this the client sends a list of formats it can handle, and the server applies with data in any of those formats that it can produce. HTTP is an Internet protocol. It is similar in its readable, text bases style to the FTP and NNTP (Network news transfer protocols) that have been used to transfer file and news on the Internet for many years.

Active Server Page (ASP)

ASP Technology basically used VB script languages to utilize active X technology in their web pages or (it is specification for a dynamically created web pages that utilizes Active X scripting). When a browser request an ASP, the web server generates a page with HTML code and then send it back to the browser. ASP's are similar to CGI scripts.

Active X

For dynamic web page we use Active X technology. Active X includes VB scripts/programmes that runs on the client machine rather than Web server. It is a client site solution for the web. To implement active X technology we make use of variety of programming like java applets, java scripts, C, C++, of Active X controls, visual basic etc.

Common Gateway Interface (CGI)

CGI is a specification for transferring information between a www server and a CGI program. A CGI program is any program written in any programming language including C, PERL, JAVA, VISUAL BASIC etc. designed to accept the data that conforms to CGI, specification. CGI programs are the most common way to interact dynamically with users. For example, use a CGI program to process the forms data when it is submitted.

PERL

PERL stands for Practical Extraction and Report Language. PERL is a programming language aimed at processing text. Because of its strong text processing abilities, PERL has become one of the most popular languages for writing CGI scripts. It is an interpretive language, thus making it easy to build and test simple programs. The web developer community widely adopts this multi-platform language.

JAVA APPLETS

These are the Java enable programs executed from within another application like browser with the advent of OOPS (name of C++ program), the applets becomes very popular for flexible components.

JAVA Server Pages (JSP)

JSP is a similar Active server page (ASP). As with active saver page, JSP operates with a pair of technologies. The client page has embedded call, and the server side provides the functionality and transfers the resulting data back to the client. The difference between the technologies is that the code embedded between the <% and %> tags in JSP is exclusively JAVA, where ASP uses Microsoft visual basis.

COM AND COM+

COM stands for Component Object Model. COM is a framework for developing and supporting program components object. It provides similar capabilities to those defined CORBA (Common Object Request Broker Architecture). A framework for developing the inter operation of distributed objects in a network that is supported by the major companies in the computer industry. It is a model for binary code that enables programmes to develop objects that can be accessed by any COM complaint application.

DCOM

It stands for Distributed Computer Object Model. DCOM is an extension of COM. It is a set of program and interface in which client programs requests the services from the server.

CORBA

It stands for Common Object Request Broker Architecture. CORBA is a distribute architecture whereby the ORB (Open Request Broker) client, different computer communication application and request the server for service for third party network independent the platform.

Visual Studio

It is high Level Language. All graphical user interface application program interface including COM, DCOM and CORBA. These technologies are application tier services that provides front end by business application.

What concepts the Web uses?

The web has become an umbrella for a wide range of concepts and technologies.

These include:

Global Hyper Text Publishing Concept

It promotes the idea of a seamless information world in which all online information can be accessed and retrieved in a consistent and simple way. To access information in this seamless world, we will need the ability to address many types of data, text files, images, sound files and animation sequences. Hypertext Publishing make use anchor Tag Web Contents on the Internet.

Universal Reader Concept

We can use one application – a universal (or common) user interface to read a variety of documents. This concept implies that once information is published it is accessible from any type of computer; in any country and that any (authorized) person needs to use one simple program to access it. This is accomplished in the web by using a core browser or application that is augmented by supporting application.

Client Server Concept

It allows the web to grow easily without any centralized control. Anyone can publish information and any more authorized person can read and download it. Publishing information requires a server programs, and reading data requires a client browser. All the clients and servers are connected with each other through Internet. The various standard protocol allow all clients to communicate with all savers.

Hyper Text Transfer Protocol (HTTP)

Protocol are the rules that describe how clients and severs comminute with each other over a network HTTP is protocol used by www. It can be defined as a set of rules that signify how the web pages are transmitted over the web.

There are various types of files like test files, sound file, music file, graphics etc. are to be transferred from one host machine to another. HTTP protocol is used to fulfill when client request to web server.

Commands that help to communicate between the browser and the web server are listed below:

- GET Command that initiates the server to retrieve the information located at the path specified in the URL
- HEAD Difference Head and Get command is that, the server retrieves only the document header to the browser. HTML document is divided into the Head and the Body. In the Head section contain information about the document and in the body section contain the actual text that is displayed within the Browser window.

POST The post method instead of reading this page writes the page. However, instead of replacing of replacing the existing data, the new date is appended to it in same generalized sense.

The main task of HTTP is to deal with the message format and transmissions of the message and what actions web browser and sever should take in response to various commands.

Uniform Resource Locators (URLs)

In practice, URLs are the strings used as addresses of objects on the web. URL marks the unique location on the Internet where a file or service an be found. URLs follow a fairly consistent pattern.

The first part describes the type of resource.

The second part gives the name of the server holding the resource.

The third part gives the full file name of the resource.

URLs are universal in such a way that they provide access range of network service, which required separate application in the past.

Format of URLs are as follows:

GRP: Ftp://server address/complete file name

Telnet: telnet: //server.address:port

HTTP: http://server, address part: /home page.html

- The URL class simplifies network connections by offering encapsulations to different protocols
- A URL has four parts: a protocol name, a host name, a port number, and a path to a file.

For example,

http://www.cis.ohio-state.edu : 80/index.html

- A computer has a single physical connection to the network, through which more than one communication can be handled concurrently. The port number identifies the application responsible for the communication in discourse.

The URL class offers six constructors and an assortment of query functions:

- URL (String spec)
- URL (String protocol, String host, int port, String file)

- URL (String protocol, String host, String file)
- URL (URL baseURL, String relativeURL)
- URL (URL baseURL, String relativeURL, URL StreamHandler handler)
- URL(String protocol, String host, int port, String file, URLStreamHandler handler)

HTTP Servers:

- HTTP servers are responsible for serving text and graphical content using Hypertext Transfer Protocol.
- An HTTP or web server runs an HTTP daemon, which is a program responsible for responding to requests from web browsers. The server may also be configured to process different types of scripts.
- An Internet web server is designed and configured to provide web content to the general public.
- An Internet Server is configured to provide web content to authorized users only. Internet servers are usually located behind a firewall within a local LAN and intended for use by only the members of the organization or company.
- An extranet server is an intranet server that also permits some limited access by the public or other authorized users outside the local area network. These servers are popular for business partners who wish to share information.
- A web server desinged to provide e-commerce services may be called an e-commerce server. These services, which are supported through special programs or scripts, may include inventory searches, a shopping cart program, credit card verification, and an automatic email confirming your order.
- There are three main HTTP daemons in use today. These are HTTPd, Microsoft IIS, and Apache. Currently the most popular is Apache, which is on over 60% of all servers.
- The web server software HTTPd (HTTP daemon), was the original HTTP server software. HTTPd was developed by the National Center for Supercomputing Applications for the Unix operating System and is free, open source software.
- Microsoft IIS (Internet Information Server) is packaged with Windows NT and Windows 2000. It provides a user-friendly graphical interface but works only on Windows NT or 2000 Servers.
- Apache is a free, open source HTTP daemon built on HTTPd. Although originally designed for use on Linux / Unix systems, it is also available for use on Windows NT and OS/2. Apache is currently the most widely used HTTP daemon on the Internet.

- If the traffic on a web server becomes too heavy, the site may be mirrored. Mirroring a site means placing a copy of the site on another web server.

FTP Servers

- An FTP Server runs an ftp daemon in order provide file services (download, upload, delete) using the FTP protocol.
- An FTP server requires a name and password from the user before allowing files transfers. For public download, "anonymous" transfers are permitted with the user name "anonymous" or "ftp" and any text for the password.
- Two popular FTP server programs are FTPd (FTP daemon) and Microsoft's IIS. FTPd is a free Unix-based program in wide use, while IIS is designed for specifically for use on Windows NT or 2000 Server systems.

SMTP Servers

- SMTP (Simple Mail Transfer Protocol) servers allow users to send and receive email through the Internet.
- An SMTP server runs a daemon responsible for locating the IP address of the recipient email account, verifying that mail has been delivered, displaying an appropriate error message if mail is undeliverable, retrying to send mail if the recipient server is busy, and generally getting the mail through.
- Mail servers may also provide SMTP relaying services, which forward email coming from one SMTP to a different SMTP.
- Mail servers may also be used as list servers, allowing email messages to be sent to all the recipients who have singed up on a list, and allowing people on that list to in turn reply to the list. The email address for list servers are often majordomo@domain.com
- The most commonly used SMTP daemon is Sendmail, another product of open source software.

Proxy Servers

- Proxy servers provide a means for workstation on a secure intranet or private LAN to access the internet the Internet while preventing Internet traffic from accessing the private LAN.
- A proxy server sits between the Internet server and the client workstation, processing the requests made by the client and determining whether to pass those requests on to the Internet server of deny the request. Similarly, the proxy server can manage

some of the requests sen from the Internet server. Proxy servers can be configured as to what types of services they permit.

- Since proxy servers can provide packet filtering, they can be used to restrict the types of file that network users access over the Internet. For example, a proxy server may be set to prohibit any MP3 files from being downloaded.
- Proxy servers may also provide caching services. With active caching, the server uses low activity periods to download and store documents that may be requested by network users, while passive caching determines whether or not to store documents as they are requested by users on the network.

NNTP Servers and Newsgroups

- NNTP (Network News Transfer Protocol) servers are used to provide access to newsgroups.
- Newsgroup servers store a variety of newsgroups, and can be configured to communicate with other NNTP servers so that server has a copy of all the messages available within the newsgroup.
- If a newsgroup is moderated, any new messages posted to the newgroup are first reviewed by a moderator, who determines whether to publicly post the message or discard it.
- Newsgroups may be configured with an expiration date, thereby automatically erasing messages after they reach a designated age.

Other Servers

- A server running a telnet daemon is a telnet server. The telnet daemon, used mostly on Linux / Unix systems, allows a remote user to log onto the server and type in commands as if he were sitting directly at that computer.
- A directory server provides access to directories of information, such as phone books, email address lists, and various other directory-type information. Directory servers are also known as LDAP servers, since most conform to the Lightweight Directory Access Protocol.
- Mirror servers are backup servers that duplicate everything that takes place on the main server so that they can immediately replace the main server if it fails.
- A single computer may run a variety of daemons and thus be more than one type of server. For example, an HTTP server may also be a telnet and FTP server.

HTML Forms:

It is not that you display your products only on the web site. You make the site interactive to have people respond to it. This response may be in the form of feed back, purshase order or just comments. For all these we use what is called the Forms. The main idea to get information from the visitors of the site. These forms are integral part of the HTML and are easy to create, as you would learn in this chapter.

HTML allows you to have the forms in such a way that the user has minimum effort to do. It usually is in the form of buttons or options to choose from. Then you have text boxes for users to fill up, or have check boxes, drop-down menus, larger text areas and even clickable images.

Creating a form

We can divide the form into 3 parts:

1. FORM tag, which includes the URL of the CGI script that will process the form;
2. Form elements, like fields and menus;
3. Submit button, which sends the data to the CGI script on the server.

Let us see how this is done.

1. Type <FORM to initiate the form.
2. Type METHOD=method, where method is either GET or POST. You would learn about them later in the chapter.
3. Type ACTION="script.url"> where script.url is the location on the server of the CGI script that will run when the form is submitted.
4. Create the form's contents.
5. Here I am using the form to get information from a possible client.
6. Type </FORM> to complete the form.

See how the text is created in Word Pad and its result in the browser.

CGI gateway Services:

CGI is the Common gateway Interface. It is a standard agreed upon by WWW server writers to allow servers to call user written programs. CGI scripts can be written in any language, but the majority of them tend to be written using the Perl programming language. Any script in your public HTML directory having the suffix .cgl can be run provided it meets the following conditions:

- It must be readable and executable by you.
- If it is writable, it must only be writable by you.

- The file must be owned by you, and it must have the same group as your primary group.
- The directory containing the file must only be writable by you.

The best way to ensure that these conditions are met is to run the following commands in Linux:

chmod 755 scriptname

chmod 755

chown –R yourusername *

Note that if you are running CGI from a Group project area in /vol/project things are slightly different:

- cgi scripts in /vol/project must be executable and readable by the group.
- the cgi script's group ownership must be the project group not the primary group of any user (cs2 or whatever.)

Files must be in Unix format, not Windows. The programmer's File Editor (Start > Programs > Editors > PEF) on Windows workstations has an option under "File/Save As" to use Unix Format, or from the Linux command line dos2unix can be used to convert Windows files. When a web request comes in that names one of your CGI scripts, and the above constraints have been satisfied, the script itself is executed as you in the normal Unix way. This means that unless it is a true compiled executable, the first line of the script should be a #!/path/to/interpreter line. So, for example, all Perl CGI scripts should have first line #!/usr/bin/perl. Your CGI script will be called with a number of shell environment variable set. If the URL that invokes the CGI script contains a '?' then anything following the '?' is passes as command line arguments to the script.

Similarly, if the invoking URL names a CGI script and has a '/' section after the name of a valid CGI script, the '/' section is extracted and placed into the PATH_INFO environment variable. Taking input from WebPages is inherently dangerous as this is often used by attackers to gain access. A good example of this being the publicized "contest" run by PCWeek Box where an NT and a Red Hat Linux box were setup (and somewhat secured.) the Linux box was quickly compromised using a CGI program that did not check user input properly. For example if taking a username in, make sure it only contains alphanumeric characters, and is of a sane length (like 8 characters as opposed to say 400K). some CGI language are as: PERL and PHP. Out of this PERL has been explained earlier. Let us understand what PHP is.